POLITICS IS FOR POWER

How to Move Beyond Political Hobbyism, Take Action, and Make Real Change

Eitan Hersh

SCRIBNER

New York   London   Toronto   Sydney   New Delhi

Scribner
An Imprint of Simon & Schuster, Inc.
1230 Avenue of the Americas
New York, NY 10020

First Scribner hardcover edition January 2020

SCRIBNER and design are registered trademarks of The Gale Group, Inc.,
used under license by Simon & Schuster, Inc., the publisher of this work.

For information about special discounts for bulk purchases,
please contact Simon & Schuster Special Sales at 1-866-506-1949
or business@simonandschuster.com.

The Simon & Schuster Speakers Bureau can bring authors to your live event.
For more information or to book an event, contact the Simon & Schuster Speakers Bureau
at 1-866-248-3049 or visit our website at www.simonspeakers.com.

Manufactured in the United States of America

1   3   5   7   9   10   8   6   4   2

Library of Congress Cataloging-in-Publication Data has been applied for.

ISBN 978-1-9821-1678-1
ISBN 978-1-9821-1680-4 (ebook)

For Julia

Contents

CONTENTS

POLITICS
IS FOR
POWER

Introduction

June 2019. On a Wednesday evening with dry summer weather, a volunteer political organization is holding its monthly meeting. Lemonade and cookies are set up in the back of a borrowed meeting room. A few young children mill around as fifty adults make their way to large round conference tables. This organization, like similar ones around the country, was formed in the aftermath of the 2016 election to support Democratic candidates and progressive causes.[1] It's now planning its next moves.

The meeting is taking place a few blocks from the center of town in Greensburg, Pennsylvania, an hour southeast of Pittsburgh. Greensburg is the seat of Westmoreland County. Over the past twenty years, Westmoreland has gone from a politically split county to a Republican stronghold. Two out of every three of the 182,000 votes cast in 2016 went to Donald Trump.

The monthly meeting is a temporary liberal oasis here. A few dozen people with left-leaning policy views briefly enjoy a sense of camaraderie that they rarely get to experience outside this room. Everywhere else they go—work, church, school, among their neighbors—their political views are abnormal.

One man, a new face to the group, lingers at the back of the room. He seems apprehensive, and serious, maybe sad. I later learn he was one of those two out of three voters in the county who supported Donald Trump for president in 2016. He's about fifty years old and has a thick beard. He wears a T-shirt with a slogan that professes his love of drinking. He chooses the rearmost chair at the rearmost table and sits down. When he sits down, I notice that he is drinking a glass

1

of wine. I notice because wine is not being served at this meeting. At some point, he has left the room and come back with a full, stemless glass, now taking slow, deliberate sips as the leaders in front make announcements.

Soon, a young organizer facilitates a discussion at the back table where the man sits. The organizer asks all at the table to introduce themselves. When his turn comes, the man says he's a Republican and a Christian, as well as the father of a child serving in the military. He also says he's pro-life.

A couple of people shift in their seats, unsure where this introduction is going, worried that this rare hour in which they are surrounded by fellow liberals is about to be disrupted.

The man continues, almost mournfully, "I'm a Christian, and there's no such thing as a racist Christian." That's why he's here, he explains. He feels that his own small community is going down a path of hatred and, as a Christian, he needs to take a stand. Even though he disagrees with the other people in this room issue by issue, he says, he's here to learn about this group and maybe to contribute to its work. He's here because Donald Trump doesn't represent his Christian values. He offers advice about how the group can better approach people who are like him. He remains visibly uncomfortable through the whole meeting, but the group is glad he came. They welcome him. He has traveled a long political distance to be here this night.

His presence is not an accident; it's a triumph. The group's leaders have been working for over two years, slowly building support and training volunteers to win over people exactly like this man. In a county that could hardly be more hostile to their views, they have had a remarkable string of successes, as we will see. The successes were hard-earned through many evenings of their lives, miles of door-to-door canvasses, and stumbling blocks along the way as they learned how to build an organization from scratch. They did this work—and continue to do it—for one reason:

They want power.

When ordinary Americans volunteer in politics, they are trying to acquire power. Each voter they convince is a small piece of that power. Accumulated votes translate into politicians and policies advancing their values. If the group in Westmoreland County can convince this man to join them—if they can help him convince other members of his family and religious network to vote a certain way— the group might be able to change dozens of votes that they couldn't change without him.

Each vote may seem like an insignificant drop in a 135-million-vote bucket, but the group labors with the knowledge that it is working in concert with like-minded organizations across the state and country each doing its part. The group also knows, and sees, that opposing groups, with very different values, are also getting supporters for the other side. They are in a pitched battle with one another, each seek- ing political control.

What they're all doing, that's politics.

I often think of groups like this in evenings on my couch. A pile of laundry sits next to me. Over some two hours I fold it half-heartedly as I watch TV and clutch my phone. I refresh my Twitter feed to keep up on the latest political crisis, then toggle over to Facebook to read clickbait news stories, then over to YouTube to see a montage of juicy clips from the latest congressional hearing. I then complain to my family about all the things I don't like that I have seen.

What I'm doing, that isn't politics.

What I'm doing I call *political hobbyism*, a catchall phrase for con- suming and participating in politics by obsessive news-following and online "slacktivism," by feeling the need to offer a hot take for each daily political flare-up, by emoting and arguing and debating, almost all of this from behind screens or with earphones on. I am in good company: these behaviors represent most of the ways that most "politically engaged" Americans spend their time on politics.

In 2018, I asked a representative sample of Americans to estimate about how much time they spend on any kind of political-related activity in a typical day. A third of Americans say they spend two hours or more each day on politics. Of these people, four out of five say that not one minute of that time is spent on any kind of real political work. It's all TV news and podcasts and radio shows and social media and cheering and booing and complaining to friends and family.[2]

Political hobbyists tend to be older than the general public, though they are found in all age groups. They are disproportionately college educated, male, and white. In the current climate, they're more likely to be Democrats than Republicans or independents.[3] Not only are they different from the general public, they also have a different profile from people who engage actively in political organizations. For example, of the people who spend two hours a day on politics but no time on volunteering, 56 percent are men. But of those who spend that much time on politics, with at least some of it spent volunteering, 66 percent are women.

Those who volunteer, such as the group in Westmoreland County that is out convincing neighbors to vote and to advocate, have something to show for their commitment to their political values. As for the rest of us, all we have is a sinking feeling of helplessness in the face of overwhelming challenge.

As a political scientist, I study the ways that ordinary people participate in politics. The political behavior of ordinary people is hard to understand. We don't often reflect deeply on why we engage in politics. However, when we step back and investigate our political lives, we can paint a general picture of what motivates us. Summing up the time we spend on politics, it would be hard to describe our behavior as seeking to influence our communities or country. Most of us are engaging to satisfy our own emotional needs and intellectual curiosities. That's political hobbyism.

This book explores the problem of political hobbyism. Voraciously consuming politics or tinkering online seems harmless, but it's a problem for two main reasons. First, we are making politics worse. Our collective treatment of politics as if it were a sport affects how politicians behave. They increasingly believe they benefit from feeding the red meat of outrage to their respective bases, constantly grandstanding for the chance that a video of themselves will go viral. In treating politics like a hobby, we have demanded they act that way.

Second, hobbyism takes us away from spending time working with others to acquire power. While we sit at home, people who seek political control are out winning over voters. In 2018, for instance, the Ku Klux Klan in North Carolina went around offering to help opioid addicts, telling addicts that their addiction wasn't their fault and that the white knights of the KKK were there to offer a helping hand.[4] This image haunts me not just because in it I see an organization I fear that is serious about power, that recognizes how service to one person at a time aggregates into power. The image haunts me juxtaposed to how most of the rest of us are doing politics.

When the KKK is out in the streets offering opioid addicts help at the same time as most of us who are supposedly interested in politics are spending hours a day on social media, and at the same time as the mainstream political parties are unleashing a deluge of clickbait ads to raise money that will mostly pay for more ads, we should understand what is happening here: we are ceding political power to people who want it more than we do. Hobbyism is a serious threat to democracy because it is taking well-meaning citizens away from pursuing power. The power vacuum will be filled.

For generations, political theorists and political scientists have worried about the average person's capacity to participate in democracy. It is not difficult to find embarrassing statistics about how profoundly uninformed the typical American citizen is: most don't know which political party is in the majority in Congress; most cannot name the three branches of the federal government.[5]

The average citizen, who doesn't spend much time thinking about politics, is not my concern here. My concern is the informed citizen who is *already* spending significant time and energy on politics, but without serious purpose. More likely than not, if you are reading this, this book is about *you*. It's about me, too.

Political hobbyism is found in all circles, but it's mainly a problem for people who are well educated and on the political center and left. These groups are the focus of the book. Scholars have noted that as the share of college-educated Americans has increased since World War II (less than 5 percent had a degree in 1940; over 30 percent do today), those with a college degree have become less likely to see themselves as special, as responsible for their communities, as trustees, getting involved and encouraging others to do the same. They will follow the news, join an email list, make an occasional financial contribution, or attend a one-off rally, but they will shy away from deeper organizational engagement. Harvard professor Theda Skocpol has argued that this change in attitude by college-educated

Americans—that they feel less special—may be the biggest reason for the precipitous decline in their engagement in local political and civic organizations since the mid-twentieth century.[6] In how they consume news, identify as partisans, and engage from the side-lines, well-educated Americans now tend to treat politics as if it were a game.

While there is no shortage of political hobbyism on the political far right, which is consumed by conspiracy theories and outrageous news, hobbyism is a particularly serious problem among those in the ideological center and on the left. Self-proclaimed independents are prone to hobbyism because activism does not fit well with the above-the-fray self-image that they want to curate. Many independents say they care about politics, but they don't feel at home in activities dominated by more partisan or ideological voices. As two leading political scientists note, independents end up plugging into politics in strictly superficial ways, angry when their favorite party does something they don't like but unwilling to lift a finger to empower their own values.[7]

Why is hobbyism a problem for Democrats? Because hobbyism is prominent among college-educated white Americans. Today, an American who is white, college educated, and interested in politics is 60 percent more likely to identify as a Democrat than a Republican.[8] They spend more of their leisure time consuming political information than those without a college degree and less time than racial minorities volunteering for political organizations.[9]

Political hobbyism on the left also stands in sharp contrast to the most successful recent political movements, which have been on the right—the right-to-life movement, the gun rights movement—which were developed around chapter-based, local organizations with thousands of volunteers willing to roll up their sleeves and, slowly and steadily, achieve modest political goals: taking over political party committees, quietly seeding judicial offices, recruiting state legislative candidates—activities that seem beneath the political hobbyist who is strictly infatuated with national political drama.[10]

Educated Democrats, fiddling around in politics online and voraciously consuming news, have a long legacy. They are reminiscent of a well-documented phenomenon from the 1950s of "amateur Democrats" who formed local clubs in major US cities.[11] These clubs, which were briefly popular in middle-class neighborhoods of New York, Chicago, Los Angeles, and other cities, were dominated by the cosmopolitan, professional class. Officially, in their meetings, the clubs had an agenda: opposition to the insiders who controlled the Democratic Party as well as promotion of a liberal ideological worldview. But club meetings were often focused on debates of broad national concerns. In long nights at clubhouses or over snacks and coffee in living rooms, participants discussed grand political issues and hosted intellectuals as guest speakers.[12]

What distinguished these clubs from the "regular" Democrats, who controlled levers of power in the Democratic Party at the time and who mobilized voters in working-class areas of these cities, were the motivations that brought them into politics. The regulars—political staffers and volunteers alike—sought recognition when they did a good job securing votes and organizing precincts. They sought *power* for their side. Achieving this goal meant doing good in the eyes of the voters. To win the voters' favor, they delivered on issues that their voters cared about. But to these party regulars, policy issues were secondary to winning and holding power.

The amateur clubs wanted to win, and in several cases their leaders made headway into elective office, but what inspired the participation of rank-and-file amateurs was a social scene where they could argue about principles. They saw themselves as worldly in comparison to the working-class party regulars; the amateurs cared about the big important ideas, not fixing potholes and helping neighbors. Whereas party regulars employed long-term precinct captains who took pride in knowing their neighborhoods, the amateur clubs, composed of younger professionals, had trouble sustaining active volunteers for more than a year or two. The lawyers and doctors and other professionals had a distaste for the parochial. They didn't have the time to organize city and suburban blocks. What they made time for was arguing into the night about the issues.

Amateur Democrats of the mid-twentieth century were, like today's hobbyists, emotionally invested in politics. They celebrated electoral wins and mourned losses much more than did the seasoned organizers who were out in the neighborhoods for the party machines year after year. The eminent political scientist James Q. Wilson, author of

The Amateur Democrat, described an amateur as someone who "sees each battle as a 'crisis' and each victory as a triumph and each loss as a defeat for a cause." The participants were in it for the emotion. One leader summed up, "The principal motivation for many of these people [i.e., active members and leaders] is the sheer fascination with politics."

The Republican side had, and still has, its own version of this. Like the Democrats, the amateur types tend to be more ideological than the party regulars. They are in politics for the big ideas rather than for the day-to-day management of a community or a state. For example, not long ago I found myself at a playground in rural New Hampshire, eavesdropping on a newcomer to Republican activism. He was ignoring his children by talking politics on his phone to a friend. I was ignoring my children by listening intently to his conversation.

This man—about forty with a trimmed beard and gentle manner—was trying to get involved in his local Republican committee. Apparently, the first thing he decided to do was to transcribe the state Republican Party's platform into Microsoft Excel. Each sentence he put on a different row in the spreadsheet. On each line, he made a check mark if the sentence abided by conservative principles, according to him. On his phone call, this man was obsessed with the degree to which the state Republican Party was Republican in Name Only (RINO) or truly conservative. For a fortysomething-year-old dad, he had an oddly Holden Caulfield grade of disdain for the hypocrites in charge. He didn't seem to think much about what could win votes. He was just dreamily concerned with being authentically conservative.

Such a desire to focus on ideology rather than on acquiring power was common among the Democratic clubs. According to Wilson, the professional class involved in the clubs tended to believe that if all voters thought through the issues as deeply as they did, their side would eventually win. The party regulars, on the other hand, who interacted daily with working-class voters, saw this view as naïve. The typical voter does not wish to think through public policy. The best thing to do is convince them, through actions, that Democrats care about them. Show voters you care, serve them, empathize with their day-to-day concerns. They will connect your expressions of concern with the Democratic brand. The Republican on the playground, like the Democrats in the clubs, brought to politics both a romantic vision of persuasion and a smug disdain for those who just don't get it.

One organizer I talked to in 2018 told me that his Democratic friends who aren't involved beyond news-following believe that their political positions are self-evidently correct. They don't volunteer in politics because if they have to convince anyone of their ideas, that means the ideas aren't self-evidently correct. So the friends don't want to struggle to move politics toward what they think is right because they think they shouldn't have to. It's a strange, utterly doomed logic, but it encapsulates the mores of hobbyists from that New Hampshire playground to social media newsfeeds everywhere.

Today's hobbyists possess the negative qualities of the amateurs— hyperemotional engagement, obsession with national politics, an insatiable appetite for debate—and none of the amateur's positive qualities—the neighborhood meetings, the concrete goals, the leadership. Today's hobbyists are even more distant from the party regulars, the workers who think about counting votes in the precincts rather than about grandiose policy fights.

Yet, citizens who want to empower their political values would be better off if they spent less time consuming politics as at-home amateurs and instead fell in line to help strengthen organizations and leaders. Rather than kibitzing with their social media friends, they could adopt some of the spirit of the party regulars, counting votes and building interpersonal relationships in their neighborhoods. If the typical engaged voters found meaning and pride in organizing ten, twenty, or a hundred voters instead of in dissecting the latest Washington controversy, they'd go a long way to empowering their values.

Democrats may resist this argument because the local Democratic organizing committees that were once powerful in this country, the ones that the amateurs railed against, were, in many cases, overtly racist. Racial minorities were kept out of politics and terrorized by hierarchical, local organizations. A call to focus on building grassroots organizations might seem nostalgic for the exclusionary party committees of old. We don't want to go back to that. As in all studies of American politics, the story of race is just below the surface of this book. Political hobbyism is and has always been largely a white phenomenon, but it will take almost to the end of this book to fully understand its racial contours.

Typical explanations for what's ailing American democracy let ordinary, engaged citizens off the hook. If we cast blame for political dysfunction on the media, on gerrymandering, on attempts at voter disenfranchisement, on wealthy political donors, on the Electoral College, on unapologetic racists, it's hard to see how ordinary citizens could do much. But that's awfully convenient: the evidence presented here will convince you that our own behavior demands at least as much reform as any political institution.

At the same time, the problem of political hobbyism is acute today because of specific changes to media, technology, law, and political parties that we can also not ignore. Technological changes have affected all forms of leisure, and it's important to see how they affect political leisure, too, but a century of political reforms—transparency laws, campaign finance laws, political party reforms—have impacted how ordinary people plug specifically into politics. These changes were meant to make politics more open to ordinary people and less dominated by political elites, but they have simultaneously weakened power-seeking organizations and strengthened forms of political engagement that play to our worst instincts.

By the end of this book, I want to have convinced you of four things. First, for the typical Americans spending an hour or more a day on politics, what they are doing is engaging in a hobby. We don't like to call it that. But when we look at the actions that constitute their political activity and, as important, the actions they are not taking, we have no choice but to face the truth that what they are doing is motivated by their emotional needs and a pursuit of personal gratification rather than a deeper commitment to the common good. Second, I want to convince you of *why* politics became something of a hobby: our persistent appetite for political information and intrigue combined with new technologies and laws that play to our baser instincts. Third, I want to convince you that political hobbyism is bad for our democracy.

Finally, I want to show you the alternative to political hobbyism:

actually doing politics. If you feel unfulfilled, melancholy, paralyzed by the sadness of the news and depth of our political problems, I hope I can show you the redemption of politics as a service to others, a form of politics where participants get power to improve their communities, present and future.

To show you, I will share stories of remarkable Americans coming together to organize effectively and making strides for their vision of what ought to be. Their stories show the stark contrast between the sacrifices a few people are making and the political engagement of the typical news-obsessed American. In many cases, the volunteers are spending the same amount of time on politics as the hobbyists, but the volunteers act to empower their political values.

Learning about the power-seeking behavior of these people will shed light on some surprising, and perhaps uncomfortable, changes we ought to make to improve our democracy, namely by redirecting our political energy toward serving the material and emotional needs of our neighbors. To convince you to do politics like this, though, I need to start from the beginning. We first need to hold up the mirror and examine how we typically engage in politics now.

PART I

All day long,
I can't shout back at the boss,
I can't shout back at the wife,
I can't shout back at the kids.

But I come here in the evenings and I shout at these people,
and I go away feeling like a new man.

—Democratic club activist,
Riverside, New York,
circa 1962[1]

When we do politics, what exactly are we doing?[2] In this first section of the book, we are going to observe five common types of political activity: news consumption, partisan cheerleading, voting, activism, and donating. How would we describe our motivations for these activities? As we'll see, we often engage in politics not to effect change, not quite for the sake of the common good, but for emotional or expressive ends. Much of the time we spend on politics is best described as an inward-focused leisure activity for people who like politics.

We may not easily concede that we are doing politics for fun. While maybe *some* portion of our political activity is for entertainment, calling politics a leisure activity does not capture the feelings we often bring to politics. Obsessively checking the news, for instance, can be neurotic, anxiety-inducing behavior. True, sports fanatics also agonize as they soak up endless minutiae of sports, but in politics the day-to-day minutiae seem much more important.

Even when we insist that we have higher motivations, our actions often betray a shallower basis for political engagement than we might like to admit. Consider a person who spends an hour a day ranting about politics on Facebook. He may genuinely feel an obligation to right the wrongs he sees in his newsfeed, to help others see the truth of his viewpoint. To outsiders, though, it can seem as if he is spending all this time not for others but for himself, because he is lonely or wants to get something off his chest. Neither he nor they could easily diagnose the true motivations in his heart. No matter the true motivations, we may want to determine whether his actions (like our own) objectively fit with the stated civic motivations: Is he really changing people's minds so they come around to his viewpoint?

Actions matter more than motivations, but thinking critically about our motivations helps us determine how much of our political activity is even meant to be a service to others and how much is meant to be a service to ourselves. While reading the coming chapters, we should both evaluate whether our motivations are mostly about personal gratification, service to the common good, or something else; and regardless of our motivations, we should evaluate whether the actions seem effective or ineffective, deep or shallow.

To build some intuition for what deep versus shallow actions look like, the chapters in part one will contrast our common behaviors with four stories of ordinary people who take power seriously. These stories will introduce key themes for the rest of the book. The volunteers who are profiled came into activism because they cared about issues or because they were upset about the direction of the country. However, rather than just spinning their wheels and feeling upset, they found ways to increase their own political power. Their energy is spent not on following political drama or debating issues, but on winning over people to their side.

CHAPTER 1

Refresh the Feed

Hobbyism and News Consumption

Late one evening, I called my father on the phone while he was watching TV in his bed. He told me he was watching cable news. I asked him why. "It's our civic duty to be informed," he said. I thought he was joking. "Every morning, you read the paper," I said. "On the way to work and on the way back, you listen to NPR for twenty-five minutes. And you think you have a civic duty to watch cable news at night?" When I pressed him, my father acknowledged that, really, he just likes watching TV before bed, and he prefers cable news to anything else on TV at that time.

Like my father, many of us use the language of civics to describe our news habit. We need to be informed to figure out how we will vote, and we need to absorb the news to be informed. Yet watching hours of cable news each day or endlessly refreshing Twitter and Facebook would be hard to describe as something required of us by civic duty. A better description is addiction. Walking around the house, we might find it difficult to resist checking our phones to see the latest political controversy. When we are disturbed by the news, we may feel that we need to do something, but the only something we can think of doing is reading more news.

Changes in media offerings since the 1970s reveal key insights about what motivates people who closely follow political news today. News choices used to be quite limited, especially on television. During the broadcast-TV era, the Federal Communications Commission required the few channels to show some kind of educational content

15

for an hour between 7:00 p.m. and 11:00 p.m. The major networks all satisfied this requirement by producing an evening news program. Up until 1987, broadcasters also needed to present politics in an ideologically balanced way, under a policy called the fairness doctrine.[1]

In this environment with just a few TV channels, lots of people, including those who did not particularly care for politics, ended up watching news. The news they watched was evenhanded, in recognition of the fairness doctrine and that the audience for the news program was ideologically broad-based.[2] In hindsight, it seems peculiar that in the broadcast-TV era many people who didn't care for politics at all ended up watching the nightly news. In fact, they just liked watching TV more than they didn't like politics, and news was the only thing on.[3]

Once cable was introduced, and with each subsequent technology, the choice set expanded. Consumers who do not like politics can watch something else. The producers of political content no longer have an interest or a legal obligation to appeal broadly. Instead they want to capture a dedicated following of viewers who will seek out political news obsessively.

To appeal to the news junkies, every venue for news—from cable to social media to newspapers—has discovered that loyal news followers like drama and emotion and provocation.[4] As scholars Jeffrey Berry and Sarah Sobieraj describe in their 2014 book, *The Outrage Industry*, cable news anchors use vicious language, mockery, insults, and sarcasm, all while looking directly at the camera and conveying intimacy and mutual understanding with their viewers.[5] The studios learned from Rush Limbaugh that they can cheaply produce content with meandering aghast reactions to current events. Through a string of tangents, the shows convey both that viewers are justified in feeling outraged and that viewers can rest assured that, any day now, their political opponents will be vanquished.

Cable news offers little investigative journalism, but the anchors put on an act that they are taking viewers on deep dives, behind the scenes, into the weeds. Rachel Maddow, for instance, will report information such as the prison identification numbers of convicted members of President Trump's inner circle (Trump adviser Paul Manafort is three-five-two-zero-seven-dash-zero-one-six; Trump lawyer Michael Cohen is eight-six-zero-six-seven-dash-zero-five-four),[6] information that is neither hard to find nor in any way useful to viewers. Reading numbers out loud, though, seems authoritative.

Shows on both sides love "proving" the hypocrisy of their opponents. From George W. Bush to Barack Obama to Donald Trump, cable news has maintained a regular trope of calling the president fascist. Of Bush, former MSNBC host Keith Olbermann fumed, "You're a fascist! Get them to print you a T-shirt with FASCIST on it! . . . You, sir, have no place in a government of the people, by the people, for the people."[7] Some of us find these rants cathartic.

Cable news has long been more popular on the right than on the left. Why? In part, this is because cable news viewers are mostly retirees, and retirees lean Republican. The median age for both MSNBC and Fox News is sixty-five, and more Republicans are around that age than Democrats.[8] Scholars have also posited that those of us with conservative dispositions are more attracted to the strength and certainty projected by cable news anchors.[9] Nevertheless, while Fox News has defined the outrage-industry genre, Donald Trump's presidency has spurred intense demand on cable news for outrage on the left. From 2016 to 2018, viewership of MSNBC doubled. When Americans were asked in 2018 about their news diets, almost as many reported having seen MSNBC (33 percent) as reported having seen Fox News (39 percent) in the prior month.[10]

News junkies who use social media rather than cable news have revealed a similar taste for outrage. The algorithms that govern our newsfeeds show us whatever content we will keep watching, sharing, and commenting on. Our demand for extreme and provocative content induces supply, a phenomenon that Facebook has finally acknowledged to be a serious problem on its platform. The more provocative the content, the more we tend to engage with it. At Facebook's scale, even Mark Zuckerberg has said this "can undermine the quality of public discourse."[11] Whereas on cable, it's conservatives who prefer to be in the outrage bubble of Fox, on social media it's liberals who prefer to be in ideological bubbles, unfriending people who convey political opinions they disagree with at higher rates than conservatives.[12]

Junkies who read newspapers have also revealed their penchant for outrage. In their research, Jeffrey Berry and Sarah Sobieraj looked at newspaper columns at three points in time: 1955, 1975, and 2009. In the first two periods, they found that columnists basically never resorted to name-calling and belittling. But suddenly, in their 2009 data, popular writers such as Charles Krauthammer and Maureen Dowd had emerged who regularly used this language.

Demand for outrage helps to explain the market for fake news that became a matter of national attention in 2016. In 2016, one in four Americans visited a fake news website, as discovered by a team of researchers who asked a sample of Americans to install software on their computers that tracked what websites they visited.[13] The researchers found that participants who were most interested in and most knowledgeable about politics consumed fake news the most. These people weren't easily duped by the lies of fake news stories. They were sophisticated consumers who sought the fake stories because they are junkies. After already reading through the comparatively tame world of real news, they wanted to up their dosage, and so they went for fantasies.

It isn't just extremes and outrage that attract us. We're also attracted to a seemingly infinite supply of news that serves no useful role to us as citizens. I have personally read articles in my newsfeed about Melania Trump's dresses, Paul Manafort's suits, Betsy Devos's houses, Donald Trump's meals, Hillary Clinton's flu, Paul Ryan's workouts, Alexandria Ocasio-Cortez's dance routines, Donald Trump Jr.'s intellect, Barack Obama's vacations, James Comey's opinions about Donald Trump's hands, and commentators' opinions about other commentators' opinions about tweets. None of this helps me be a better citizen.

The increased number of media choices has not only revealed that we demand outrage and celebrity political gossip, but that we do not demand news about our local communities.[14] The typical readers of this book may intensely follow the news yet not know the issues or candidates in local races. They might say they don't have enough information to know how to vote in local contests, and so they abstain in those elections. Thus even as they consume the news, the most basic *civic* reason for why anyone would consume the news (to know whom to vote for) does not explain why they are doing it.

Just from 1990 to 2014, regular newspaper readership and local television viewership plunged from over 70 percent to under 50 percent of the population. Online news consumption increased, but online readers opt for national news sources rather than local ones.[15]

The decline of local news consumption has multiple sources of blame.[16] Part of the story, for newspapers, anyway, is the loss of classified sections as a source of revenue. Part of the story are the economies of scale in national news distributed online. But another part of the story is simply that local news, however important, doesn't inspire the clicks and likes and shares that national news does. Local news is tiresome. It is especially tiresome for college-educated Americans. Among TV-news watchers, college-educated Americans say they get their news from national programs, whereas non-college-educated Americans get their news from local programs. According to a nationally representative survey from 2016, those with a degree were 58 percent more likely than those without a degree to say they get their TV news exclusively from national programs.[17] According to 2012 data from the Pew Research Center, while over 60 percent of daily-newspaper readers are not college educated and over 70 percent of local TV-news viewers are not college educated, a clear majority who say they are regular consumers of the *New York Times* or the *Wall Street Journal* have a college degree.[18] While some of these educated consumers are surely getting both national and local news, many simply skip the local stuff and read from sources that cater to the educated class interested in the national drama.

To the political hobbyist, news is a form of entertainment and needs to be fun. In the past, local news, even when not itself fun, was bundled with sports and weather and national scandals that drew us to local news broadcasts and local newspapers. We ended up learning about local politics accidentally, when we were waiting for the local station to tell us the weather report. Now that all of these separate items have been decoupled, our lack of interest in local news shines through. We have collectively shown that what's fun is the scandal in Washington that seems big today and will be replaced by another drama tomorrow. That's what keeps us coming back to cable news anchors and keeps training our newsfeeds.

CHAPTER 2

Staten Island, Staten Island, Take Me In

Empathy and Authenticity in Political Power

I n 2017, Lisa Mann was alone riding the subway in New York. Lisa is in her midfifties, an architect. She and her husband, who is also an architect, are in business together. The couple has two teenage sons, whom they raised in the Windsor Terrace and Park Slope neighborhoods of Brooklyn.

Lisa was hesitant to speak with me, not just about her subway ride, but about the political work she has done since then. She is reserved. She doesn't like to talk much about herself. Yet, she participates in a form of political activism that seems absolutely least conducive to her guarded personality. I wanted to understand her.

Lisa was riding the New York subway when two teenagers got on her train car. They approached a third teenager and started to taunt him aggressively. The third kid may have been developmentally disabled, Lisa first thought. The altercation felt ominous: something dangerous, something ugly, was going to happen, and as soon as the train pulled in to the next station and opened its doors, other riders quickly shuffled out to switch to another train car, away from the brewing fight.

Without thinking, Lisa stood up at the subway door near the teenagers and put her foot up against the sliding door, preventing it from closing, which prevented the train from moving on. "I let the door thud against my foot again and again and again," Lisa remembered, "more of a sensation than a sound."[1] What was she doing? Not escaping the car like the others. Not calling for the police. She just stood there, stopping the train from leaving the station. She inserted herself into the story of this brawl, changing the pace of this scene from dangerous and fast to dangerous and slow.

One of the "almost men," as Lisa called them, got in her face, stared her down. Lisa's mind went to a recent tragedy on a train in Oregon, where three riders intervened in an altercation. A man was harassing other riders. The men who tried to talk him down were stabbed, two of them to death. Lisa stood fast, resolutely, now eye to eye with the teenager. Their faces were inches apart and she could see that he was about the age of one of her sons.

Something about Donald Trump's election, which had shaken Lisa, made her want to be less anonymous, to take more responsibility, to intervene in her community. "I didn't want them to hurt each other. . . . Can we *please* stand down," she thought. The aggressors said to Lisa that the third boy had said something to them that made them mad. Lisa responded, "Do you think you could be the bigger person here? Can you be the bigger guy?"

The boys were surprised. They sat down. They stayed seated, keeping to themselves. A few stops later, they were still on the train when Lisa got off at her stop. As she passed them on her way out, she looked all three in the eye, as if to say, "*Please*. Don't hurt each other."

Intervening like this isn't natural. Diffusing a fight. Assuming responsibility, respectfully, for the children around you whom you don't know. It was hard for Lisa. She reflected about this experience in writing, in words she couldn't as easily say out loud. "It is time to be . . . very brave. Brave enough to speak with people we fear, to face the nuances of our bias, to recognize the frailty of humanity, and to forgive."

Lisa told me, "I really started feeling that if we are going to save our democracy, we all really need to work, to do hard things."

The way she does politics *is* hard. She doesn't do it because she loves it. She sees it as something she must do.

Before 2016, Lisa was a voter, read the newspaper, but otherwise practiced "benign pseudo-engagement," as she put it, sometimes dropping references to her friends about token political activity "as a kind of liberal currency." In other words, she was a hobbyist.[2]

After the 2016 election, she wanted to do in politics what she did on the train: intervene, participate, take responsibility. She found her way to a meeting in her Brooklyn neighborhood. Small activist groups were popping up, one focused on racial justice, one on protesting Trump's cabinet appointments, and others. Lisa volunteered with some of these groups for a while. By temperament, though, Lisa didn't like protests and shouting. She didn't like showing up confrontationally to the office of her member of Congress. She was more comfortable in one-on-one dialogue than in large groups. She also didn't have any good friends doing these activities with her. After a few months, she took a step back.

Then a close friend received an email about a new group forming called Changing the Conversation Together, founded by professional organizer Adam Barbanel-Fried. Adam had adopted a strategy called deep canvassing, in which volunteers usually undergo hours of training before they face voters. They don't just talk to likely supporters who need a mild nudge to show up on Election Day, which is the focus of normal canvassing. Volunteers talk to voters who are likely to oppose the volunteers' side or have strong misgivings about their side. The volunteers don't get into arguments with these voters. Instead, they focus on building mutual understanding, on listening and taking each person seriously. There's not a robotic script, no forced thirty-second conversation that both the canvasser and voter can't wait to run away from.

In training for deep canvassing, volunteers are asked to think of intimate stories from their personal lives. They share these stories at the doors of strangers to help to convey why they have reached the political conclusions they have reached and allow the strangers to open up about themselves in turn. Together, maybe the volunteer and the stranger can learn from each other.

Along with her friend, Lisa went to one of the first trainings that Adam led for this group. She is not one to share intimate details of her personal life with strangers, but here she was in training to do just that. "This was deeply uncomfortable," she said.

I talked to Lisa on the phone and to several others in Adam's group, but I wanted to see them in action. I made my way to Brooklyn to attend a training the group was hosting. Dave Fleischer, the organizer who is credited for inventing the strategy of deep canvassing, was in town from Los Angeles to speak to the group at the home of one of the regulars. I RSVP'd.

• • •

I arrive at the condo building on the edge of Prospect Park, in Park Slope, a liberal, wealthy neighborhood in Brooklyn. A doorman greets me. Upstairs, the apartment, and the event's hosts, are warm and unpretentious. Snacks are on the table. Folding chairs are set up in the living room between a comfortable deep couch, a scratched-up brown upright piano, and what looks like a broken television. Potted plants sit by the windowsill.

Around six o'clock, thirty people crowd into the living room. They are professionals, arriving from offices still dressed for work. They are almost all white, probably two-thirds women, and range in age from late twenties to late sixties. A couple of high school interns are also present. Lisa, now a leader in the group, introduces Dave Fleischer.

Dave stands up in the middle of the crowded living room. He has a shaved head, is sixty-three years old, looks younger. He's originally from Chillicothe, Ohio, and has been canvassing since he was fifteen, a professional organizer his whole adult life.

Dave's work with deep canvassing is a scientific breakthrough. At first, it was the subject of an unfortunate academic scandal. A researcher who published a paper about Dave's work earned a lot of publicity, but the researcher had faked the data. The study was retracted. Soon after, other researchers, political scientists at Stanford and Berkeley, orchestrated a new experiment. Some voters were subjected to a deep-canvassing conversation about transgender rights and some weren't. The placebo group was canvassed about recycling. Months after these conversations, voters who were subjected to deep canvassing still had significantly more pro-transgender views than the placebo group. Dave's technique is possibly the most successful mode of political persuasion ever measured.[3]

Dave is skeptical about how normal political campaigns work. Even though campaigns in the last twenty years have recruited volunteers to do door-to-door canvassing and phone banking, they do them in a mechanical way. The volunteers are given scripts and told not to deviate too much from them. For getting out the vote, a scripted reminder can increase participation by a couple of percentage points. Campaigns have not found as much success in using volunteer-based techniques for persuasion, durably changing voters' minds about how they should vote on issues or candidates.[4] Persuasion is hard, which is why campaigns mostly focus on turning out their base voters.

Sometimes, though, a campaign lacks sufficient supporters to just mobilize the base and win. Sometimes, the only choice is to persuade voters to join your side. Dave cares about those situations. Also, in deep canvassing, volunteers focus on being good listeners and on making a human connection to someone they might disagree with. They are emissaries from one party to another, looking for good-will. Dave doesn't just think deep canvassing is effective, I believe he thinks it is virtuous.

He stands up in the living room, and his workshop this evening feels like a religious space. The audience is rapt. Dave learns names, looks you in the eye. He is patient and kind and always trying to give everyone the benefit of the doubt. I think, as I sit watching him, that anyone from any political walk of life could come into this living room and feel connected to Dave's message. People would feel that they should, in their own lives, try harder to be a better listener and a more decent person.

Dave shares as an example one of his own stories that he tells voters at the door when he canvasses. He talks about his high school girlfriend. Dave knew he was gay from the time he was six. In high school, still in the closet, he had a girlfriend. Sometimes, he would suggest they have sex, knowing that she was committed to not having sex until marriage. He didn't want to have sex with her, but as a high schooler he thought, in his role as boyfriend, he should tell her he wanted to have sex with her. That he could always ask knowing she would always refuse was the perfect situation for him. Once, though, she didn't refuse. Dave panicked. He started making excuses for why they couldn't. Dave thought she must have felt terrible about this— why didn't her boyfriend want to have sex with her all of a sudden? Was something wrong with her? But he couldn't have sex with her because he wasn't attracted to women.

In this story, and in every story Dave tells to voters at the door, he is not the hero of the story. There is no hero. In this story, he presents himself as a jerk, even though the listener realizes how tricky this must have been for Dave in the early 1970s in high school. But, he says, he wasn't honest with his girlfriend. He hurt her feelings.

This story, like all of his stories, is also not a thinly veiled political parable. He's not telling a story to score points in an argument. He's telling about a bit of his life that has always stuck with him.

Dave tells these intimate details to make a connection that maybe the person at the door can, in some way, relate to. Maybe they connect to the idea that sexuality is complicated. That high school is complicated. That people make mistakes. That people hurt others whom they care about.

Dave has told this story while canvassing on behalf of abortion rights. He might say how the memory of the story helps him understand some of the complicated reasons why a woman may face the decision to have an abortion. What if Dave had had sex with his girlfriend and she got pregnant? He tells a stranger at the door that his pro-choice position comes from a place of respect for the people he loves. Dave hopes voters may reciprocate by thinking through how they arrived at their own position. Maybe if they think about it the way Dave does, they'll come around to his position. And maybe not, but even if not, he hopes they can understand him better than before.

The audience in the living room is transfixed by Dave's stories. Some are in tears.

Dave says, "You know what issue we're canvassing on? It's love. It sounds corny. We are showing voters love when we canvass. We're trying to teach them that voting is a gift we give people we love. We want to connect our love of our family and friends to policies we think support those who we love."

The language of love is foreign, almost off-putting. To many of us, it doesn't naturally mix well with politics. It reminded me of the religious language commonly used by leaders of the civil rights movement. I think of James Lawson, a civil rights hero who served as a mentor to the student protesters who staged sit-ins at white-only lunch counters. In 1960, groups of students gathered in Raleigh and started the Student Nonviolent Coordinating Committee. Lawson spoke. "Love," he said, "is the central motif of nonviolence. Love is the force by which God binds man to Himself and man to man. Such love goes to the extreme; it remains loving and forgiving even in the midst of hostility."[5] Dave is now orchestrating a system where door-to-door canvassers talk to their opponents with a message of love.

Everyone has questions for Dave. A woman who has been canvassing before, but never *deep* canvassing, says she tends to get angry when people disagree with her about politics. She asks Dave how she can tolerate it better. Another asks whether this technique, telling stories and building rapport, is manipulative. Another asks how to connect a personal story to a conclusion about politics. One is simply exasperated about how awkward it is to share personal details about one's life to a stranger. "Deep canvassing," Dave tells the assembled group with a smile, "is inherently socially awkward."

In the 2018 election, Lisa worked with the Changing the Conversation Together organization in New York's Eleventh Congressional District—covering Staten Island and a small portion of Brooklyn. The Eleventh District is the most conservative area of New York City, the only area of the city to have voted for Donald Trump and the only area, until 2018, with a Republican member of Congress. The Democratic candidate in 2018, a young decorated war veteran, Max Rose, won the race by five points, winning the Staten Island portion of the district by eleven hundred votes.

"I spent more time in Staten Island than I ever expected in my life," Lisa told me. During the 2018 election, she canvassed eighteen shifts on Staten Island, plus a couple of shifts in South Brooklyn. On weekends, volunteers from different parts of the city would carpool over the Verrazzano Bridge. Some took the ferry over from Manhattan. Forty or fifty volunteers would show up, twenty of whom were regulars such as Lisa.

"My stereotype of Staten Island," says Lisa, "was that it was very white, a combination of middle class and maybe more affluent, and deeply Republican." But she found this image changed over time. "In the neighborhoods we focused on, Staten Island was so mixed from one door to the next: about political persuasion, ethnic background, diversity of views, about everything. On a given street, from door to door, you didn't know who was the next person you were going to meet."

Sometimes, a volunteer could spend the morning in training, practicing telling a story and eager to open up to a stranger, and after a whole day of walking around would have had no transformational, inspiring conversations. "Even when it didn't work," says

26

Lisa, "there's something good about what we are doing." Another volunteer told me, "We talked to people who were raving Republicans and they didn't bite our heads off. We all [the volunteers and the strangers] walked away feeling better." By debriefing afterward, canvassers who had an unlucky day got to hear the good conversations that other people had had.

Lisa told stories at the door about her mother, about her Japanese American in-laws who had been interned during World War II, about her biracial children. Following Dave Fleischer's model, her stories aren't political parables nor does she play the role of hero protagonist. The stories are just ways to explain sincerely why the political climate is troubling to her, why she holds the views she holds. If Lisa went to a Trump supporter and told him that Trump is bad and the voter should vote against Trump, it wouldn't work. But she goes to the doors of Trump voters and says where she is coming from. Because she is sincere and respectful, some of these strangers will let her make her case.

Storytelling in deep canvassing is like Lisa's foot pushing against the subway door, preventing it from closing, slowing down the pace of the interaction to allow for space between people, a moment of humanity. She felt she made progress even when a Trump supporter didn't radically change his or her mind but might have thought, "Wow, you are a decent person. And you're a Democrat. I was scared to talk to you before. I thought you were going to yell at me."

One day, Lisa approaches a house. Her list says three registered voters are there, two older and one younger. She discovers the younger person lives with and is caretaker to his grandparents. At the house Lisa sees an old campaign sign for a Republican politician. In addition, something about the house, Lisa couldn't remember what, suggests to her that a military family lives here.

The young man opens the door and is unfailingly polite but "so unwilling to share anything with me." He keeps saying, "I don't talk about politics, I don't talk about politics." Lisa wants to convey to him how important his vote is in the upcoming 2018 election. For fifteen minutes they talk, he too respectful to end the conversation but quiet, she too persistent to cut off the conversation herself.

Off the cuff, Lisa tells him about a park near her home in Brooklyn that was recently renamed in memory of a veteran of the Iraq and Afghanistan Wars who was killed in Fallujah. She attended the dedication ceremony. Lisa has a personal connection to the ceremony: she and her husband had bought their home from the parents of this soldier soon after he was killed. "I raised my kids in that house." That dead soldier's childhood bedroom became her children's bedroom. The ceremony and park dedication were important to her.

As soon as Lisa tells the man this story, he, a veteran, opens up to her. "All of a sudden, he trusted me." He tells her that he always tries not to draw attention to himself. He tells her that he has found people don't react well to his opinions. He's half-Ecuadorean, in the military, in a home with grandparents who are staunch Republicans. Nonwhite friends of his, he tells Lisa, have had issues when wading into political conversations. So he keeps his profile low.

By the end of their conversation, they talk again about the importance of the election. "I felt absolutely confident that he would vote. And in fact he did. I followed up with him."

In the 2018 election, Lisa's group had deep-canvassing-style conversations with two thousand voters. The group's follow-up analysis suggests that voters they talked to were significantly more likely to vote, and to vote Democratic, than neighbors who weren't canvassed.

Lisa is good at canvassing not because she is eager to talk to anyone about politics. That's not her. She is good at it because she is resolute and honest. She would tell strangers at the door that she had come over from Brooklyn on a Saturday or Sunday to talk to them. If they suggested that someone from Brooklyn had no business on Staten Island, she might tell them, "[I] felt so strongly about the power of the vote in [your] district that it led me to leave my kids, their basketball game, their track meet, to talk to [you] about how important this is." Many of the days she canvassed, she would truly rather have been with her kids at their track meets. She told the voters that. They understood that this was important to her. Maybe they should give her a chance. She was so willing to respectfully give them the chance, maybe they could return the favor. More often than you might think, they did. She multiplied her vote, her democratic power.

CHAPTER 3

Rooting for the Team

Hobbyism and Partisanship

I live two miles from Fenway Park. On a beautiful summer night, there's no other place like Fenway, especially during a Red Sox–Yankees game. My kids are little, and I sometimes wonder about what I'll do when I take them to a Yankees game at Fenway. A couple of them are old enough to know that we love the Red Sox. They are not old enough to know that we hate the Yankees. They're certainly not old enough to know about people shouting "Yankees suck!" over and over at Fenway, a chant that has echoed through the park for most of my life.

I will someday have to explain to my children that this is all a joke. We don't mean it when we say we hate the Yankees. We don't actually hate Yankees players or fans. When we chant "Yankees suck," it's a friendly taunt. And, okay, yes, at Fenway, drunk people sometimes actually brawl about the Red Sox–Yankees rivalry. But we're not egging on these brawlers nor are we in any way responsible for their violence. They are just using the friendly rivalry as an excuse to do what they wanted to do anyway, which is fight. The rest of us are just having a good time being part of a crowd, rooting for our team.

As with rooting for a team, at the core of our political identity is partisanship. We are Democrats or Republicans. (Or we are independents who pretend not to align with a party but secretly and consistently support one party over the other; you know who you are.)[1] Nearly every way that we engage in politics, from voting to activism to debating with our friends and family, is colored by our identity as a Democrat or a Republican.

Sometimes, it seems as if Democrats and Republicans hate one another. Is it play hate, "Yankees suck" hate? Or is it real hate? The Pew Research Center reports that the other party makes us feel afraid. Many partisans think ordinary people in the other party, not just politicians, are closed-minded, immoral, dishonest, and lazy. About a third of each party thinks members of the other party are unusually unintelligent. About a third of members of each party say that if a new person moved into their neighborhood, they'd have a harder time getting along if they were from the other party. Survey respondents say they are less willing to socialize with, be friends and neighbors with, and marry members of the other party.[2] Some political scientists read survey evidence such as this and conclude that partisans *loathe* each other.[3]

People do sometimes lose friends over political disagreements. One activist I talked with, Krystle, had a colleague at work she was close with; they had lunch together every day. Krystle hated Donald Trump and knew the colleague liked him. In the midst of Trump's child-separation crisis at the southern US border, Krystle, upset, asked her friend, "How do you feel about this, as a Christian woman, children being taken away from their parents?" The friend shrugged it off and said that the parents shouldn't have brought their children to the border in the first place. Krystle felt the tension grow between them; she doesn't loathe her colleague, but the friendship deteriorated. Krystle has other friends, Republicans, some of whom voted for Trump, whom she has kept. But some friends, some family members even, she hasn't been able to keep close. With those broken relationships, partisanship doesn't feel like play animosity, like "Yankees suck" teamsmanship. It feels serious.

But step back from the heat of the Trump era. Step back to the Obama era, not so long ago. Then, too, survey researchers were measuring record-level feelings of partisan animosity toward ordinary people on the other side. When, in 2008, political scientists asked Americans if they would be upset if their son or daughter married someone of the other political party, 27 percent of Republicans and 20 percent of Democrats said they'd be upset. When the same question was asked forty-eight years earlier, in 1960, only 5 percent of either party's supporters said they'd be upset. That's a significant shift.

When Americans were asked in 2012 if they saw important differences between the two parties, 81 percent said they did. When the same question was asked forty-eight years earlier, in 1964, only 55 percent said they did. In hindsight, maybe the 2012 election between Barack Obama and Mitt Romney feels like nothing compared to the current political climate. But try to recall how you felt at the time. Maybe you felt it was the highest-stakes contest of your life. A lot of Democrats and Republicans genuinely felt that way. In 1964, the presidential candidates were Lyndon Johnson and Barry Goldwater, who were unquestionably more extreme in their policy differences than Obama and Romney.[4] Yet survey takers did not respond as if the stakes were as high. What changed?[5]

In part, what has changed is that Americans have started to treat political parties as they treat sports teams. When I identify as a Red Sox fan, it reflects a connection I have to the people who live in my area of the country. Yankees fans feel some geographic camaraderie around their team, too. While I would not think or say that New Yorkers suck, it's somehow quite easy for me to say that the Yankees suck. Once I decide to rally behind my team, I focus on the team identity rather than any underlying reasons for why I chose that team in the first place.

Increasingly, Americans look around at their social groups, at their racial and religious groups, and they see an alignment between those groups and a political party. Their party identity, in turn, helps them feel grounded, connected to their groups, and it gives them something to rally around.[6] They will say things and feel things about their team and its rival that they would not otherwise say or feel about the underlying groups. When answering surveys, they will offer responses to showcase their loyalty to their party. People who are otherwise intelligent will even suspend their commitment to the truth for the sake of the team.

Consider a moment from 2017, which made headlines at the time. President Trump's first press secretary, Sean Spicer, told the media that Trump's inauguration crowd was the biggest in history. Side-by-side photos comparing the attendees at Trump's inauguration with President Obama's inauguration show Trump's crowd to be a fraction of the size of Obama's.

Researchers showed the side-by-side pictures to a random sample of Americans and asked them a simple, factual question: Which of these pictures shows more people? Two percent of Clinton voters got the factual answer wrong. Eight times as many Trump voters (15 percent) got it wrong. Among Trump supporters, the ones with the *highest education levels* got it wrong the most often. It's not that these people couldn't grasp the truth. It's that they gave the answer that gratified them, regardless of the facts. The educated ones, who were more likely to be informed about Spicer's claims, knew what answer to give to cheer for their side.[7]

We see a similar phenomenon in sports. One famous example comes from a controversy surrounding the New England Patriots in 2015, called Deflategate. Star quarterback Tom Brady was suspected of being involved in an effort to deflate footballs to make them easier to grip. He was suspended for a few games. Researchers surveyed Patriots fans, and fans of other teams. Patriots fans reported that Brady was innocent. Everyone else thought he was guilty. Patriots fans were three times as likely to strongly believe that the NFL punished Brady "in order to distract people from the league's other problems."[8]

The difference between Patriots fans and nonfans was especially stark among fans who were the most interested and most knowledgeable about football. If people reached conclusions about Deflategate based on the facts, then those most aware of the facts should have been the ones most likely to agree with one another. The more informed people—the listeners to sports radio, the readers of sports commentary—should have seen eye to eye on what happened. But informed Patriots fans and informed fans of other teams were the least likely to agree.

When it comes to sports, we are fans first, not fact finders. Hardly anyone knows what actually happened in the scandal, but we don't need to know to take a side. As a Patriots fan, I am convinced enough of Tom Brady's innocence. It's not because I trust in Brady's personal integrity, but because the stakes are low enough that I don't care if I'm wrong. If taking my team's side feels good, that's all I need. In sports.

• • •

To showcase loyalty to one's team, partisans will not only report believing false claims, but otherwise kind people will say unkind words, just in the way that tens of thousands of people will put on a smile and shout "Yankees suck" at the top of their lungs. When Democrats and Republicans report on a survey that they hate the other side or that they'd be upset if their child married a member of the other political party, are they being serious? How do we know whether it's play hate or real hate?

That question led me to conduct a study in 2016. Using identical wording, I asked Democrats and Republicans how they feel about partisan intermarriage, and I also asked Red Sox and Yankees fans, and Phillies and Mets fans, how they would feel if their kid married a fan of their rivals.

If the record-high levels of Democrats and Republicans reporting they'd be upset about their kids marrying one another is due to a genuine level of partisan loathing, then Democrats and Republicans ought to express greater concern about partisan intermarriage than sports fans express about fan intermarriage. Except for a tiny number of extreme fans, sports allegiances couldn't possibly cause people to be genuinely upset about their child's marriage partner.

In a representative sample of the Northeast, almost 20 percent of Yankees fans said they'd be upset about their child marrying a Red Sox fan, the same percentage in this sample as Republicans who said they'd be upset about their child marrying a Democrat (more Democrats, 32 percent, in this Northeast sample said they'd be upset). Four times as many Yankees, Red Sox, Phillies, and Mets fans said they'd be upset about marriage to the opposite team than Democrats and Republicans reported in 1960.[9]

Red Sox and Yankees fans whine about their kids marrying their rivals almost as much as Democrats and Republicans do. That sports fans and political partisans whine at similar rates tells us that the survey respondents aren't being entirely truthful. In these surveys, people are mostly just shouting from the bleachers that the other side sucks.

Outside of surveys, we see little hatred between ordinary Democrats and Republicans. We may see tension at family reunions (in families that are politically engaged), but little hatred. Even in today's heated political arena, the norm against partisan animosity persists. It was tested in the summer of 2018. President Trump's press secretary at the time, Sarah Huckabee Sanders, was denied service at a Virginia restaurant because the restaurant owner thought the Trump administration is "inhumane and unethical."[10] From liberal members of Congress to Barack Obama's senior adviser David Axelrod to the *Washington Post*'s editorial board, leaders across the political spectrum came to Sarah Sanders's defense. Those who supported the restaurant owner[11] argued that denying service to a public official such as Sarah Sanders is acceptable, though denying service to ordinary people is not. Even the restaurateur's defenders acknowledged that ordinary Republicans and Democrats should not be subjected to partisan discrimination.

Political scientists have worried about partisanship spilling over into everyday life. When they perform real-world tests of partisan bias, they don't find much. A few years ago, two scholars collected essays about politics written by Democratic and Republican college students.[12] They then recruited Democratic and Republican teaching assistants to grade the papers but didn't tell them about the goals of the study. Did the Democratic and Republican graders favor or punish students in grading based on whether they were politically aligned or unaligned? No, there was no partisan bias in grading.

Knowing that Democrats and Republicans will say on surveys that partisans on the other side are unintelligent and lazy, another team of researchers investigated professional interviewers.[13] These people are hired by survey firms to conduct lengthy in-person interviews with voters. The researchers asked the interviewers what they personally thought about the respondents whom they'd just spent time with. When asked about the intelligence of the people they just talked to, or how hardworking they are, there were no partisan differences. Researchers have found some counterexamples, studies in which partisans favor in-partisans or punish out-partisans, but the evidence is much less convincing.[14] Overall, in real life, we don't shout at people, penalize them, or treat them badly because they support the other party.

Dave Fleischer, the deep-canvassing pioneer, offers a useful perspective on partisanship, very different from what we would surmise from surveys showing how much partisans loathe one another. Dave says that having knocked on many doors of Republican voters, he has often heard opinions he finds repugnant but rarely people he found repugnant. The people are so much better than their opinions, he says. He believes that voting for Trump was a terrible choice some people made, but that the Trump voters he talks to—and he talks to a lot of them—are so much more than that one choice they made. For Dave, and for many people who get out of their bubbles to connect with the other side, it's not uncommon to have strong negative feelings about policies and leaders while having generous feelings for the ordinary voters who empowered them.

If Dave was asked on a survey if he loathed ordinary people who call themselves Republicans—if he was asked if he thought they were stupid, immoral, closed-minded, lazy—I can't imagine him saying so. It's not that he doesn't see high stakes in elections. He sees very high stakes. But he approaches each voter as a person who is not defined by the votes he or she casts. You know what many voters are thinking in the voting booth? Dave asks. "How inadequate they feel about the task of voting. What are these offices? Who are these candidates?" That's what they're thinking about. You don't approach them with vitriol.

What's pathetic about partisan teamsmanship is that it is most prevalent among those of us who have the least need for it: the well-informed. Political parties are useful brands for voters who don't pay much attention to current affairs. If all that you care to know about politics is that the Democratic Party wants to use government to help people who have less and that the Republican Party wants to limit the power of government, then partisanship is a quick short-cut for one's political values. You might expect that less-informed citizens focus on cheerleading for their party and adopt their party's positions like automatons.

In fact, just as the most informed sports fans are the most committed to their teams, it is the news-following educated people who act like partisan automatons[15] and who think the voters on the other side are horrible.[16] Fandom is a central component of their political identity. They could enthusiastically lend their support to a party and its candidates without so much visceral emotion. They *could* talk to neighbors the way Dave Fleischer and Lisa Mann do, with an open heart. But if politics is a sport, then the only way worth watching it is as a fan embracing the rivalry. Rather than thinking of a neighbor as someone who needs to be treated with dignity if one hopes to convince him of anything, we treat him as a distant villain not worthy of our time. The less we talk to him and interact with him, the more we can preserve a lazy form of political engagement where we purport to loathe people we don't know.

CHAPTER 4

Precinct 206

Party Organizations and Political Power

Mecklenburg County is the largest county in North Carolina, with Charlotte at its center. The northern end of the county is considerably more Republican than Charlotte, and much whiter. It includes the communities of Huntersville and Cornelius, and at the northern edge of the county, sitting on the shore of Lake Norman, a small liberal enclave, the town of Davidson. Hillary Clinton won the 2016 vote in Davidson by thirty points. Every precinct adjacent to the town went for Trump. Davidson is home to Davidson College, an elite liberal arts school with just under two thousand students.

In January 2017, a meeting took place seven miles down the road from Davidson, in Huntersville. An organization called the Democrats of North Mecklenburg was founded there in early 2016 by local activists. Until the Trump victory, it was a relatively small organization. But then people started showing up to see how they could get involved. This meeting in January 2017 was meant to showcase volunteer opportunities right at the time when the Trump administration was beginning to govern.

The Dems of North Meck, as they are sometimes called, invited Drew Kromer to give a presentation. Drew was a sophomore at Davidson College, who grew up in South Charlotte, forty minutes south of Davidson. From the time he was in high school, Drew was a political junkie. He volunteered on campaigns and got to know local Democratic leaders. If that's all you knew about him, you might think that he'd be the stereotypical political science student—he knows a lot of political facts, maybe harbors political aspirations, the kind of person who might lead a College Democrats or College Republicans chapter. I see students like that in my classes.

Drew came to speak to the Dems of North Meck about something specific: starting precinct organizations as affiliated groups with the state Democratic Party. In a competitive area such as North Meck, Drew said, volunteers should focus not on one-off events and independent organizations, but on building sustainable Democratic committees. If folks start these groups within the structure of the Democratic Party, they get resources from the party that they couldn't otherwise get, such as access to the national Democrats' voter database and computer system, which the state party pays for and shares with its local affiliates. Plus, a sustained organization gives volunteers time to meet neighbors and form deeper relationships with voters than they otherwise could do from one-off volunteering.

In several respects, this was a strange pitch. Drew was a college student and unlikely to stay in any precinct long enough to follow his own advice in the near term. The organization he was speaking to was not part of the Democratic Party's official structure, but an independent group. Maybe the group would be skeptical of ceding independence and becoming a formal affiliate of the party. Also, a lot of people whom Drew respected in North Carolina Democratic politics had advised him against getting involved in the party. One leader called the party organization "a building that had burned to the ground." He told Drew the party is feckless, tired, and can't get anything done. But Drew thought he saw an opportunity.

Drew's speech piqued the interest of a professor at Davidson who was in attendance: Greg Snyder, chair of the religion department, a twenty-year veteran of the school. He teaches such classes as Introduction to the New Testament, Jesus and His Interpreters, and Letters and Thoughts of Paul. "Drew was talking about precinct organizing," Greg told me. "I heard Drew talking about it and it clicked for me."

Greg joined Drew and next did something that not many people would have thought to do or known they could do. They formally organized a precinct as a committee of the state Democratic Party. "We got five people in a room. We had a chair, a treasurer, and a secretary." Eventually, the group would have to post a notice and hold elections for their new organization, following rules stipulated by the bylaws of the state party, but at first, few people knew or cared they existed.

"I went through the official process to be the official organization. And no one was doing that before so we could just do it," Drew explains matter-of-factly. "I had a conversation with the chair of the county party. I love to read the rules and know the rules. So I read the forty-page document outlining how to do this. You get to understand how the power flows from the state party down to the voters."

I asked Drew why he was so focused on the rules, on the formal structure. Most precincts in the county that Drew knew of did basically nothing. They got five people together, assigned roles (chair, treasurer), and that was it. Why was he trying to replicate that? "I wanted to create something," he said. "But . . . I knew quickly it didn't mean anything if we didn't do something with it. . . . While the party organization provided structure, it might not provide power."

Most formal precincts, he tells me, "don't do anything except the minimum to get a comical amount of power." The precinct chairs in Mecklenburg County become members of the county executive committee for the party. Maybe they like the title. Maybe they like to go to meetings. Maybe they aspire to move from the rank of precinct chair to the rank of county chair. "The most impressive thing a county chair does is take interviews by newspapers," Drew tells me. "The papers still don't know that the county party doesn't do anything."

Greg, the religion professor, and now treasurer of this nascent precinct organization, took the group a step further. "We wanted to become a recognized entity where we could solicit funds and spend money." Typically, precincts are just part of the county party. They have no money themselves. "I applied to the state to get an Employer Identification Number. I got recognition from the state to set up a bank account." Keep in mind, this is a *precinct* committee; precincts are small, like neighborhoods. But this one, Precinct 206 in Mecklenburg County, wanted its own bank account.

The main thing they imagined doing with money was eventually hiring their own organizer. Greg and Drew never liked how state or national campaigns swoop into North Carolina towns such as theirs with organizers right before an election and then leave right after. Greg said, "All these groups come in with their data and their people, and then they're gone. There's no structure to support emerging candidates, to keep the conversation going. . . . We need a persistent organization on the ground between elections."

Having obtained his Employer Identification Number, Greg tried to open the bank account. He didn't really know what he was doing. "I'm a religion professor. What do I know about accounting or anything like that? I walked into a bank on Main Street. They seemed confused. I went to another bank. They accepted the ID number." And that was that.

I asked why Greg and Drew didn't just join with the Dems of North Meck and work with the existing organization down in Huntersville. In addition to the benefits the precinct organization got from being an official party affiliate, such as access to the voter database, they had other reasons to focus on a precinct committee in Davidson. Greg and Drew wanted to get the students at Davidson College involved in politics beyond the campus. The Dems of North Meck met monthly, seven miles away in Huntersville, a distance that would pose a barrier for the students.

Many College Democrats and College Republicans clubs, not just at Davidson, are "kind of insular pizza-eating clubs," Greg says. They host forums, debates, discussions, all on campus, away from the political world around them. And they order pizza. And these are some of the most engaged students on campus. Greg and Drew thought a local precinct organization with students in leadership positions could draw students in a way that existing political organizations could not.

Other groups around Davidson formed after the Trump elections, groups focused largely on protesting the Trump administration. Drew and Greg didn't want to go that route, either. They wanted to focus on state legislative, even municipal, elections, in which a neighborhood organization could have an impact.

"We don't talk much about Trump," Drew says. "The arguments we find most effective are advocating for basic fairness in voting, gerrymandering, and the racial dimension of it. When I make a pitch . . . I talk about democracy here in North Carolina." Drew's approach is local, but in North Carolina, it's easy to see the connection between local, state, and national politics. The state legislature, for instance, plays an important role in determining polling places, voter ID laws, and gerrymandering. "It's all connected," Drew says.

Almost immediately, the Precinct 206 Democrats had a following. They had built-in constituencies of students, whom Drew brought in, and community members, whom Greg recruited. Almost immediately, a turf battle ensued with the older guard of the town's Democrats. That battle soon reached a dramatic crescendo in what the students call the Massacre on the Green.

Here's how it went down.

Drew formally organized a precinct that wasn't organized. But the old guard of activists in the town thought this was their territory and that they should have been involved, as Drew explains it. Some seemed to think that these transient students, obviously not homeowners in Davidson, shouldn't be in charge of a precinct committee, even though the committee wasn't active with anyone before. "People think zero-sum. That's why other groups feel threatened. But it's not like that. We're creating . . . new activists." Greg and Drew said they wanted to work alongside other groups, and nobody was doing what they were doing, so why not?

Complying with state party rules, the Precinct 206 committee needed to have an official election of officers, just a couple months after they formally created themselves with the initial group of five. For $20, they rented a room in the town's public library, which sits beside the quaint town green, surrounded by charming shops and cafés and a Presbyterian church. Per the rules, they publicly posted the time and place of the election.

According to Greg and Drew, a leader of the old guard quietly recruited friends to stage a coup. The leader planned to bring ten, maybe twenty, people to the meeting. For the election of precinct chair, Drew might have the support of the four other people who showed up to the first organizational meeting. But now the old guard could reassert control. They could vote in one of their own as chair.

It's a small town. Greg and Drew caught wind of the coup. Drew brought forty students with him. The two groups of activists arrived at the library as it was getting dark. Ominously, the library suddenly lost its power, so they needed to meet somewhere else. They walked out onto the town green beside the library. Drew quickly got some chairs from his nearby fraternity house. They set up on a platform on the green. Two opposing factions met in the darkened public green of a small North Carolina town.

The old guard stood in the back and "made a scene the whole time," Drew says. "Some of [them] struck me as Trumpian. They were aggressive. They got in people's faces. One of them told a kid who was of Colombian origins, but a US citizen, that he shouldn't vote." One of the college students made a comment about the "gray hairs" in the back of the crowd. Drew made the student apologize.

The Massacre on the Green was tense but its conclusion was foregone. Drew had rallied more people than the old guard. His term as chair of an organization that had structure, but no power, a hollow party as scholars would call it,[1] was secure.

This fight between old-guard activists and new activists is reminiscent of the tensions between "amateur" Democrats and "regular" Democrats in the 1950s. At that time, the regulars controlled the political process in many cities and were motivated by the desire to stay in power. The amateurs were issues-oriented newcomers. In Drew's story, it would be a mistake to think of the old guard as the regulars and to think of Drew and Greg as the amateurs. In many communities, the current old guard in local party politics is more like the amateurs, in that they are not actively working to court votes and control offices. Rather, they tend to be more like amateur social clubs, possessing, as Drew put it, "a comical amount of power." Unlike the amateurs of the 1950s, Drew and Greg are not focused on issues and ideological purity, but on taking the reins so they can use the party apparatus to get power for their political side.[2]

The Precinct 206 Democrats got their feet wet with a local, nonpartisan election in the fall of 2017. They practiced using the voter registration database, organizing and training volunteers for canvassing. They put together a voter guide and invited all the local candidates, even independents and Republicans, to send in a picture and a brief statement. The voter guide raised eyebrows among the old-guard Democrats. Why was a Democratic organization giving free press to

Republicans who were running for these nonpartisan offices? Greg says, "We believed in conveying an open attitude. A lot of volunteers who came to the group came as unaffiliated voters. And they came because we were more expansive in our vision." The precinct committee grew.

During the 2018 election season, twenty to fifty people, students and a growing number of community members, would attend monthly meetings. At the meetings, they'd plan the next events. They'd debrief about the last ones. They'd solicit ideas for how to do better. Drew gave educational presentations. He once lectured about how the elected judicial system of North Carolina works.

At the end of the meetings, the group served tea and cookies. "It helps to have something," Drew says. "It helps people linger after and socialize." For some retirees, Precinct 206 has become their primary social network. "This group serves a really important social role in the lives of our members." People send Drew notes saying they've met more friends in this town in the last year than in the previous twenty.

Canvassing for voter turnout is the group's bread and butter, but they also put on huge events for a precinct committee, such as a forum for mayoral candidates attended by two hundred people. Another event, sort of a rally, a state senator called "the Woodstock of precinct organizing." Seven hundred residents of Davidson showed up.

Christy Clark, a 2018 Democratic candidate for state representative in North Mecklenburg, was not considered by the state Democratic Party to stand a chance at winning. In 2016, the Republican candidate in the district won by six thousand out of about forty-five thousand votes cast. The state party maintained a ranking of candidates, prioritizing those it would financially support in 2018, and Clark just didn't have enough of a chance to get funding from the state party, according to Drew.

Drew learned of a way to help convince the state party that Clark was a viable candidate. Clark had raised about $40,000 on her own. Under Drew's leadership, Precinct 206 held an event and got her another $8,000 or $9,000. As Clark was hard at work convincing the party and the electorate that she was a viable candidate, this influx of grassroots financial support was a significant boost. It moved her up the rankings in the state party's tabulation, which triggered the state party to throw in a whopping $680,000. Money, plus a lot of canvassing work by Precinct 206, by other groups in the district, and by the candidate herself, launched Christy Clark into the legislature, winning a Republican area by 415 votes.

The group's successes extend beyond electoral victories. The committee has also worked to bridge racial divides in Davidson. Out of six thousand registered voters, about five hundred are black and live in a poorer area divided by railroad tracks from the wealthier area of town that contains the college and town green. The black voters make up 15 percent of the registered Democrats.

Greg says that the feeling on the black side of town has long been that white people only come by during elections, to ask for votes. The precinct group wanted to change that. "We're not just some group that would like to have diversity," Greg tells me. "[The Democratic precinct committee] represent[s] these people, too." Greg says he's spent more time on the other side of town in the last five months than in the previous nineteen years. Black and white residents are meeting each other. White residents are learning about some of the challenges black residents face that the whites weren't previously aware of, such as how uncomfortable black residents sometimes feel while shopping in the town's stores.

Interracial programs didn't have much success in other community organizations. Greg mentions that the two Presbyterian churches in town are mostly divided by race. The churches differ in worship style and philosophy and there isn't much interaction, even though you might assume there'd be opportunities for collaboration. The precinct Democratic group, Greg says, "doesn't start with those built-in divisions."

Precinct 206 hosted an event on the black side of town the likes of which hadn't before been seen. A picnic barbecue on a beautiful day in a park on the other side of the tracks. A band played. Face painting for the children. Dozens of people showed up, half white, half black. A black pastor has since become involved in the leadership of the precinct committee.

In December 2018, the precinct organization hosted a Christmas party at one of the wealthier, white homes. Five or six African Americans from other side of town came to the party. "That's a huge accomplishment for us," Drew says. "That would never happen before, anyone coming across the train tracks for a Christmas party. It might not seem like a huge achievement to you, but given the history in this town, this was a big deal for us."

Through his work, Drew has raised his profile in the state. He's now on the invite list to the governor's Christmas party. He has shown the rest of the state how to take the formal structure of a party and actually infuse it with political power. That's pretty good for a twenty-two-year-old with political ambition. He has proven himself in a way that's exceptional for a college student—for anyone.

What's going to happen to the precinct committee now that Drew has graduated? The organizers are mostly not students anymore, and the more permanent residents are taking the lead. But Drew wants students to stay involved. He's thinking through the rules—the institutional design—to help encourage them. He made a rule that the president of the College Democrats club automatically has a seat on the board of the precinct committee. If he can set a new norm in the student Democratic group, then within a year or two, students might come to assume that the student group and the community group have a long-standing relationship. Even though students come and go every four years, plenty of campus organizations, from fraternities to a cappella groups, have traditions of group participation that are passed down, one four-year generation of students to the next. Maybe the involvement of student Democrats in the local precinct can be a tradition passed down, and students can make a difference off campus, building—and deploying—their power.

CHAPTER 5

Voting, or Not

Hobbyism and Elections

I f surveys are to be believed, Americans love voting. On surveys many more people report that it's a duty to always vote (90 percent) than report that it's a duty for adult children to take care of their elderly parents (74 percent).[1] If you ask Americans what political activities they enjoy, by far the most say voting. I asked about this recently on a survey. About 50 percent of Americans say they *enjoy* voting in *local* elections, many more than who say they enjoy watching presidential debates or following campaign news. They also say they participate in voting more than any other form of politics. Three in four say they vote in presidential elections. Two in three say they vote in local elections.

Sadly, when it comes to voting, surveys cannot be believed. One of the first studies I ever conducted as a political scientist was called a validation study.[2] Whether a person votes in the United States is a public record. Along with my graduate adviser, I linked several national surveys to public records of who actually voted. We first asked people on the survey if they voted. Then we validated their answers with the government. We discovered that up to 50 percent of confirmed nonvoters say that they had voted in a recent election. Incidentally, almost none who are validated in the public records as having actually voted say that they didn't vote. All the "misremembering" (aka lying) is among those who didn't vote but say they did.

What kind of person lies about voting? People who are well educated and who profess an interest in politics. If you think of yourself as a person who likes politics and ought to vote, you tend to say on surveys you voted even when you didn't. Based on surveys, college graduates appear 20 percentage points more likely to vote than non-college grads. But half of that difference is attributable to nonvoting college grads lying on the surveys.

In spite of all the professed interest and engagement in elections, electoral participation is low. In the 2014 federal election, participation dropped to 36 percent of eligible citizens, the lowest since the 1940s. It spiked in the 2018 federal election, a point we'll return to later. In local elections, turnout is often below 20 percent.[3] For offices such as school board, turnout can dip into single digits.

If we articulate such a strong belief in voting, why is participation so low, particularly in local elections? A first reaction might be that lower-tiered elections have low turnout compared to presidential elections because they are uncompetitive. But that's incorrect. An uncompetitive race for president draws higher turnout than a competitive race for governor or senator. An uncompetitive race for governor or senator draws higher turnout than a competitive local race.

In Massachusetts, as an example, in 2008, Barack Obama beat John McCain by twenty-five points. The race was never expected to be close. Yet three in four registered voters cast a ballot. Just fourteen months later, the state saw a tense special election for the US Senate. Stakes were high. At the time, Democrats held sixty votes in the Senate, enough to prevent a filibuster from Republicans. Compared to the presidential blowout in the state, the vote mattered in the special election. But turnout dropped twenty percentage points, and it fell especially steeply in Democratic areas.[4] The Republican, Scott Brown, won the race.

If turnout isn't driven mainly by competition, maybe it's driven by the media. Turnout is low, so goes this explanation, because the lower-tiered races get so much less media attention than the presidential race. This mistakes a symptom for a cause. State and local elections generally feature noncelebrity politicians competing with one another over sensible policy differences dealing with the practicalities of running a government. Yawn. There are often televised debates for state elections, but few people watch them. There are often points of conflict and drama, but most people aren't interested in them. News follows demand, and for local elections demand is low.

The real explanation for the dynamics of voter turnout is that we treat politics like a game and follow the spectacle. Turnout is high in presidential elections compared to other US elections in the same way that football viewership is high when the Super Bowl is on. Many people who do not like football or even know the rules of the game end up at a Super Bowl party. They're there for the commercials, the guacamole, and to be part of a cultural moment. That's why turnout is high in presidential elections. Without the spectacle, even people who say they care about voting don't show up.

In the fall of 2016, when I taught my regular college course on US elections, I noticed something was different from when I taught the same course four years earlier. As the November election approached back in 2012, several students told me that they were missing a class here and there to go canvassing for President Obama's reelection campaign. In 2016, not a single student missed a class to canvass for Hillary Clinton. On the other hand, the class in 2016 was committed to their election-night parties. They gathered in dorms, bought liquor, and projected cable news on the wall. I later saw a pin with a slogan that perfectly captured the feeling on the political left leading up to the 2016 election: I BELIEVE THAT SHE WILL WIN. The slogan does not implore anyone to vote or to help. It just says to believe. That's what my students believed. At the next class meeting, several of them cried through the lecture.

Why did so many students volunteer for the Obama campaign but not the Clinton campaign? With Obama, the students had a candidate who was exciting, young, dynamic, especially compared to his competitor Mitt Romney. With Clinton, Democrats believed they had a candidate who stood between Donald Trump and the White House, but not someone as fun to support as Obama. And so they didn't. If voting is about supporting someone you think is fun, then 2016 just wasn't fun for Democrats. It was only fun for Republicans.

If you were a twenty-year-old Democrat in 2016, it might be hard to take this point, as I have learned from my students. Maybe you didn't go all out for Hillary Clinton. But at the same time, you don't have much memory of the political conditions in 2008 (when you were twelve), nor did you actively engage in the 2012 election (when you were sixteen). You came of age around the Trump-Clinton race. Are you the kind of person who would have gone knocking on doors (and gone voting) for Obama even though you didn't do this for Clinton? If nearly your whole college was enthusiastic about Obama and planning bus trips to swing states and phone banks and letter campaigns, you might have joined in. But few people around you were doing that in 2016 and so you didn't, either. And the reason you didn't, and others didn't as well, is that the candidate in 2016 just wasn't as exciting and dynamic and inspiring as the candidate in 2008 and 2012.[5] Through most of the fall 2016 campaign, the youngest voters—specifically those who were not yet eligible to vote by the 2008 election—were, according to polls, far less enthusiastic about the Democratic candidate and Democratic Party than those who came of age during the early Obama years.[6]

For some political junkies, the biggest spectacle is not even the presidential general election. If you love the game of politics, nothing beats months of live debates followed by a season of Tuesday-night state-by-state showdowns that constitute the modern presidential primary.

Most democracies do not have primaries such as ours, in which ordinary voters vet candidates for their party's endorsement. We have only had this system since 1972. Before that, as in other countries, political insiders had a strong say in which candidate ran as the endorsed candidate of their party. In our current system, candidates are not vetted at all by party leaders. They are only vetted by primary voters.

Without much reflection, this sounds like a good idea—the process should be open to all. However, in the decades since the primary reforms, we have heard warnings of the dangers of our system. Nelson Polsby, a political scientist, wrote back in the 1980s that not only are primary voters completely unrepresentative of the electorate in general, primary voters also lack the ability to engage in "peer review," to judge candidates for the presidency on their "intelligence, sobriety of judgment, intellectual flexibility, ability to work well with others, willingness to learn from experience, detailed personal knowledge of government, and other personal characteristics that can best be revealed *through personal acquaintance*" (my emphasis).[7] There is value, according to Polsby, in senators and governors working with one another and learning each other's styles, learning who is equipped to be president.[8] They should have a say in vetting candidates for the party nomination.

Without the input of a party's leaders, primary voters could be seduced by inexperienced celebrities and demagogues, Polsby warned in the eighties, and not because the voters are incompetent but because they get sucked into the sport of politics. If voters are making decisions based on who's best at making speeches, who has the best zingers, who makes the most outrageous promises he or she can't keep, we might not be making good decisions. That's why Polsby and other experts thought we should not choose candidates through a nomination system that looks like a reality show, with state-by-state battles in which losing candidates drop out one at a time; with TV networks keeping voters engaged by hosting a dozen debates; with postdebate spin rooms giving the spoils to candidates who are the most aggressive and offer the most stinging rebukes. The primary system we have is perfectly designed to delight the political junkie, by creating valuable media events, and poorly designed for vetting future presidents.

But for political hobbyists, the spectacle is captivating. As Donald Trump often noted on the campaign trail in 2016, his presence—crude and unhinged—drew record audiences for televised primary debates. Did you catch one of those in 2016? You probably did. How about the respectful and very hinged debate in the last gubernatorial election in your state? Did you miss that one?

CHAPTER 6

Voice of Westmoreland

Protest, Community Building,

and Political Power

I f you spent some time with her, you'd quickly surmise that should
you ever end up in a hospital, you'd be lucky to have Angela
Aldous as your nurse. She is compassionate and funny and full of
energy. She has a great Wisconsin accent. She had worked as a nurse
at the University of Wisconsin hospital system in Madison. Then her
husband got a job in Greensburg, Pennsylvania, and she moved away.

During the 2016 election season, she mostly stayed at home in
Greensburg, quietly following the news. *PBS NewsHour*, FiveThirty-
Eight, and RealClearPolitics were the preferred outlets. The couple
had two girls, and during the fall of 2016, Angela was mostly home
with them, one two years old, one newborn.

Angela says she's an introvert, but she had a story to tell. In 2010,
then in her twenties, with no kids, working full-time at that hospital in Wisconsin, Angela was diagnosed with multiple sclerosis. Her
labor union, the SEIU, was instrumental in getting her the time off
she needed to manage her care. She was out for three months before
she could return to work. The next year, newly elected Wisconsin
governor Scott Walker planned to do away with collective bargaining for public sector unions. Angela knew she had been able to keep
her job after such a long time off because of her union. Now the
SEIU needed her help.

For over a month, Angela joined in protests in the state capitol in the morning and then went to work a 3:00 p.m.–midnight shift at the hospital. While protesting, she told her story to show why the union mattered to her. She told other people's stories, too, about how the union helped fight for them, for the safety of nurses administering chemotherapy who were exposed to toxic chemicals, for the safety of patients put at risk because of mandatory overtime nursing shifts.

On February 26, 2011, a Saturday protest in Madison drew somewhere between seventy thousand and one hundred thousand people. Surrounded by coworkers, firefighters, police officers, other union workers, and many supporters, Angela felt the energy of the crowd. Angela—the introvert, the newly diagnosed MS patient who not long before couldn't come to work because her right leg stopped working and her vision was impaired—took the stage.

Snow was falling, accumulating on her red poncho, her long hair half-covered under a winter cap. She wore props—purple hospital gloves on her hands and a stethoscope dangling around her neck. She spoke on behalf of the nurses. With a big grin, she asked the crowd if they'd like to have a catheter inserted by a nurse who was forced to work a sixteen-hour-plus shift due to the mandatory overtime. "Trust me, guys," she said in her Wisconsin don't-ya-know accent, "ya don't."[1] The crowd loved her.

But then she moved to Greensburg, Westmoreland County, a place unlike the liberal enclave of Madison. The county gave Trump a thirty-point victory over Clinton in 2016. When she moved, Angela was still a nurse but no longer in a union. She worked shifts in a hospice facility in Pittsburgh and no longer received emails from the SEIU with political updates.

She followed the 2016 election campaign, watched the online polls showing Clinton would be a shoo-in, juxtaposed with all those Trump supporters around the county, and she queasily remembered back to the Wisconsin protests. The protests that she was so committed to ended in defeat for her. The camaraderie of the initial months of anti-Walker mobilization felt inspiring to Angela. Energized, she and other volunteers worked to get petitions signed to recall the governor. By January 2012, the organizers had collected almost a million signatures, which triggered a recall election in June. But the energy dissipated after the protests morphed into an election. Tens of thousands of people showed up to protests, but once the canvassing for signatures and then canvassing for votes began, volunteers stayed home.

"We thought we were going to win," Angela tells me, "but we never really built anything long-lasting." Maybe the organizers overreached. Maybe a recall election was the wrong strategic move. But, Angela wonders, what happened to all those union workers and supporters who were so angry at Walker? Why didn't they care enough to knock on doors? Why didn't they want to do something that would mean real change for the policies they cared about? Those who had been knocking on doors, such as Angela, watched in shock when Walker won the recall election by six points. "We had our 2016 moment a few years before 2016," Angela tells me.

On the day of President Trump's inauguration, in January 2017, Angela looked at her daughters and felt that she needed to find a way to do something. "I'm so lucky," she tells me in a quiet voice, her baby crying in the background of our conversation. "I have this shitty disease, but I have the medicine I need. I have privileges, so I have an obligation. This is a time in history people are going to read [about] in history books. My kids are going to read about it. For a lot of us, we don't want to look back at the end of our lives and say we did nothing."

On Inauguration Day, Angela could have used a glass of wine. Since she was nursing, instead she downed an entire container of Oreos. Then she started a journal.

Inauguration Day was day one. For 1,461 days, the entirety of a presidential term, she planned to write down one thing she did each day to make a difference. In recalling the beginnings of this, she blushes at how small some of those first entries were. Getting two kids dressed and out the door, over to the post office to buy stamps, which she'd later use to send postcards to voters—the post office trip was an accomplishment for a day. On one night, at 10:30 p.m., it was time to write in her journal, but she hadn't yet done anything that day. So late at night, she called the office of her Republican congressman to—I would guess respectfully, Wisconsin-ly, hopelessly—complain on the voice-mail service. She logged it in her journal.

At this time, Angela had few friends in Westmoreland County.

She was still new to town. She had just had two kids in quick succession. She was making friends with other hospice nurses, but the facility where she worked was all the way in Pittsburgh, thirty miles away. She worked there per diem on the weekends, when her husband would stay with the kids. On weekdays, she was with the kids in Greensburg.

In Pittsburgh, people her age were organizing in activist groups that were, at the time, largely focused on protests. She joined them a few times, but she had mixed feelings about it. It was good to see people who cared and were excited to be involved. But the focus on protests reminded her too much of what hadn't worked in Wisconsin. "Constantly calling or standing outside your congressman's office or the Women's March, is that long-lasting? They have funny signs, but so what? I saw that in Wisconsin. That stuff doesn't work."[2]

Westmoreland County felt isolated, different from Pittsburgh or Madison. This is a 95 percent white enclave, once a union area, but now deeply conservative. Early in Trump's term, winter 2017, when protesters in liberal areas were flooding airports in opposition to the president's ban on Muslim travelers, Westmoreland County's mood felt to Angela like cold indifference.

At the height of Trump's Muslim ban, Angela was in the car with her children, in the center of Greensburg just a few blocks from her home. In the center of town is the Westmoreland County Courthouse, a large, gray, imposing, domed, circa-1900 building with statues honoring justice on top and memorializing Civil War heroes below. A public plaza at the footsteps of the courthouse bustles during the day with workers on break. Jurors coming in for jury duty or lawyers preparing for court may sit at the outdoor tables or lean against the raised flower beds and scroll through their phones.

As Angela drove past, she saw a small group in the court plaza holding a sign in protest of the Muslim ban. Seeing them, she started to cry. In Pittsburgh, maybe this kind of protest would have felt less useful to her, like preaching to the choir. But driving through Trump territory in Westmoreland, she finally saw this group, an oasis, who cared as she cared. She was overcome with emotion. She stopped and thanked them and offered to buy them all coffee to warm them up from the cold.

From this brief interaction, introductions were made, contact information was shared, and a new group was formed: a community organization to support progressive causes and candidates in Trump country. Six volunteers sitting around a kitchen table beginning in April 2017. An empty-nester, stay-at-home mom. A retired Catholic schoolteacher. A former lawyer, now in her fifties, heading back to school to go into nursing. Another attorney in his fifties. A recent college grad. And Angela.

The group started small, and from the beginning their priority was to have a long view of change. "In this area," Angela told me, "I knew we would lose most elections for many years. We could make gains and we'd still lose. But I wanted to build something sustainable that would survive when we lost elections."

The group started by learning. They found videos posted by graduate students at Harvard, a training program called the Resistance School. Experts gave lectures about how to organize, hold meetings, recruit others, knock on doors. Angela's group watched the videos together and took notes. Organizations in Pittsburgh—the Sierra Club and a nonprofit umbrella group called Pittsburgh United—helped train them more. They chose a name for themselves—Voice of Westmoreland, VOW for short, pronounced "vow," like the word, like an oath—that would be welcoming to skeptical neighbors who would have shut off conversation at words such as *resistance*, that would be welcoming to people such as the evangelical man with the glass of wine who showed up to one of those monthly meetings in 2019.

The group was conscious about what could work in this conservative area. They couldn't focus just on elections but instead needed to focus on issues. They felt they could have better conversations with voters about gerrymandering and the environment, and especially about health care, than they could about Trump and electoral politics. Plus, a focus on issues would sustain their energy during the lulls between elections.

VOW held protests, but only as deliberate tools to recruit other volunteers. Angela comes back to those memories of Wisconsin rallies. "You need to have conversations with people who aren't already convinced. At rallies, you might think you're drawing attention, but your snarky signs aren't going to persuade anyone." But in an area where liberals were in hiding, lonely at home and in church, demonstrations served the specific purpose of recruitment. Angela and her team would stand in that plaza next to the court, her kids in a carrier and in a stroller, and new allies would approach them, just like how the first small group found Angela in the same plaza. Between the heckling yells from afar of "Build that fucking wall!" a few people would come over and write down their contact information. They would start coming to monthly meetings. The VOW contact list started to grow.

Angela knew about the power of her story from her experience in Wisconsin. Now in 2017, when the federal government was on the brink of dismantling Obamacare, Angela talked about her MS again. She talked openly about the medicine she took, how it cost $7,000 a month, how she needed MRIs and frequent care. Without insurance, she would be incapacitated and impoverished. More supporters joined. From six to forty.

Angela learned about organizing. In addition to the video tutorials and outside organizers who came to Greensburg, she went to a training conference in Harrisburg for new Pennsylvania leaders. She participated in a "resistance" program put on by MoveOn. She and another VOW leader would learn about a strategy and would then teach what they learned to a group of twelve who showed up back in Westmoreland.

Just as VOW was getting off the ground, an opportunity dropped in their laps. The local congressman, Republican Tim Murphy, who had been in office since 2003, was caught having an affair.[3] Text messages revealed that this antiabortion legislator had asked his extramarital partner to have an abortion. He resigned from office in the fall of 2017. A special election was called. VOW got volunteers to knock on doors in their ultraconservative area on behalf of the Democratic candidate. That candidate, Conor Lamb, won by 755 votes in February 2018.

The VOW contact list grew and grew, to four hundred by the time of Lamb's election, to a thousand by the end of 2018. Fifty people started showing up to monthly meetings. Door-to-door canvassers went out weekly. The volunteers who joined them were mostly Democrats, but also anti-Trump Republicans and independents and socialists—anyone who wanted to pitch in. Nuns and a pastor joined for a canvass. One all-star canvasser was eleven years old. When she knocked on a door, you could see the person at the door relax, Angela told me. Angela liked canvassing alongside her. The girl would say that she was there to talk about seniors. "How crazy would it be if seniors couldn't afford insulin and stuff they need? That's not right," she would tell them.

Many volunteers who showed up were scared of knocking on doors. One person came to canvass in a Kevlar vest, afraid of what he might encounter at a stranger's door. Angela helped them all practice telling their stories, talking about issues, empathizing and connecting with people who disagree with them.

Some volunteers only showed up once. Some came all the time. Few did what Angela did, putting in twenty, thirty, forty hours some weeks, organizing the operation. Many older volunteers couldn't go up to houses and knock on doors because the walking was too much, so they served as drivers, shuttling canvassers from door to door in the spread-out neighborhoods of Westmoreland County.

The most active volunteers became a community. For the retirees, VOW became a primary social scene. For young families, too. They call the kids running around the meetings the VOW cousins.

Community begets good deeds. VOW doesn't talk about this part, would never brag about it. They take care of their growing community of friends and neighbors. Angela has driven undocumented immigrants in her VOW community to doctors' appointments. Some are too afraid of being deported if they get pulled over that they won't drive at all, even to the doctor's. One woman in the community was about to be evicted from her home, and the group quickly came to her assistance. When the federal government shut down in 2019, the group chipped in for gas cards and diapers to help those not making ends meet. All quietly and behind the scenes. "This is the most powerful thing I've ever done," Angela says about creating VOW. "It's the thing I feel called to do."

Every week during the summer and fall of 2018, before the volunteers went out canvassing, they gathered in a room. Each person was asked to tell the group his or her story about why he or she was there.

This is an organizing tactic: having volunteers reflect on their own stories openly can motivate them to face a stranger, to remember why they are doing this.

Angela's story, about her illness, is a powerful motivation for her action. But, she said, when she heard everyone else's story in going around the circle—a couple without health insurance canvassing, a Muslim family facing religious discrimination canvassing, a teacher without school supplies canvassing, a Latina mom who so badly wanted to canvass but instead drove other canvassers because she felt her English wasn't good enough—Angela remembered that she was doing this for all of the stories, not just her own. She starts to weep as she tells me this over the phone. How can she not try her hardest, knowing everyone's story about why he or she is there, Angela tells me. And through her tears, through her illness, through the cries of a baby in the background and a preschooler loudly demanding a *PAW Patrol* action figure as we talk, I realize I am talking to an American hero.

CHAPTER 7

Like, Share, Click

Hobbyism and Activism

"He's the biggest celebrity in the world, but is he ready to lead?" That was the tagline in a viral presidential TV ad, but not an ad about Donald Trump. In 2008, the Republican presidential nominee, Senator John McCain, ran this ad against Senator Barack Obama, accusing him of being a celebrity. The ad showed massive crowds chanting Obama's name. It also showed clips of Britney Spears and Paris Hilton.

Candidate Obama certainly had a lot of fans in 2008. Millions of Americans signed up for campaign email lists, knocked on doors, and made small financial contributions. Many people dedicated weekend after weekend of their lives to his campaign. Many more shared inspiring YouTube videos with one another. Nearly 2 million people attended his first inauguration. They believed in him and embraced his mantra, "Yes we can."

By John McCain's accusation, all of this energy was just a form of political fandom. Was it? Or was it the foundation of a political movement?

Obama was counting on the movement. He believed that his presidential power was tied to the grassroots support and the energy that he had accumulated during his campaign. That's why he created Organizing for America, a group aimed at taking the campaign's lists of volunteers, donors, and fans, and mobilizing them not just to win presidential elections but to win policy fights in Congress.[1]

The first big policy fight was over health care. With control of

Congress and the White House, Democrats pushed through the law that became known as Obamacare. On March 22, 2010, the day before Obamacare was signed into law, Republican leaders gathered together in a room on Capitol Hill to choose a messaging strategy. They brainstormed different slogans that reflected their opposition to the new health law. They coined "Repeal and replace." "We were enjoying ourselves," Republican Senate leader Mitch McConnell said about the meeting.[2]

Obama's army had its moment on the campaign trail. Once he was elected, it was the Republicans' turn to enjoy themselves. At the center of their fun were town hall meetings that members of Congress hosted during the Obamacare debate to solicit feedback from constituents. The town hall meetings started in 2009, just months after Obama's election. Newly energized Republicans booed, cheered, chanted, and yelled about their opposition to health care reform. They felt the wind at their backs of an emerging anti-Obama movement.

Democrats were hard to find at those town halls. Where were those millions of Democrats who shared the YouTube videos?[3] Democrats had already done their part; they had won the presidency and Congress. Maybe this made them feel safe. Maybe they were motivated by the electoral win rather than by the policy change that the win was purportedly intended to usher in.

They continued to stay home. They stayed home in 2010 and again in 2014, midterm election years when Obama's name was not on the ballot. His supporters were energized by Obama but not, evidently, by the policy agenda he advocated. That policy agenda required Democratic votes in Congress. Voters under thirty years old, who adored Obama, made up 17 percent of the electorate in 2008. They made up just 11 percent of the electorate in 2010, the year Democrats lost control of the House.[4] Obama was exciting to them. But the federal and state representatives who were necessary to translate his vision into law were not so.

The hibernation of Democrats during the Obama years was both a top-down story and a bottom-up story. Political and academic observers argue that the Obama team and the Democratic Party made strategic errors in failing to harness the electoral energy into sustained policy activism.⁵ That's the top-down story. The bottom-up story is that most of the citizens whom Obama inspired in an electoral context just couldn't be bothered between presidential election cycles.

Was McCain's "celebrity" ad right after all?

In 2011, the Obama administration rolled out an initiative perhaps more suited to his supporters' tastes. The administration embedded the most popular form of online activism, petition signing, in the White House website. The program, called We The People, was modeled after a similar initiative set up in England, home to such successful crowd-sourcing endeavors as a boat named Boaty McBoatface and a ballot initiative called Brexit.

The White House committed to responding to any petition that met a certain threshold of signatures. Online petition drives were already popular before the White House got involved. Change.org, for instance, and Democratic-aligned groups such as MoveOn and CREDO, circulate petitions online. But the White House website promised a response from the president, which made it alluring.

Along with a colleague, Brian Schaffner, I investigated the kinds of topics that racked up signatures on the White House site. We gathered data on 13 million signatures from eighteen hundred petitions over about twenty months.⁶ With the help of a team of students, we categorized every petition by its topic. Off the bat, 15 percent of the petitions (weighted by their number of signatures) were jokes, of the Boaty McBoatface variety. Petitions calling for creating a *Star Wars*–style Death Star and for changing the national anthem to an R. Kelly song garnered signatures. So did a number of "venting" petitions, calling for states to secede from the union or for the TV anchor Piers Morgan to be deported to England. That kind of thing.

Of the petitions that weren't outright jokes, something about their topics was startling. Only 5 percent of them were focused on big items such as taxes, health care, education, maternity leave, or other "redistributive" issues. We label issues "redistributive" if they call for tax money to be taken (mostly from rich people) and redistributed via government services to the public (who are mostly not rich). The big domestic issues in American politics are generally redistributive issues.

Petitions, instead, focused on narrow issues ("Recognize Dia-phragmatic Hernia Awareness Day!") and issues of second-order concern ("Crack Down on Puppy Mills").

It isn't that the petition writers didn't try to get traction for redis-tributive issues. "Renew Tax Cuts for 98 Percent of All Taxpayers." 1,519 signatures. "Create Public Sector Jobs and Put Americans Back to Work." 1,819 signatures. "Extend Unemployment Benefits." 3,057 signatures. "Create a Single-Payer Health Care System." 3,147 sig-natures. "Forgive Student Loan Debt to Stimulate the Economy." 32,008 signatures.

Thirty-two thousand signatures to support student-loan forgive-ness doesn't seem so small, until you realize which petitions did bet-ter. How about to prevent the FDA from regulating premium cigars? 37,513 signatures. Free online access to scientific journals? 65,704 signatures. GMO labeling? 77,106 signatures.

The petitions with large numbers of signatures were primarily addressing legitimate policy concerns, but minor ones. Petition-gathering organizations such as MoveOn see the same phenomenon. Saving dolphins generates enthusiasm among petition signers. So does demanding funding for PBS and NPR. Aid to the poor? Not so much.

Schaffner and I looked closer at the White House data. We obtained the zip code of every petition signer, which we linked to the income level of their neighborhoods. Not surprisingly, people in wealthy neighborhoods were more likely to sign online petitions than those in poor ones. More surprising is that those in wealthier neighborhoods were especially likely to sign petitions if the petition was about issues that were frivolous and narrow. Academics refer to this behavior as postmaterialist. For citizens whose material needs—food, shelter, health—are met, politics can be focused on frivolous and nonmaterial issues. Politics can be more of a game.

What Schaffner and I saw in the petitions follows a larger trend in policy activism. Since the 1960s, experts have measured a steep drop in advocacy groups caring about economic inequality, job train-ing, and blue-collar workers. The focus has shifted to postmateri-alist issues that felt more comfortable to well-to-do supporters of DC-based advocacy organizations.[7]

• • •

The promise of the Internet for politics was to make participation easy. Just as shopping on Amazon is frictionless compared to shopping in stores, online petitions are a frictionless way to participate compared to, say, attending a community meeting. Precisely because the cost of participating in an online petition is so small, we don't evidently use them for serious things. We use them as another form of self-gratification. The surge of digital petition signers who flocked to the digital White House in the Obama years reflects the shallowness of engagement that we collectively bring to American politics.

The same is true for various forms of online *consciousness raising*, which is a euphemism for sharing and arguing on Facebook, on Twitter, and on comments sections of news websites. Why do we argue online and share articles? We do this not necessarily to convince anyone but to convey an image of ourselves and to pass the time in an intellectual-ish way. We click and post and share not to take a civic action (a concrete action to advance politicians or policies we think are in the common interest). Mostly, we click and post and share to convey an image to our social networks and ourselves. It's the modern-day equivalent of showing up to a house party of the 1950s Democratic clubs. Some of those clubs' leaders were serious about policy, just like many of those who circulate petitions. But the typical person who showed up to the meetings to debate, to be seen, to gossip, to have cocktails, was much like the petition signer today, except at least the club member had human contact in his or her neighborhood.

CHAPTER 8

The Russians of Brighton

Bossism and Political Power

H e's been called the Ukrainian boss.[1] An old-time ward boss in modern-day Boston.[2] Some say he directs four hundred voters to the candidates he wants. Others, himself included, say it's closer to a thousand voters. He boasts about his influence, about all the politicians who love him. He controls enough votes to get candidates elected in close races. Politicians visit him. They send him birthday greetings. He has pictures and gifts from mayors, governors, and senators. One year even the US president sent him a letter offering best wishes. State representatives and city council members have shoveled his walk and escorted him to the grocery store. A local blogger wrote back in 2007 that he has heard ugly stories about the Ukrainian boss, but the stories couldn't be printed because nobody is willing to go on the record.[3] I heard he was the subject of a federal inquiry into election tampering. We'll get to that later in the book.

He's a legend in his small community, and well-known to politicians, but to the public he is obscure. I had never heard of him. When I was hunting for stories of political organizers, a Boston insider tipped me off that I should look into Naakh Vysoky and the Russians of Brighton. So that's what I did.

Based on what I initially heard and read, I was nervous to talk to Naakh Vysoky. Once I learned that he was now ninety-eight years old, I was still nervous, but I knew I wanted to meet him in person while I still could. I called the building he has lived in since the mid-1980s and asked to speak to the resident services coordinator for the Russian-speaking residents. She told me Naakh Vysoky was well enough to talk and was ready to meet with me.

As you drive up a hill in Boston's Brighton neighborhood, up Commonwealth Avenue, with the Green Line streetcar screeching up the middle and brick row houses along the carriage lane, a winding side street at the top of a hill is called Wallingford Road. I approached on a winter day with gray-white clouded skies that looked as if they were about to unleash a blizzard. Naakh Vysoky's home, in a low-income senior housing complex, is a sterile concrete-and-brick rectangle of a building. Old-fashioned television antennae that I didn't think existed anymore sprout from the roof. Maybe it's because I had been watching *The Americans* on TV around this time, but the only thing that came to mind when I saw this place was that it felt Soviet, a fitting home for a Ukrainian boss.

At the entrance, next to a locked sliding door, at wheelchair level, a large metal-box intercom system with a telephone keypad hangs on the wall. It is decades old, probably original to the building. To use it, you press down the pound button hard to scroll through each resident's name, unit by unit, on a small display screen that's difficult to read. I get on my knees to press the button and squint at the names, half of which are Russian, the other half Chinese. After five minutes of pressing the pound button on my knees, I find Naakh Vysoky among the fourth-floor names. He tells me to come up, but he doesn't buzz the door. So I wait until another resident eventually leaves and I sneak in. I ride the cramped and creaking metal elevator up to his floor. I walk alone down the long hallway of gray walls and worn carpeting, past the heavy apartment unit doors painted offensively bright yellow. The place doesn't feel or smell quite like a nursing home. It's more like a college dorm that has not been renovated for several decades.

The apartment unit is exceedingly modest. Medical equipment is strewn everywhere, a walker, a stethoscope, pills, oxygen. There's a stack of VHS tapes. The walls are a collage of political memorabilia, pictures of current and former politicians with Naakh, Democrats and Republicans both, handwritten messages for Naakh. Some are in frames, some aren't. There are plaques and awards. The apartment is maybe three hundred square feet.

Naakh sits in a wheelchair, wearing a faded blue-and-white plaid flannel shirt under a heavy black coat. He wears a baseball cap with the campaign logo of the current Republican Massachusetts governor, Charlie Baker. Naakh slowly rolls up to the table, which is crowded with papers, more memorabilia, more medicine, a bowl of grapes. His wife, Klara, sits on the couch behind him, resting with her eyes closed during much of my visit. In front of Naakh on the table is a folder with papers he's going to show me. I'm not sure if they were brought out because I am here or if they are kept on this table all the time.

I came to see him because I wanted to know how he became the Ukrainian boss. Already, though, the image I had of the Ukrainian boss was changing. For one thing, I couldn't think of him as a *Ukrainian* boss. He's not Ukrainian, he's Jewish, with a mezuzah on the doorpost of his apartment. He's a refugee, a survivor of German and Soviet persecution, a nomad across Eastern Europe. His first language was Yiddish. He picked up Russian, Romanian, Moldovan, English, and Ukrainian along his way because he had to. That's the first thing he told me, that he speaks six languages. At the beginning of our meeting, he is pretty reserved. But he builds up to ask me, "Are you a Yid?" I said I am. He starts to talk.

Naakh was born in 1921 in Kishinev, in Romania.[4] The Germans invaded when he was twenty. Nazis killed his mother, sister, brother-in-law, and nephew. The family lost contact with Naakh's father. Naakh fled to the Soviet Union and was sent to a camp in Siberia. Then he was forced into the army, where he was injured. In an army hospital, he recovered and began caring for others who were wounded. He learned a bit about medical care. After the war, he found his father in Chernivtsi in Ukraine. Naakh moved there, became a doctor, and married his wife, Klara, a schoolteacher. They had a daughter, Fay.

Fay later tells me that in Ukraine her parents were always helping people in their community. When a student at school was being treated unfairly, Klara would go to war for the student, Fay tells me. When a patient was being mistreated, Naakh would go to war for the patient. That's how Fay put it. They were often going to war for Jews in town, who were facing increasingly threatening anti-Semitic discrimination. In 1979, because of the anti-Semitism and given the opportunity to leave, Naakh and his family moved to New York and in 1985 to Boston. He was sixty-four then.

In Boston, Naakh and Klara got involved in the community of retired Russian immigrants in the Brighton neighborhood. They had settled in Boston ahead of many more immigrants from the former USSR who would come in the years that followed. Naakh and Klara were there earlier and spoke better English, so they became leaders. They liked to help people. Klara helped new immigrants learn English. Naakh drove people to doctors' appointments and on other errands. They gained the trust of these new neighbors, nearly all poor living in low-income housing. Many of them relied on $500 a month in Social Security payments, food stamps, and Medicaid. Most didn't speak English. Most could not work.

Naakh became a leader of their community association.

"I vus elected president of the da people of da immigrants," he tells me. "Ven I vus elected, I vus fast guy. I didn't sleep."

He's telling me he was strong and full of energy. Talking in his apartment, Naakh is hard to understand. His English is difficult to follow. He also throws in Yiddish from time to time, a language I do not know.

Naakh had never been particularly political, but then something happened. The Republican Congress in 1996, along with President Clinton, passed a welfare reform bill. The bill stipulated that most legal immigrants, even those in nursing homes, would be denied disability and food stamps. If they wanted to retain those benefits, immigrants would have to apply for citizenship. Across the country, the *New York Times* reported, some five hundred thousand legal immigrants were going to lose income and food stamps because of the new law.[5]

Naakh, as volunteer leader, alerted his neighbors that they had to take the citizenship test fast or they were going to lose their benefits. They were scared. What would they do if they failed the test? How would they study for this test?

"Dey said, 'I go to suicide,' you know. Dey had Parkinson's. Dey had Alzheimer's. Dey said to help and I had to help." Naakh wasn't exaggerating about the suicide. Aid groups across the country including Catholic Charities warned of a potential epidemic of suicides among elderly immigrants who would be cut off from government benefits.[6]

Naakh and Klara started arranging study groups. Of the 150 possible questions on the citizenship test, which assessed knowledge of the workings of government, test takers would see 20 questions. Most immigrants could take the test in their native language, though Yiddish wasn't an option. The immigrants in Naakh and Klara's study groups took it in Russian. They also had to write a couple of sentences in English and face an in-person interviewer. Naakh and Klara helped them study. Others helped, too. Wendy Wang, a naturalized citizen from China and a neighbor of Naakh's, helped the Chinese residents.[7]

Throughout 1996 and 1997, the cutting of aid to legal immigrants was a major point of contention in Washington. Bill Clinton, who signed the welfare bill, opposed this part of the law. Democrats were angry that Clinton willingly sacrificed elderly immigrants for the sake of the larger bill. Republicans were split on the matter. Moderates, including many Republican governors, thought it was unfair to legal immigrants. George Voinovich, governor of Ohio, wanted changes: "Are we going to throw those people [legal immigrants in nursing homes] out on the street and wipe our hands?"[8] Many Republicans in Congress who had voted for the welfare reform bill answered yes. Said Majority Leader Dick Armey, "We do not want to encourage people to come here for benefits."[9]

Clinton tried to pressure Congress to make changes to the initial law. He talked about it in the 1997 State of the Union address. To further raise public concern and force Congress to fix it, Clinton started sending letters to a million immigrants telling them that they were about to lose their benefits.[10]

Naakh got to work, too, not just preparing neighbors for the citizenship test. He raised alarm in the media in Boston, sharing with the public how the law was affecting his community. "I vent on television, on radio, vif my bad, bad language. I became known." The *Times* wrote about him. In a forgiving, water-under-the-bridge way, he tells me, "The Republicans in Congress, then they made a mistake. I like them. I like Democrats, too. I like everybody. But the Republicans made a mistake."

January 8, 1997. As part of a national media push, Naakh was asked to speak in Washington at the National Press Club. I can't figure out who asked him. He says a minister. He was seventy-six years old at the time. "I vus vith a cane," he says. "I vus sick"—nervous he means. "Dey vohn't understand me. . . . [But] dey help me to make a speech."

He arrived at the airport in Washington. He saw someone holding a sign: "'Naakh, we are waiting for you.'" I am not sure if Naakh means a chauffeur was holding up a sign to find him or if a supporter was holding up a sign to encourage him. Either way, he was impressed by the way he was treated on this trip. "Dey put me in a very nice hotel for a simple man."

During his speech, he was nervous, shaking, as he recalls. The minister there had told him, "All of this depends on you." Naakh shows me clippings from the event, in the mess of papers on his table, a picture of him at the podium at the National Press Club.

He says he saw two girls in the front row as he talked. "Two correspondents. Do you know what this is?"

"You mean reporters?"

"Yes, reporters. Dey begin to cry during my speech. My speech is going good. I have more courage."

He shows me the crumpled pages of the speech he gave. Big font, faded paper, no staple, one page out of five missing among the scattered files, maybe under the bowl of grapes. With a pen, he had added pronunciation markings above the letters to help him read the English. I ask him if it's okay if I take a picture of the last page of the speech with my phone.

It reads, "I ask the Congress on behalf of all réfugees, old and sick people, to be more sensitive to the terrible situation they are in, and to take care of them. I pray for a change in the new law to give old people comfort, people who had lived with hardships, beatings, and threats in their native country. They cannot work. Many cannot really learn English. I ask our government to help them to live their lives in peace in our démocracy. Thank you."

After a public uproar from governors, the president, and Naakh Vysoky, Congress eventually eased some of the restrictions on aid to immigrants. "Dey make for amendment. That speech, dey tell me, I help five hundred thousand people with my speech.

"Ven I get home, I vahs at home the big *eitza*, the big *macher*"—a problem solver, I think he says in Yiddish, a big shot. "My people trust me. I saved their lives."

Over a few years' time, amid the uncertainty in the welfare law and its amendments, Naakh helped three hundred people practice for the citizenship test. "I study with them. I took them to the test. I translate. I help. I made them all citizens. This was my begin."

Now Naakh was ready to become the boss.

Not long after, in 1998, Brian Golden, a candidate for state representative for the Brighton neighborhood, starts hanging around the lobby of Naakh's low-income housing complex. He tells Naakh that he'd like to be in office, "'but I have who to be for me.'"

Naakh tells him, "'Don't vorry, I go to help you.'

"I made a committee of forty people. They work for me."

Golden gets elected and becomes close with Naakh. "He's like a son to me. And after [Golden] comes, comes his friend, comes another. We have six hundred, seven hundred, a thousand voters."

Golden remembers the story in more detail. I meet him in his current office, a huge corner office on the top floor of Boston City Hall, with views overlooking the harbor. Golden is now the director of the Boston Planning & Development Agency, maybe the most powerful job in the city. I asked for thirty minutes of his time. He spends nearly three hours telling me about Naakh. He loves Naakh. Golden visits him once a week and gets sad thinking about the end of an era as Naakh gets weaker with age. Golden paces around the office as he talks to me. I sit and take notes.

Golden grew up in an Irish Catholic family in an overwhelmingly Irish Catholic neighborhood of Brighton. He was a conservative Democrat and an Army Reserve officer when, in 1998, he entered a five-way race in the primary for the state legislature. During the campaign, he wanted to make inroads in the Russian community, but he didn't know anything about them. He didn't know if they were internally organized or not. He couldn't find out who the go-to person was.

Not until a few days before Election Day did Golden finally learn about Naakh. It was too late to get his endorsement, but Golden won the race by ninety-two votes. "My first order of business was to see Naakh." Naakh and Golden formed a tight relationship from then on. Naakh helped Golden in his subsequent races. With Golden as his first candidate, Naakh began developing a political machine in his apartment complex.

After September 11, Golden, still a reservist in addition to a state legislator, was called for multiple tours overseas. In 2002, a challenger announced his campaign against him right as Golden was leaving with his unit to be stationed in Bosnia. He returned in June of 2002 just a few months before the primary. His challenger was David Friedman, a former president of the *Harvard Law Review*, university debating champion, and Supreme Court clerk. Friedman is now senior vice president of the Boston Red Sox, a role that sometimes sends him to Golden's office to get approval for redevelopment. In the 2002 race, according to Golden, Friedman was appealing to the wealthier and more liberal areas of the district. The district was getting more liberal and more affluent. The position of conservatives such as Golden in the Democratic Party was getting shakier.

As representative, Golden had focused on constituent services in the poorer areas. That is what the voters he talked to cared most about. He responded to requests. A woman wanted Golden to help her son "[get] a job on the Pike," meaning as a tollbooth operator. Neighbors wanted streetlights and potholes fixed. Naakh once complained to Golden that the seniors were having trouble getting to the bus stop and the subway because the sidewalks weren't always shoveled between the senior housing and the public transit stops. Along Wallingford Road, a number of absentee landlords owned buildings and they didn't shovel their sidewalks. The Public Works department regularly fined these landlords, but the landlords would rather pay the $50 fine than deal with shoveling. After Naakh raised the issue, Golden and his staff personally cleared the sidewalks from Naakh's complex down to the subway line on Commonwealth Avenue. For a Christmas present one year, Golden bought his staff their own shovels.

Returning from his tour of duty in the middle of the campaign, Golden realized he was in trouble electorally, and he told Naakh.

The educated, liberal voters in the district cared about policy more than constituent services, and Golden wasn't a liberal policy maker. Naakh called him in. Naakh was lying in his bed in his apartment. Naakh's lieutenants, the volunteer assistants who helped him get out the vote, circled around the bed, along with Golden. Naakh's chief deputy was Phillip, who had served as a factory supervisor in the Soviet Union. Whereas Naakh charmed and smiled, Phillip barked orders, Golden tells me. Together, the team planned how they were going to knock on all the doors, talk to all the voters. They delivered to Golden overwhelming support in the Russian community.

Golden won reelection by three hundred votes. Naakh expanded beyond Golden to other candidates for local and state races. Naakh endorsed candidates. "He would not understand even today what *grassroots* means, but that's what he did," Fay, his daughter, tells me. In 2009, someone outside the community found a copy of a sample ballot that Naakh's committee had distributed in their building. A blogger posted it online, along with a translation. The bubbles next to the names of endorsed candidates were filled in. A message in Russian reads, "On September 22, elections will be held in our city, and we ask you to show your support for the candidates involved with our community. You may address them if you need any help. Please mark in the bulletin the names printed in bold."[11]

Did Naakh make enemies?

"Mister Hersh," Fay tells me in her accented English, "the only way not to make enemies, you know that, is to sit at home and watch television." She says her father never campaigned against anyone. He only campaigned *for* people. But, yes, she imagined that the politicians on the other side of Naakh's vote bloc resented his organization.

Ward 21 in Brighton has twelve precincts. In 2005, the average turnout *outside* Naakh's precinct was 19.8 percent of registered voters in the local elections. In Naakh's precinct, located in the low-income, immigrant, senior housing complex in which he lives, it was 44.8 percent. In 2007, the other precincts had an 8.2 percent turnout rate. Naakh's precinct: 29.9 percent. This is all the more impressive because he has a higher registration rate among eligible voters than any of the other precincts.

Naakh does favors for his community. He didn't stop helping after the welfare fight or the shoveling. He helps people get better apartments. He helps with funeral arrangements. "'I need this, I need this,' I help them. They trust me. They come kiss me." In return, they give him their votes. He tells them whom to vote for. His fellow organizers, all old Russian volunteers, the lieutenants, make sure everyone gets reminders.

Naakh doesn't intimidate. "Nobody fears Naakh in that building," Golden tells me. Fay says of her parents, "It is not in their nature to force anyone to do anything. They lead by example." The voters simply respect Naakh's judgment and believe, as Naakh does, that their community is better off when they vote together as a bloc.

From the politicians' view, Naakh makes their lives easier. Instead of talking to one thousand voters, they come to Naakh. Naakh enjoys their attention. From the moment I set foot in his apartment, I can see the pride he takes in being close to politicians. I can see how much he enjoys it, receiving phone calls on his birthday and plaques and honors.

A man of modest means, he has not benefited materially from any of this, but cherishes being a macher, a big shot, on Wallingford Road. And he has power to deploy. When he asks politicians about government services for the community, politicians give him full attention. "What underlies the recognitions and commendations he gets," Fay tells me, "is the profound passion for helping one person at a time."

Trained as a doctor, Naakh learned how to be an organizer, which he was from his midseventies until he was ninety-two. "Then I became a little sick." At ninety-eight now, he leaves the electioneering to others. But even today, he spends Election Day in the lobby of the building, making sure everyone knows he is still there and expects them to vote. Yet most of his people are now dead. "Sometimes I want to die, too, you know."

I asked him if he has any advice for younger people before he dies. He said, "Just work with people. Help the people. Be interesting." I think he means be interested in other people. Take interest in their lives. But maybe he does mean to be interesting.

CHAPTER 9

Selfish Donor, Selfie Donor

Hobbyism and Campaign Finance

By the edge of the golf course, waiters serve lemonade, iced tea, and Arnold Palmers in sleek tall glasses. The lunch buffet offers five different types of little sandwiches, plus heaping bowls of salads. At dinner, the buffet is bigger and the drinks are stronger. Most people stick with gin, whiskey, and wine, but at one of the weekend's evening events, an eccentric man orders a peppermint schnapps on ice with a glass of milk on the side, and I make a mental note that I'd like to try that sometime.

The donors at this retreat have each paid about $10,000 to be here. Over the weekend, beneath starry summer skies, they'll hear a lecture from a noted expert on national security, insider gossip from a few members of Congress, rousing patriotic speeches, maybe an earnest rendition of "America the Beautiful," and expressions of gratitude for their financial contributions at this critical moment for our country. Along the way, they'll take selfies with the electeds and they'll talk politics and business among themselves.

What are these donors doing? Why are they here? Why did they give $10,000 to be here? In the public's mind, wealthy donors shell out money to politicians to get something in return, such as business-friendly laws and regulations.

But political scientists who have studied campaign donations have not seen much evidence that the typical big-money donors are giving money in return for favorable policy. Lobbyists aside, the typical high-dollar political donor doesn't have transparent financial motivations. Consider that 98 percent of donors give money to candidates from only one political party. If they wanted to influence those in power, they might instead donate to both sides, the way a lot of big corporations do.[1] Or consider that donors to congressional campaigns are not more likely to give to politicians who are committee chairs, who are on the powerful finance and appropriations committees, who are members of the majority party, or who are long-term incumbents who wield power in Congress.[2] The money doesn't seem directed to maximize donors' influence.

Brian Schaffner, my political science collaborator, and I wanted to dig deeper into motivations expressed by donors. In 2016, we surveyed a random sample of 676 donors who gave the maximum allowed donations. We asked them lots of questions about why they gave. Donors exhibit a general desire to help their side, or to be "party boosters."[3] A party booster doesn't try to strategically allocate money to candidates who are in toss-up races and doesn't care primarily about advancing specific policy items, but just wants to express a commitment to a political party through a donation.

Party-boosting donors use the language of duty in articulating their motivations. When asked about their donation, 85 percent of all max-out donors agreed that their contribution advanced the common good. There's no reason to doubt the sincerity of their view. They have money to spare. They could spend it on anything they want. They choose to spend it on candidates and parties that they believe serve the country well.

But motivations are tricky. Consider that most max-out political donors report making contributions in conjunction with a campaign event: fancy dinners and cocktail parties, box seats at sports games and orchestra seats at exclusive Broadway shows. Just as charitable organizations put on lavish galas or sponsor bicycle rides to support their causes, campaigns and parties host events to draw donors in. Political donors are political junkies. They like having their picture taken with political celebrities, gossiping about politics, and reporting back to their friends about the latest intrigue from Washington.

What do these events tell us about donor motivations? Donors don't generally want their dollars to be strictly transactions of money in exchange for influence. They also don't want the money to be used as efficiently as possible, allowing the politician to spend more time on policy and less time with them, or allowing the money to go to campaigning rather than having a third of it spent on the cocktail party. The donors are motivated to give when they get a chance to party with politicians. Some of these donors are strategists who want to cozy up to politicians at the events so they can call in a favor later on. But for many donors, the campaign event is the reward for the donation. It's fun, exclusive, and political, and it's targeted to people who enjoy leisure time spent in fun, exclusive, and political ways. A high-end donor to 2020 Democratic presidential candidate Pete Buttigieg compared the experience of hosting an event for Buttigieg to "getting a reservation at the best restaurant opening." The donor went on, "It is bragging rights. It's [being able to tell friends] that I've met him."[4]

An extreme example of this comes from the 2016 Republican primaries. During the primaries, wealthy donors traveled around the country to attend the live presidential debates. They would fly in, attend a cocktail party, then watch the debate in the arena with the locals. The donors traveled to Iowa and New Hampshire and all around the country to attend multiple debates in person because, as Republican donor (and future failed gubernatorial candidate) Foster Friess told the *Washington Post*, "It's the same thing as going to a football game. If you're in the crowd, you can hear the cheers, unfiltered by microphones. The chemistry is so much more exciting."[5]

Part of what's motivating donors such as Mr. Friess is party boosting. Donors both want to help their side and to satisfy their appetite for political intrigue. Part of what's going on, for some donors, anyway, is the desire for influence. But wealthy donors also seem to be motivated purely by the entertainment they derive from politics. For the extremely wealthy, spending $10,000 to eat, drink, golf, schmooze, and take selfies is not a bad price for a summer day's entertainment. Some rich people will spend thousands of dollars on hunting expeditions or weekends in Paris. Others have a taste for politics.[6]

On our survey Schaffner and I asked donors about a hypothetical scenario. We asked half of the donors how likely they would be to give $1,000 to a political party to attend an intimate dinner with a prominent elected leader. In this scenario, a donor gets to support their party plus gets the entertainment value of the dinner. Forty-nine percent of the donors said they were somewhat or very likely to make a contribution with these terms.

For the other half of the donors, we modified the language of the hypothetical. We asked them if they'd pay a $1,000 *fee to an event planning company* to attend the intimate dinner with the politician. In this scenario, a donor gets to have a fun dinner but the money does not serve the party. Nor does it benefit the politician's campaign in a way that would make the politician feel beholden to the donor. But even here, 38 percent of the donors said they would pay up, which is not much lower than the percent eager to donate to the party. For a sizable chunk of the donor class, it seems as if the motivation is not party boosting, but entertainment.[7]

Ego stroking is probably the best explanation for why a kind of extremely wealthy American funds a narcissistic super PAC or self-financed political campaign. Take Howard Schultz, for instance, the Starbucks founder who explored a short-lived independent bid for the presidency in 2019. Schultz opposed President Trump but felt that the Democrats were too liberal to support.[8] As a successful businessman, a billionaire, maybe he could put his skills and money toward a political movement. After all, other billionaires, such as the Koch brothers, have done just that.

If Schultz was serious about this, he could have replicated his retail business model. With Starbucks, he spent years building the brand, first in Seattle, then in the rest of the Pacific Northwest, and year by year getting bigger and more national. He hired local workers in every city to sell his brand, who in turn showed ordinary people how his product compared to its competitors'. But when it came to politics, Schultz had a different idea: an independent bid for presidency, planned and executed in less than two years. He took to cable news and talk shows to make his case.

I like to imagine Howard Schultz appearing before a roomful of business school students. A naïve student says, "I want to enter the cola market. I'm not happy with Coke or Pepsi. I've never made cola before, but in eighteen months, I want to have the biggest share of the market. I'm willing to invest hundreds of millions of dollars. How do I do it?"

I imagine Howard Schultz responding, "Don't be an idiot. You can't build a national brand and get a plurality of the market in eighteen months. With Starbucks in the coffee business, it took me years. I convinced consumers through grueling retail sales. I hired a huge workforce. If a novice could beat Coke and Pepsi at their own game in eighteen months with a few hundred million dollars, a lot of people would have done it already."

That Schultz took the slow-and-steady approach with his own business, when his own financial stakes were high, but took the implausible talk-show-circuit approach to the presidency when the stakes were high only for other people, is a good indication that political activity may just be a hobby for him.

Some donors aren't in it just for entertainment or for ego or for their own financial enrichment. Some donors give money to politicians to push them on a policy issue the donor cares a lot about. According to our study, many congressional donors think that in return for their contribution they will get access to politicians to talk about issues. Even if access isn't their motivation, donors acknowledge that their money buys them the chance to talk policy with a politician. About half of the congressional donors think they could approach the politician they supported about a policy they care about.

At first glance, this seems different from donations motivated by party boosting or entertainment. But even lurking in this motivation is a form of hobbyism. Consider this explanation of why one donor gave to a member of Congress, as reported to Schaffner and me in the 2016 study:

[Congressman X] is one of the brightest people in Congress. He takes time to reach out to me, and we have great conversations that are often very helpful in explaining what is going on. He always seems to have time to chat when he calls me although I know he has so many calls to make.

I have observed this phenomenon while watching politicians chat with donors. Conversations about policy often don't look like lobbying but rather look like opportunities for donors to get the inside scoop or to feel heard. For some donors who love politics, receiving a call from a sitting senator or representative who gives them the latest news from the Hill and asks for their take is thrilling. And it affords the donor the opportunity to tell his friends and family, "My good friend Congressman so-and-so called me last week to wish me a happy birthday and to ask my take on Iran." A lot of the advice that politicians are getting from donors is meant to give pleasure to the donors—entertainment, a psychic boost to their egos that confirms their importance in the world—rather than meant to give input to the politicians.

Just as in the nonprofit sector, a political campaign tasked with raising money ought to solicit donors' advice and host lavish events if these strategies raise the most money. And if some donors are motivated by the spectacle of politics, what's so bad about that? Maybe it's better than if they were motivated by a desire to mold policy to their preferences.

Even when the intentions of the donors are harmless and the strategies of the campaigns are sensible, the combination of the strategic motivations of campaigns and the hobbyist motivations of donors can create at least three problems. One problem also arises in the nonprofit world: with extravagant galas, organizations can blow a lot of money on expenses. If they aren't responsible or competent stewards of their cause, the cause isn't left with much money.

Second, just as with nonprofits, some organizations cannot compete when it comes to galas. The *New York Observer* in 2014 helped its readers sort through gala invitations, suggesting the best ones were those that supported the French Heritage Society, Lincoln Center, the American Museum of Natural History, Alvin Ailey, the Metropolitan Opera, the YMA Fashion Scholarship, and so on, not exactly the who's who of poverty alleviation.[9] In politics, this kind of disparity means that candidates and organizations that aren't centered in wealthy social networks cannot put on the same kind of entertaining display as those that are.

The hobbyist motivation among wealthy donors is also problematic for a reason that doesn't have a parallel in the nonprofit world: partisan asymmetry. Unlike Democratic donors, Republican donors typically support politicians whose policy priorities align with a wealthy person's financial interests. The donors can view donations as an investment. When Schaffner and I asked max-out donors why they made their contribution, many more Republicans than Democrats said that a very or extremely important reason for their gift was that the politician could affect the donor's own industry (37 percent of Republicans versus 22 percent of Democrats).

This asymmetry puts Democrats at a disadvantage. Not motivated by their own bottom line, Democratic donors instead have to be motivated by ideology, issues, or even by the entertainment value that a donation provides. For entertainment value, state legislative races and other low-level offices don't offer donors much. Maybe this is a reason that over the last decade, Republicans more than Democrats have invested in the offices that, however small and unexciting, are the key to congressional redistricting and consequential state policies.[10]

It's relatively easy to see why a hobbyist motivation could inspire a wealthy donor to give a few thousand dollars in exchange for an invitation to an exclusive dinner party. Harder to see is how personal gratification inspires the growing cadre of small-dollar donors. After all, these donors aren't lavished with champagne and scallops wrapped in bacon. In return for their contributions, they are rewarded mostly with email.

Prominent candidates from Barack Obama and Elizabeth Warren and Bernie Sanders to Rand Paul and Donald Trump have all raised millions from small donations. During the 2016 Democratic primary, Bernie Sanders regularly mentioned that the average donation to his campaign was just $27. Ordinary Americans, not wealthy elites, were supporting his campaign, Sanders proudly declared.[11] But actually, Donald Trump was most successful with small-dollar contributions. Raising $239 million from donors giving less than $200 each, Trump raised more from low-dollar donors than Sanders and Hillary Clinton combined. Trump raised even more from low-dollar donors than President Obama in 2012, who was considered especially adept at this kind of fund-raising.[12]

When politically engaged Americans shell out $27 or $50 to a political candidate, what are they doing? Their motivation is clearly not individual-level influence or access, so what is it? If you yourself have ever contributed a small donation to a politician, you probably think of it as motivated by duty: doing your part to advance a vision of the common good. You donate to a candidate who is offering a vision for the country that you endorse. Your contribution is meant to make the vision a reality.

This picture of the dutiful small-dollar donor is compelling and has motivated reformers to experiment with laws that encourage more Americans to make small contributions, such as through government matching programs.[13] But two other features that define small-dollar donors are worth considering.

First, small-dollar donors tend to be ideologically extreme, even more so than big-dollar donors.[14] For better or worse, big donors tend to be comfortable with the status quo and resistant to extreme liberal or conservative platforms. They value keeping the ship of state afloat, not rocking the boat too much in either direction. Small-dollar donors don't come from the pool of business leaders who want stability but from the pool of activists. When small-dollar donors give money to campaigns, particularly to the campaigns of members of Congress, they tend to support politicians who offer strong ideological positions.[15] To the extent that Americans think polarization is a problem, small-dollar donors probably exacerbate it.

More concerning, small-dollar donations flow to candidates who make crude, vicious, and provocative appeals. Small donations are commonly solicited online or through email, in messages sent out to thousands, if not millions, of potential supporters. The solicitations lend themselves to scientific investigation about what works and doesn't work. Campaigns and their consultants test and tweak messages, running experiments on small samples of potential donors and learning which appeals do the best job at attracting donations.

Through experimentation, they have learned to taunt. The Obama campaign, for instance, found that its appeals were most effective at raising money when they focused on competition and took a nasty tone that "Obama himself was not enthused about."[16] According to a leading expert on campaign finance data, the candidates who can attract the most small-dollar donations are not just those who are strongly ideological, but who can use media to heckle.[17] For example, Representative Joe Wilson, who famously screamed that President Obama was a liar when Obama was speaking before Congress in 2009, raised $2 million in the days following his outburst.

This isn't new. Advocacy groups see the same thing. Harvard professor Theda Skocpol has reported the rise of solicitations "tak[ing] dramatic, polarized positions—ideally identifying an immediate threat to which their positions are a response." That's what gets the donations coming in.[18]

It is no surprise that President Trump so ably fund-raises among small-dollar donors. What likely keeps them engaged are appeals where Trump attacks his opponents and makes outlandish claims. His aptitude for provocation is one of the reasons why Trump is so popular at rallies and in fund-raising appeals. Though Democratic donors may be uncomfortable admitting it, what makes them click a button to donate is not much different. The video that raises money is the one featuring a politician in attack mode, such as a debate clip from the 2019 Democratic primary of Senator Kamala Harris going after Vice President Joe Biden for his position on busing.

What, then, do we make of small-dollar donors? Is a $50 donation about dutifully investing in a vision of the common good or is it entertainment for the donor? It's both. Case by case, it looks like civic duty. But in the aggregate, we often see donations flowing to candidates who are offering a spectacle of ideological purity and provocation.

So there it is. What news do political junkies demand? Outrage and gossip. Why? Because it's alluring. What news do we avoid? Local news. Why? It's boring. What do we think of our partisan opponents? We hate them. Do we really hate them? No, but politics is more fun if we root for a team and spew anger at the other side. It's easier to hate and dismiss the other side than to empathize and connect to them. When do we vote? When there's a spectacle. When do we click? When politics can be a frivolous distraction. When do we donate? When there's a cocktail party or a viral video. *What are we doing?* We're taking actions not to empower our political values, but to satisfy our passion for the sport of politics.

Not like Angela or Lisa or Naakh or Drew.

When I look at myself, at my history of political engagement, I wish I identified more with the stories of Angela, Lisa, Naakh, and Drew and less with the news-obsessed, retweeting, snarky, aloof-from-my-community hobbyist. I wish I could even say I identified with the hundreds of people in the background of the organizers' stories, the helpers who put in a few hours here and there to make their visions a reality. Maybe you identify more with the organizers than the hobbyists. If you do, that's great. If you don't, welcome to the club.

If we are twenty-one years old, are we like Drew or one of the students who helped him start a precinct organization in North Carolina? If we are in our thirties, maybe with young children, like Angela, are we doing anything like what she has done building a sustainable organization like the Voice of Westmoreland in Pennsylvania? If we are in our fifties, soon-to-be empty-nesters, are we like Lisa, creating space for conversation with those who are different from us on Staten Island? And if we are in our nineties like Naakh, can we look back and say we've done anything quite as interesting, as powerful, as what he has done organizing his neighbors in Brighton?

The charge of hobbyism is stinging because we have higher motivations and deeper values in our hearts than show in the hours we spend on political consumption each week. Maybe we don't reflect often on what we actually do in politics. Maybe we don't have a clear sense of what we are supposed to do instead. But we do care. Don't we?

PART II

And as the machine itself became, as it were, more active and human, reproducing the organic properties of eye and ear, the human beings who employed the machine as a mode of escape have tended to become more passive and mechanical. Unsure of their own voices, unable to hold a tune, they carry a phonograph or a radio set with them even on a picnic: afraid to be alone with their own thoughts, afraid to confront the blankness and inertia of their own minds, they turn on the radio and eat and talk and sleep to the accompaniment of a continuous stimulus from the outside world: now a band, now a bit of propaganda, now a piece of public gossip called news.

—Lewis Mumford, 1934[1]

CHAPTER 10

Political Leisure

The philosopher Aristotle argued that without leisure time, democracy cannot thrive. If a citizen's entire day is dedicated to labor, no time is left to learn civic skills or actively engage in political debate.[1] Modern sociologists have examined a different connection between democracy and leisure: political values can affect how we spend our time and money. The products we buy, avoid, or boycott, as well as the leisure activities we choose, are influenced by our political views.[2] Nike enters the political fray with advertisements featuring quarterback Colin Kaepernick's decision to protest during the national anthem; Chick-fil-A enters the fray because the company owners advocate against gay marriage. We sometimes react by adjusting our purchasing habits to align our choices with our politics.

The political scientist Robert Putnam revealed another connection between politics and leisure in his 2000 book, *Bowling Alone*.[3] Putnam's idea was not that politics affects leisure choices, but the opposite: our leisure choices affect politics. The way we spend our free time affects how we participate in democracy. In a bowling league or at church, we get to know people in our communities. When we stay home and watch TV or watch our laptop screens, we have fewer connections to the community and become unpracticed at the skills necessary for getting things done together.

Politics requires leisure; politics affects leisure; leisure affects politics. Yet another important connection is at the core of this book. Politics itself is, or can be, a leisure activity. Probably the only people who naturally think of politics this way are self-described "junkies"—insatiable consumers of polls and political gossip. An extreme class of people even attend Politicon conventions or spend their vacations on liberal or conservative group cruise ships.

For the non-self-identifying junkies, the term *political hobbyism* can be insulting. Given how important politics is, it doesn't feel good to call one's political activity a hobby. The term is also insulting, I have learned, to *real hobbyists*, who see hobbies as activities with much more depth than the online bickering or addictive news consumption I'm calling a hobby.

A friend of mine named Clayton, a *real* hobbyist, explained the kind of person who comes to his mind when he thinks of a hobbyist. Clayton grew up in the 1980s and '90s in Sheboygan Falls, Wisconsin. Seared in his memory is a group of mostly retired men who spent five years' worth of evenings together in an old factory in Clayton's neighborhood, building a lightweight airplane, for fun. Clayton would pass the men on jogs. On evenings, he and his father would walk over to the factory to check on their progress. Clayton admired the group's long-term, imaginative project.

Until I met Clayton, about ten years ago, I was unaware of the hobby that was Clayton's passion. In the office we shared when we were both writing our doctoral dissertations, he would sometimes tell me about it. But I couldn't fully appreciate ham radio until I saw Clayton doing it.

One afternoon, Clayton and I took a break from our work and walked across campus. I followed him up an old creaky staircase through a cramped space to a dark radio studio. He showed me how he made contact with strangers in faraway places, using both voice commands and Morse code. He used call signs and a strange manner of speaking that was unknown to me. Right after my visit to the radio station, I went home and committed to memory the phonetic Alpha Bravo Charlie alphabet that he spoke, sensing that it was the kind of thing I ought to know.

To an onlooking cynic, what exactly is Clayton doing up there in that radio studio? He is talking in a serious tone, reminiscent of an airline pilot, or tapping out Morse code as if he were in a war taking place a hundred years ago, employing old-fashioned tools when he has a smartphone in his pocket, acting almost as if there were an emergency to report. Yet, watching Clayton tap out Morse code or confirm his receipt of faint communications is mesmerizing. He practices skills, and he is part of a community of interesting people.

Clayton occasionally spends his weekends climbing mountains with his ham radio friends, establishing emergency radio communications in the wilderness. They do this in preparation for the unlikely event of an emergency that would require Morse code transmissions from mountain peaks. Mainly they do it because it's a hobby: this ragtag group of army vets, engineers, survivalists, A/V nerds, and college professors come together as a team and build radio stations on mountaintops, and they drink beer along the way. And it's cool. That's a hobby; and admittedly, it doesn't feel analogous to the obsessive at-home consumption of political news.

In the next few chapters, we're going to try to understand how politics is and isn't like a hobby. Learning how people use their leisure time generally will help us better understand the ways that political engagement fits into our lives as either leisure or a form of service to others, or maybe both.

Drinking. Smoking. Gambling. Almost nobody would describe these common activities as a hobby. Even though, it should be noted, they meet the criteria by at least one dictionary definition identifying hobbies as activities done regularly, in free time, and for pleasure.[4] Scholars who study leisure have tried to discern what makes an activity a hobby. They have classified hobbies into such categories as collecting objects, acquiring knowledge, making crafts, and engaging in group activities (e.g., softball leagues).[5] Hobbies can fall into more than one of these categories. Birders take interest in learning facts about birds (knowledge acquisition), but also logging sightings and acquiring photographs of birds (a collecting hobby).

Politics can fit in every traditional category of hobbyism. Most prominent among them is learning facts. The study of political science—the acquisition of political knowledge—has been classified as a hobby since at least the 1930s.[6] Today, some people obsess over polls and polling averages for months, years even, preceding an election. In 2018, the *New York Times* started to run polls of competitive races and publish, in real time, the results as they trickled in. Showing the real-time results of telephone polls ("person 1 says she's voting for this candidate," "person 2 says he's voting for that candidate," "person 3 refuses to take the call") serves no purpose other than to delight junkies and educate them on how polls are conducted. Some people find it interesting. Soon after the *Times* launched this feature, a betting firm, PredictIt, began accepting wagers on how the *Times* polls would come out.[7] Who would place a bet on the outcome of an inconsequential telephone poll? Some people, apparently.

Politics is not only a hobby of knowledge acquisition, it is also a craft of sorts, typically practiced from behind computer screens. Consider the discussion of politics on Facebook and Twitter and the sharing of memes (i.e., pictures circulated online with user-generated captions). Much of the time, what is happening on social media is collective, cultural production. For fun. It is wry commentary, it is a flash mob, it is a fleeting work of art.

An example: In June of 2018, Scott Pruitt, then administrator of the Environmental Protection Agency, had reportedly sent his security guards to locations of Ritz-Carlton hotels because the hotel chain sold a brand of moisturizing hand lotion that Pruitt enjoyed. The story was juicy and weird because Pruitt had such strong preferences about lotion. The story was newsworthy, too; it came after numerous other allegations of Pruitt's misusing government resources. Moisturegate, as several news outlets called it, made headlines. *Vox* even published an explanation about how men are less likely to need lotion because their skin doesn't get as dry as women's skin.[8]

The news item unleashed the creativity of hobbyists. Some social media users found images from the movie *The Silence of the Lambs*, wherein the villain famously says, "It puts the lotion in the basket." They created memes connecting the movie scene to Pruitt and posted them online. Democratic US representative Adam Schiff composed a version of "My Favorite Things" that began, "Ritz-Carlton lotion and Trump hotel mattress," which he shared on Twitter to the delight of his followers (eleven thousand retweets). When Pruitt eventually resigned from his office, one Twitter user said the reason he resigned was "so he can spend more time with his lotion," which I think is pretty funny. Many people shared details and their own quips about the lotion. They were contributing to a collective moment, tangentially political, just for fun.[9] Political activity is often like this, one silly news story after the next to comment on. It could involve endless hours of reading articles that have been shared, sharing articles that have been read, and commenting on articles that have been posted.

Less common than politics as knowledge acquisition or a craft is politics as an in-person group leisure activity, where the goal is coming together, and where actual political objectives are the excuse for coming together rather than the goal. James Q. Wilson wrote extensively not just about the amateur Democrats of the 1950s but also about a variety of other political and civic organizations in the 1960s and 1970s. Wilson found in many groups at that time, including fraternal orders and political clubs, participants' real objective seemed to be "the quest for status or the search for conviviality."[10] Groups would go to lengths to describe their goals as having a higher purpose than just fun, but Wilson thought they were often for companionship and curiosity.

To me, the most relatable contemporary analog for these groups may be the university speaking circuit. Any given semester in any major university, politicians and political advisers come and share their perspective with audiences. If you've been to some of these, and I've been to many, you might find Wilson's assessment compelling: rare in the self-congratulatory war stories of politicians on college campuses is inspiration or education; attendance by students is more aptly explained by that "quest for status or the search for conviviality," especially when it's Instagrammable.[11]

To be sure, both in social clubs and at campus events, the activities might serve civic functions even if the motivation for attendance is merely entertainment. These settings are potential breeding grounds for political activism. From time to time, they might inspire. Nevertheless, if participants attend events or meetings mainly for personal enjoyment, we would call it a leisure activity. If it's part of a larger quest for knowledge in a specific area, which politics is for many people, then that larger quest we'd call a hobby.

According to historian Steven Gelber, who wrote a brilliant scholarly book on hobbies in 1999, hobbies are "socially approved leisure activity," which is why drinking, smoking, and gambling don't count.

If, however, instead of merely drinking, you become a wine, beer, or whiskey aficionado, or if instead of merely smoking you gain specialized knowledge of cigars, or instead of merely gambling you get serious about poker, you can alchemize these activities into hobbies after all.

Even mundane activities can be elevated into hobbies. The cultural development of the foodie is a paradigmatic example.[12] Instead of treating grocery shopping and cooking as a chore, people can turn it into a hobby. The foodie has television programming, books, online reviews, clubs, and competitions. The foodie can collect objects (cookbooks), acquire knowledge (restaurant reviews), and practice kitchen skills. Foodies can start talking in the language of artisanal handcrafted mouthfeel. Like in other hobbies, food hobbies have strange and extreme variants: seekers of exotic tastes, competitive eating, and, a personal favorite from the rabbit hole of food-related websites, mukbang videos on YouTube, which are popular lengthy webcasts of people noncompetitively eating large quantities of food.[13]

Watching TV, the most common of all leisure activities, can be a hobby, but usually it isn't. The way a foodie watches food shows as part of a larger quest for knowledge on a specific subject can make TV a hobby for her. A child who lives in my home consumes TV almost exclusively insofar as it provides him with facts about animals, facts that he also gets from books, *National Geographic*, and the zoo. TV can also be a hobby for people who study the details that most of us don't notice of production and camera angles and plot twists. But TV watching in general, even binge-watching whole series, is not a hobby because it's not goal oriented or in search of specific knowledge.

Politically interested citizens typically fit the class of hobbyists engaged in learning about a specific subject and collectively working on a craft of generating political "content." They may take pleasure in knowing the latest news developments. They may read, listen, or watch because they want to mimic the arguments of their favorite pundits. Politics, when done in this way, is a mostly private hobby, similar to the activities of sports fans or at-home foodies. Though it's less common, politics can also be a social hobby, done in groups and outside the home, with parallels to amateur sports leagues or ham radio clubs. In either case, we would call politics a hobby if it's done for personal development and enjoyment rather than as a power-seeking activity done to multiply the people who vote or who take political action or who hold a certain set of policy views.

In short, when people engage in political hobbyism, power is often the topic; power is the reason that politics is exciting to them. In contrast, when people do politics, power is not just a topic, it's the goal.

CHAPTER 11

Whose Hobby?

In observing how Americans typically spend time on politics, in news consumption and social media engagement, it seems as if what they are doing is a hobby. In observing *who* does politics and *why* they do it, it seems even more as if what they are doing is a hobby.

Political scientists have long tried to figure out why some people engage in politics and others do not. One reasonable hypothesis is that political engagement relates to self-interest: people whose self-interest is most dependent on political outcomes—people who need political power the most—should engage in politics the most. The bulk of evidence conflicts with this view. For example, even though the stakes in politics for poorer citizens are higher than for richer citizens, and even though poorer citizens report having more leisure time, poorer citizens participate in nearly all forms of politics at lower rates.[1]

Participation, instead, is high among people who, because of a number of factors we will explore in this chapter, happen to find politics interesting. The factors that lead to their interest in politics are notable because these are the factors that are at the root of any hobbyist passion. The same story of why some people, and not others, are interested in politics can be told about why some people, and not others, are interested in soccer.

Interest in politics often starts with parents. In households where parents are reading the daily newspaper and talking about politics with each other and with friends, kids are more likely to find the topic interesting.[2] Interest usually persists for one's entire life.

It is dispositional (an individual trait that stays with some people from a young age on) rather than situational (interest rises and falls in response to current events or campaign appeals). If you ask a random sample of Americans if they are interested in news and politics, the number of people who say they're very interested is pretty much the same in presidential election years as sleepier midterm years.[3] The circumstances—world events, the stakes of a particular election—have hardly any effect on the percent of the public who say they're interested in politics.

Interest in politics gels early in life, writes Princeton's Markus Prior, not just because of parents but also because of cognitive skills and personality. Our personal traits can lead to our fascination with politics and, in turn, to professions where these skills and personalities are valued. Consider lawyers and doctors. Why is political participation so much higher among lawyers than doctors, who have similar incomes and education levels? In a recent midterm election, 80 percent of lawyers told the Census Bureau they voted compared to only 62 percent of physicians.[4] The difference is not because politics matters more to the economic self-interest of lawyers; doctors are in a highly regulated field that can be impacted by political decisions. Rather, people who take an interest in politics from an early age disproportionately end up in careers in which they use skills and engage topics closely tied to politics.[5] When they aren't at work, these people are the most interested in following political news.

Sociologists have found that people who are in fields that they chose on their own (these tend to be higher-status professions) seek *catharsis* in their hobbies.[6] In a cathartic hobby, you utilize similar skills that you employ in work, except in a low-stakes environment. For example, interviews with surgeons revealed a frequent interest in hobbies such as model ship building. Why would surgeons want to spend their free time working with tiny tools and doing intricate handwork?[7] Because they get to use the skills they are good at but without any pressure. That is the catharsis. Unlike in the operating room, it doesn't matter if they make a mistake or leave the job half done.

Fields such as law, teaching, social work, and public policy have been called "politically impinged" fields.[8] Like the surgeon with his model ship, an attorney can take a break from debating minutiae in legal contracts and instead apply his debating skills to something more fun. From the perspective of this attorney, the political debate he may engage in online or among friends is of little professional consequence. In a hobby, he can bloviate about political issues he knows little about. If he tried that at work, he would get fired. That's what can make political debates fun and cathartic.

Personality and parental socialization will affect our career choices but also our social choices. Our social networks then directly affect our interest in leisure activities. We may vote, petition, or protest to gain our friends' approval. We also may bowl, dance, or play the ukulele to make ourselves look good to others. We may drink, use drugs, or brawl in bars, too. We succumb to social contagion because we want to convey an image that makes us look good to our peers.[9]

If I am in a peer group that likes soccer even though I don't, I might feign interest and pick up a few scraps of information that will allow me to participate in a conversation. The political equivalent of this is not uncommon: students on politically active campuses walking around with Urban Outfitters shirts such as one saying VOTE VOTE VOTE EVERYONE IS DOING IT. According to the student newspaper at the University of Michigan, these popular T-shirts felt, in 2016, like a form of overcompensation for those who didn't actually care much for politics and maybe weren't even registered to vote but wanted to fit in.[10]

Social contagion can explain why some hobbies—or forms of political engagement—go through fads. Playing the ukulele was suddenly, and temporarily, popular in Brooklyn.[11] Presidential candidates running in primaries can have fifteen minutes of fame when they become the object of fan obsession—an obsession milked by the media—then can recede into the background.[12] For a brief moment in November of 2015, surgeon Ben Carson led Donald Trump in the polls for the 2016 Republican nomination; then his polling collapsed.[13] For a brief moment in March of 2019, former congressman Beto O'Rourke appeared to be among the top contenders for the 2020 Democratic presidential nomination. Annie Leibovitz photographed him for the cover of *Vanity Fair*. Then the buzz went away.

Social contagion, plus the force of traditional gender expectations, can help explain the gendered nature of hobbies as well as of political activities. The gender associations of hobbies have long been a point of scholarly interest; boys and girls tend to collect different kinds of items, they choose different after-school activities.[14] Political activities have long been gendered, too. From 1960 through 2008, when respondents to the American National Election Study were asked about their overall interest in public affairs, men were over 30 percent more likely to say they were very interested than women. That question wasn't asked after 2008, but another question was, which gauged interest specifically in elections. This was asked from 1948 through 2016. A gender gap persists every year, including 2016, when men were 13 percent more likely to be very interested compared to women. In gender studies of politics, the average man has been found to know more facts about politics than the average woman, too.[15]

In actual political behaviors, as opposed to just survey responses gauging interest and knowledge, the gender gap often goes in the other direction. For a number of years now, women have been consistently more likely to vote than men.[16] The progressive activist groups that have emerged since 2016 are overwhelmingly populated by and led by women.[17]

Once an activity has a lopsidedly single-gender membership, that alone, through social contagion, affects whether men or women want to participate further. Participation could just take the form of bloviating about political news online, in the case of men, or it could be organizing neighbors to vote, in the case of women.

In political hobbies, as in all other hobbies, rich people participate differently from poor people, both because of social networks and resources: rich and poor alike might both like carpentry and have a home workbench, but the rich hobbyist's tools will be better;[18] $2,000-a-head fund-raisers can be an opportunity for socializing, learning, and debating for the rich, but will be closed off to the poor. The language that is used and the topics that are discussed in political debates will be different in wealthy circles than in working-class ones.[19] Political activities that focus on the skills and the tastes of the wealthy are, like polo and skiing, liable to create class biases in participation.[20]

• • •

Let's briefly investigate three additional important influences: technology, government, and business. These factors affect political engagement in much the same way as they affect the activities we normally think of as hobbies.

Technology. Technology affects the increments of time that we are able to dedicate to leisure and the place where leisure happens. For the person who is always available online to their colleagues, bosses, or clients, leisure time must be spent in short stints. We toggle back and forth between work and leisure all day long, checking political statistics or sports scores or watching a cooking video, then clicking back to work. At home, we can make dinner and do the laundry and bathe children and toggle over to Facebook or Twitter and then over to email. We can spend hours on leisure each day without ever spending more than a few minutes at a time.

Collectively, we create an astonishing amount of material online when we can do so a few minutes at a time. For free, we will create product reviews, political commentary, and viral memes.[21] We will also have lengthy conversations with other people so long as we don't have to coordinate our schedules with them. I can post something, return to what I was doing while others post responses, and then I can read and post again at my leisure. A conversation such as this is cheap to coordinate compared to organizing friends to have a conversation face-to-face, even in an online video conference.[22] Projects that require meeting others face-to-face or setting aside large blocks of time will be left undone.

Those of us who are still willing or able to set aside larger blocks of time or coordinate meetings can do politics in group settings. Who is most able to do that? The same group that are the most prominent participants in nearly all hobbies and leisure activities: retirees. Seeing how active retirees are in politics, we might naturally think first about their self-interest: retirees depend on Medicare and Social Security to get by. They have a more immediate stake in politics than other people do, so that's why they participate so actively. But participation also generates feelings of accomplishment, new knowledge, and a human connection that come out of all serious leisure activities. These gratifications, combined with free time, yield high rates of political participation among senior citizens.[23]

Government. Governments have always played an important role in shaping leisure.[24] Governments impact leisure through advocacy but mainly they impact leisure through the regulation of space and time. Whether a government builds one big central park in a city or a dozen neighborhood parks and what structures it builds inside those parks will affect how citizens engage in physical leisure. Similarly, regulation of the forty-hour workweek can expand opportunities for leisure just as nonregulation of hours for contract laborers can result in a contraction of leisure.[25] Regulatory decisions about TV, Internet, and radio communications can affect leisure time as well.

Politics as a leisure activity is influenced by government regulation, too. Many of the ways we engage in politics as a hobby today, from online petitions to small-dollar donations to watching C-SPAN clips, are directly attributable to government rules about how ordinary people can participate. Tweaking those rules would change the way Americans treat politics like a hobby. The reason we should not expect political hobbyism to flourish in repressive regimes such as China is that the government suppresses attempts by citizens to use social media or in-person events to engage in political activity.[26]

Importantly, governmental involvement in leisure is not always aligned with the interests of citizens. For example, in the United States, state and local governments have often built recreational opportunities only for white neighborhoods;[27] local governments have made decisions about park development based on the value of side payments from developers;[28] state governments' role in gambling as an expedient way to raise revenue may not serve citizens well.[29] For political hobbyism, we should not blindly assume that the government is currently serving the interests of the citizenry when it nudges us to spend time on politics in certain ways and not others.

Business. Solitary forms of leisure are typically mediated through corporations. That's true in politics and other forms of entertainment. Social critics have long worried about businesses exerting control, suppressing insubordination, and reinforcing existing social divisions through their influence over leisure time.[30] Reality TV glorifying the worst human instincts, news fare demonizing racial minorities, or college athletics earning millions off the free labor of poor students all enrich the producers but maybe at the expense of the consumers' best interests.

The criticism of business influence over leisure is worth noting because so much of how we "do" politics today is mediated by corporations: endless streams of YouTube videos, cable news, political infotainment on Comedy Central or HBO, and Twitter and Facebook feeds that always scroll down to more new content. Companies keep us engaged so that we spend more time on their platforms, which gives them more advertising revenue. Leisure time does not need to be spent by way of corporations, but in practice it commonly is.[31] When politics is done in leisure time, for fun, when it is focused on learning new information, on the craft of producing political "content," and on the competition between sides, it is a hobby but a passive activity typically performed via corporate sponsors.

Why, then, do some people participate in politics and others don't? We see that the idea that politics is a leisure activity, a hobby, gives us some answers. Parents nudge us toward certain interests, and our desire to look good to our friends nudges us some more; those who have interest and skills in a subject matter choose professions, friend groups, and leisure activities that allow them to engage those interests and skills, but in a cathartic, low-stakes setting; retirees participate the most since they have the most time; certain activities tend to be more popular with men and others with women; our activities are influenced by government regulations and by corporate sponsors; the increments of leisure time we have will dictate the activities we can do.

From this perspective, politics isn't special at all. Which is a hard thing for a political scientist to write. I think about politics all the time. Maybe you do, too. It is the central activity that enables us to live in a peaceful civilization. But when you look at it as a leisure activity, the same story about who does it and what exactly they do can be told about any run-of-the-mill hobby.

CHAPTER 12

Politically Spiritual, but Not Religious

Some political actions are like passive hobbies: shallow, technology-mediated activities that satisfy the short-term emotional needs or intellectual interests of participants but do nothing for anyone else. Other political actions are like active hobbies, similar to my friend Clayton's mountain-climbing, emergency-preparedness ham radio club; they're deep. They place participants in a community where they build relationships, earn trust, and cultivate skills.[1] The stories of Lisa, Drew, Angela, and Naakh were examples of deep political actions. By building real relationships, they won supporters and accumulated power. By cultivating skills, they influenced governments and pushed neighbors to take actions they wouldn't otherwise have taken.

Religious behavior also exhibits this dichotomy of shallow and deep activities.[2] Religion, like politics, is not a realm of life we usually classify as leisure; many people reluctantly perform religious and political acts because they feel they must. Yet, neither religious practice nor political engagement are merely guilt-ridden chores. Participants spend time on these activities happily learning interesting information and seeking personal enrichment and community. For some, these may be the sole reasons they participate. For others, these activities are means to a greater end of service to God or to the common good.

The last decade has witnessed a dramatic decline of traditional religious affiliation in the United States and a rise of Americans identifying as "spiritual but not religious." College-educated Americans and political liberals are disproportionately found in the ranks of the nearly one-third of the population that now identifies as spiritual but

101

not religious. They have been a source of both interest and frustration for traditional religious leaders who have seen their congregations dwindle.[3]

The way that religions in the United States are currently grappling with the replacement of religious participation with the spiritual-but-not-religious identity is instructive for our understanding of deep versus shallow political engagement. The spiritual-but-not-religious ethos illuminates the hobbyist ethos from the perspective of power-seeking political organizations. Let's briefly consider it.

Spiritual-but-not-religious identifiers seek out religious-themed activities but reject communal or institutional religious settings. They typically engage in one-off events, solitary activities, or the anonymity of being another mat in a darkened yoga studio. These activities do not typically involve long-term commitments to other people.

Spiritual-but-not-religious Americans may look for meaning in the secular observance of Lent—a time of self-deprivation "reimagined as another opportunity for a kind of spiritual wellness 'cleanse,' "[4]—a social-justice mission trip, a mindfulness exercise, and sunsets on the beach. A Jewish organization called Reboot produces a "Jewish-ish" podcast, a cookbook, a series of six-word Jewish memoirs, and an app that activates on Friday afternoons: "your phone recedes into a blissful twilight and serves up a short thought-provoking story and question to prompt a pause for personal reflection and lively discussion."[5]

Spiritual-but-not-religious participation is finding opportunities to briefly help others and then move on (a onetime volunteer shift at a food pantry) or seeking personal gratification absent any sense of duty to serve others (as in the Jewish-ish podcast). Some of these are genuine attempts at moral self-improvement, but they share a common feature with shallow online political behavior, which is a focus on the self rather than a commitment to others. One religious critic, the Reverend Lillian Daniel, describes the spiritual-but-not-religious ethos as "comfortably in the norm for self-centered American culture, right smack in the bland majority of people who find ancient religions dull but find themselves uniquely fascinating."[6]

In the 1970s, the sociologist Herbert Gans wrote about the trajectory of Americans losing their religious and ethnic cultures through assimilation. Assimilating Americans begin searching, wrote Gans, "for easy and intermittent ways of expressing their identity, for ways that do not conflict with other ways of life." He continued, "They refrain from ethnic behavior that requires an arduous or time-consuming commitment, either to a culture that must be practiced constantly, or to organizations that demand active membership." Over time, ethnic connections become less a means to an end (the end, for instance, being mutual aid) and instead become, in Gans's words, a "leisure-time activity."[7]

Reverend Daniel, senior pastor at the First Congregational Church in Dubuque, Iowa, harbors an acute frustration toward the spiritual-but-not-religious ethos, a descendant of the assimilation ethos described by Gans. She writes, "Any idiot can find God alone in the sunset. It takes a certain maturity to find God in the person sitting next to you who not only voted for the wrong political party but has a baby who is crying while you're trying to listen to the sermon. Community is where the religious rubber meets the road. People challenge us, ask hard questions, disagree, need things from us, require our forgiveness. It's where we get to practice all the things we preach."[8]

In shallow religious engagement, as in shallow politics and shallow hobbies, participants are looking for instant gratification, the equivalent of drinking green beer on St. Patrick's Day as a symbolic gesture toward one's Irish identity.[9] In religious communities, political organizations, and serious hobby clubs, participants are in it for the *delayed* gratification that comes from sustained relationships and concrete goals.

Reverend Daniel emphasizes that some regular church attendees in her own community say they are spiritual but not religious, and she has no issue with them.[10] Even though they say they aren't religious, they act as part of a community and serve others. A person who seeks only secular benefits from religious participation—personal growth, moral improvement, opportunities to do good deeds—can find those benefits from joining a church and actively participating in a community. These benefits cannot be realized, goes this critique, through one-off events, solitary sunsets at the beach, or spirituality iPhone apps, which do not place individuals in a real community.[11]

In much the same way, a political volunteer could support the work of deeply committed people such as Lisa, Drew, Angela, and Naakh because he or she finds it personally enriching, fun, and for no other reason. A deep political hobbyist could be the person who works with others in the community to organize a block party and does not have a political—a power-seeking—motive. Regardless of the motive, the action fosters relationships that are important for political work. When meeting neighbors, organizers will learn about their community and the needs of others. They will also practice civic skills—planning an event, obtaining permits from the government, organizing a team.

However, just as it is hard to sustain an atheist church community,[12] deep political hobbyism without a dose of civic duty, at least among the leaders, may be hard to sustain for long. For the introverts to talk to their neighbors, for the fatigued to attend an evening meeting, for the frail to make it to the polls, we probably need a combination of deep actions and a sense of duty.

We also need duty to act in ways that sacrifice our interests for the benefit of future generations, to have a time horizon that extends beyond our lives. Nearly every political activist I have talked to in researching this book explains his or her motivations for action in terms of a duty to the future. A version of the Golden Rule attributed to the philosopher John Rawls is to "do unto future generations as you would have past generations do unto you."[13] Such a rule resonates on climate-change policy, where the consequences of decisions today will mostly affect later generations, and any policy we make now is clouded with uncertainty about whether it will work, what other nations will do, and what new technologies the future holds to address environmental problems. Environmental action requires a sense of duty to the future.

If the retired aviation amateurs who were tinkering with an airplane in Clayton's neighborhood were told it would take a hundred years to finish their craft, almost certainly they would not do it. In hobbies, we derive gratification from a culminating event, from seeing the task to its end. They wouldn't build the hundred-year airplane. In politics, though, we need to build hundred-year airplanes. That requires deep actions plus a commitment to present and future citizens.

• • •

We have thus arrived at a more nuanced understanding of what is meant by the charge of political hobbyism. We can now see why the most common forms of engagement described in the first section of the book (e.g., obsessive news consumption, partisan teamsmanship) are akin to a rather shallow hobby. They are knowledge-acquisition and collective cultural experiences and token one-off actions and emotional discharge. They are done for sheer amusement or as an un-thought-through, cathartic, politically-spiritual-but-not-committed stab in the dark at fulfilling a civic duty.

These common forms of engagement do not obligate participants into long-term relationships. They can be turned off anytime. Even deep hobbies cannot be turned off so readily as politics. If one of those airplane craftsmen in the factory in Sheboygan called it quits or if Clayton was expected to be at a ham radio mountain retreat but bailed out at the last minute, other participants would be disappointed, hurt even. If he didn't show, they'd call him up and find out where he was.

In shallow hobbies, we are emphatically not being relied upon. When people quit Facebook, nobody likely calls them up or sends an email to convey concern or disappointment that they are no longer offering their political hot takes. The relationships are not serious enough that anyone would care to make such a call. That no one is relying on you is a great sign that the activity you are doing is a shallow hobby.

PART III

You have to know how to arouse passions to fuel the fight, and then how to cool everyone down so they'll accept the deal on the table. . . . You have to control and direct the passion, or else it can burn down everything you've worked hard to build.
—Marshall Ganz[1]

CHAPTER 13

Hobbyist Provocateur

It's one thing to wish we spent less time passively reading news and more time actively participating in politics. It's quite another thing to claim that political hobbyism is a serious problem for our democracy. Is it worthy of our condemnation? What are the harms? The next few chapters get to the harms, of which there are three, and they all follow from the idea that in hobbyism we are not taking actions aimed at acquiring power. Instead, we're taking action to satisfy our short-term desires. As with many other forms of entertainment, we become focused on conflict and drama.[1]

The evidence for our attraction to drama is clear. Take Facebook. At the end of 2018, Mark Zuckerberg published a lengthy explanation of how Facebook was trying to make things right after the many scandals the company dealt with that year. Robert Mueller's investigation confirmed that Russia used Facebook to try to influence the 2016 presidential election; a whistle-blower revealed that the firm Cambridge Analytica had accessed, without permission, personal Facebook data to target campaign ads; the Myanmar military used Facebook for a propaganda campaign in its violent attacks on Rohingya Muslims. The list goes on. *Wired* identified twenty-one big scandals altogether that year.

"One of the biggest issues social networks face," Zuckerberg wrote, "is that, when left unchecked, people will engage disproportionately with more sensationalist and provocative content."[2] When an advertiser sponsors an outrageous ad or a Facebook user shares a provocative news story, it generates attention, and that's true whether a Russian operative, Cambridge Analytica, your crazy uncle, or you were the one who shared it.

Users tell Facebook they don't want to see clickbait and fake news items in their newsfeeds, but Facebook's internal data show that this stuff attracts us. We all might come to Facebook to reconnect with high school friends and make them feel jealous with pictures of children, vacations, and restaurant meals; but we stay on Facebook for the juicier stuff—for the sensationalism.[3] Issie Lapowsky, one of the sharpest reporters covering technology today, suggests that this phenomenon "undergirds most of Facebook's problems the past few years."[4]

Our penchant for political scandal and controversy isn't just facilitated by Facebook. Or by the news media, as I discussed earlier. Politicians and their campaigns feed off our outrage, too. In recent election cycles, the Democratic Congressional Campaign Committee has regularly sent emails with subject lines such as "Doomed" and "It's too late."[5] A candidate campaign sent emails titled "tragic end" and highlighted that President Trump had ATTACKED the candidate.[6]

These Democrats were using a consulting firm, Mothership Strategies, to solicit donations. Mothership has raised eyebrows for its lucrative strategy to solicit low-dollar donations. Emails with flashing red icons and exclamation points, alerting users that the Republicans are taking away Medicare and Social Security, telling recipients that donations are being matched and double-matched and quadruple-matched by wealthy supporters if you contribute right now. (This is somewhat deceptive because a donor can only give a maximum of a few thousand dollars; no donor can legally match contributions beyond his or her own limit.)[7]

Critics of Mothership allege that these strategies take advantage of Internet-unsavvy elderly Democrats in particular, which is maybe why messages on Social Security and Medicare seem to come up a lot. Politicians who use Mothership say that they're just trying to do what works. These emails work, as the firm's internal testing no doubt shows. This is what we respond to. The emails are intended to rile the base. It's not the politicians' fault, so goes the reasoning, it's our fault. We respond with cash when we are riled up by provocative messages.

The first reason hobbyism is a problem is that our small actions, when aggregated, affect how leaders behave. Politicians want to keep their activist base engaged, the core supporters who will vote for them in primary elections (or vote for their opponents if they stray off base) and donate. When we indulge our attraction to drama, they respond by acting dramatically. Politicians who lack the taste for drama are replaced by those who do have a taste for it. Our actions seem small and harmless, but *their* reactions to our actions are not small or harmless. Email solicitation strategies are the tip of the iceberg.

It's January. A group of activists is about to mount a protest against Democratic leaders. In two days, thousands of them will gather not in Washington but in Brooklyn to protest in front of Democratic Senate leader Chuck Schumer's family home. Targeting politicians at their homes is a step beyond a protest at a legislative office: spouses and children become part of the target. The event's Facebook page describes its mission: "No appeasement, no dealmaking, no collaboration." They are angry.

The protest will be on a Tuesday night. On the Sunday before, activists gather to make final preparations. A little girl, maybe three or four years old, stands in a room of adults. She has messy, shoulder-length, straight, light-brown hair. She wears a purple polka-dot dress. Behind her, adults are decorating the signs that they will carry in the streets. She holds a sign almost as big as her and poses for a picture. Her sign shows a couple of animals, but mostly it's taken up by a message in giant colorful letters: FUCK SHIT UP. She doesn't look old enough to read it or understand it, but she holds the sign that someone, a parent probably, made for her, and she smiles big for the camera. The Facebook group at the center of this protest will later post this photo on its public page.

The protest against Chuck Schumer, which took place on January 31, 2017, was mounted by the political left, not the right. The protest was organized on Facebook and titled "What the Fuck, Chuck." In front of the senator's house, thousands chanted, "Filibuster everything!"[8] Their signs read HEY CHUCK, GIVE A FUCK and CHUCK'S A CHICKEN. The protesters demanded that the Democratic leader oppose the new administration's nominees for cabinet positions. "Vote no! Vote no!" they chanted.[9]

On the same night as the protest, just as the event in Brooklyn was winding down, President Trump held a live broadcast in Washington where he introduced perhaps the most controversial of all his initial nominees, Judge Neil Gorsuch.

Gorsuch was the nominee to fill the Supreme Court seat formerly held by Justice Antonin Scalia, who had died almost a year earlier. The nomination was stinging to Democrats because after Scalia's death, then-president Obama had chosen his own nominee, Merrick Garland, to fill the seat. But the Republican-controlled Senate refused to consider Garland's nomination, saying it would wait till after the 2016 election to confirm a new justice.

The Republican maneuver was the latest in an ongoing fraying of norms surrounding judicial confirmations in the US Senate.[10] The previous milestone in that fraying happened in 2013. Until 2013, when a president nominated someone to fill a judicial vacancy, the Senate required sixty votes to confirm the nominee. In 2013, the Democrats, who had controlled the Senate since 2006, had grown frustrated that the Republicans held more than forty Senate seats and were blocking the judges whom Obama was nominating. Democrats reacted with the "nuclear option" as it was called. They voted by a mere majority to do away with the sixty-vote threshold for judicial nominations for any judgeship except to the Supreme Court, a move that some Democratic senators, such as Amy Klobuchar, would later regret.[11] They preserved the sixty-vote threshold only for the Supreme Court. The nuclear option allowed Democrats to confirm a number of judges to important positions with only a fifty-one-vote majority.

When President Trump nominated Judge Gorsuch in January of 2017, Democrats had a choice. They could filibuster Gorsuch or give him enough votes to be confirmed. If the Democrats filibustered Gorsuch, it would deny him the votes needed to surpass the sixty-vote threshold. But if they did this, the Republicans then had to decide to let the nomination die or to go "nuclear" themselves, changing the Senate rules again so that only fifty-one votes were needed to confirm a Supreme Court nominee. Republicans reasoned that, under the circumstances of the denial of Merrick Garland and the election of Donald Trump, Democrats would oppose any nominee the president put forth. Republicans said they would do away with the sixty-vote rule if the Democrats filibustered Gorsuch.

A group of Senate moderates tried to preserve the filibuster rule. Republicans Susan Collins of Maine and John McCain of Arizona and Democrats Michael Bennet of Colorado and Chris Coons of Delaware proposed a plan: Several Democrats would vote for Gorsuch to get him sixty votes. In exchange, several Republicans would commit to preserving the filibuster the next time President Trump was able to nominate someone to the Supreme Court. At the next Trump nomination, stakes might be even higher because, unlike Gorsuch, who was replacing a conservative, the next nominee could be replacing a liberal or replacing the court's swing vote, Justice Kennedy.

Before a deal could be struck, though, the negotiations fell apart. The Democrats made the decision that they had to filibuster Gorsuch. Why? According to the *New York Times*, it was because the Democrats were afraid of the "base voters who were furiously demanding unyielding resistance to Trump."[12] Writing in *Slate*, Dahlia Litwick said the Democrats filibustered because they were "beginning to realize that their base wants to see them fight for something."[13] The protest in front of Schumer's home, and the expressions of so many others online and in calls into congressional offices that Merrick Garland's treatment was unfair, that Trump's presidency had to be resisted, and that Gorsuch should be filibustered, apparently had an effect. The Democratic congressional leaders were afraid not to filibuster.

A filibuster felt good for the base, but was it the right decision? Not according to Senator Bennet, one of the Democrats who was trying to negotiate an alternative. As he told the *Times*, "I never understood the strategy. . . . We achieved nothing by filibustering Judge Gorsuch except giving Mitch McConnell the opportunity to strip us of our ability to filibuster a nominee who will cause a dramatic shift in the balance of the court." Progressive law professors took to *Vox* to call the move a "strategic blunder," which will only "mak[e] it easier for President Donald Trump to fill a future Supreme Court vacancy with a conservative justice who will swing the balance on issues such as abortion, LGBTQ rights, and affirmative action."[14]

It wasn't hard to foresee a future when the judicial filibuster would come in handy for Democrats, even if it meant giving Gorsuch approval in the short term. Foreseeing that future required Democrats at the time to focus less on what would make them feel satiated in the moment and more about the values they wanted to empower. That future came for them not two years later, in July 2018, with the nomination of Brett Kavanaugh.

Not only was Kavanaugh considered to be more conservative than Gorsuch,[15] he was replacing the court's moderate justice, Anthony Kennedy. Kavanaugh's ascent to the court, unlike Gorsuch's, would substantially affect the ideological balance of the justices. Plus, Judge Kavanaugh was accused of sexual assault, allegations that struck the Democrats in the Senate, but not as many of the Republicans, as a big deal. In short, if Democrats in 2018 could have flown in a time machine back to 2017 and hatched a plan to let Gorsuch through the Senate with sixty votes in order to stop Kavanaugh from replacing Justice Kennedy, they would probably have done it.

What would have happened had that group of Senate negotiators brokered a deal?

We'll never know, but the logic, laid out by the law professors in *Vox*, goes like this: Some moderate Republican senators would have had a hard time voting to end the filibuster with Kavanaugh. Two Republican senators at the time were pro-choice. Kavanaugh's nomination, not Gorsuch's, put the future of reproductive rights on more uncertain ground. Also, several Republicans were indeed concerned about the sexual assault allegations. They may not have voted to do away with the filibuster under the circumstances presented to them with Kavanaugh. For some Republicans, that might have been too much for them. Several conservative analysts agree with this, arguing Kavanaugh would not have been seated if Democrats hadn't filibustered Gorsuch.[16]

We'll never know. We'll also never know what would have happened if Kavanaugh was successfully filibustered and President Trump nominated a new candidate in his place. Maybe in the long run that would have been an even worse outcome for Democrats. It's mind-numbing to go too far down this path of what-ifs.

But we do know that Democrats went with their supporters who were demanding a fight. Politicians were afraid of their wrath. If they didn't go along with the base, would they face a primary challenge? Would they never be a viable candidate in a Democratic presidential primary? The base was energized in a way it wasn't energized in the 2016 election (when its energy would have come in handy), and now it wanted to see a fight. They wanted to FUCK SHIT UP in Brooklyn; MAKE SOME FUCKING NOISE. "You need to fight! You need to lead! Show us what you have Or you will lose your seat!" "We are the resistance And you work for us! We are the resistance Get on the bus!"[17]

Is it possible to keep these two things in our heads at the same time: that it was unfair that Obama was denied this nomination *and* that filibustering Gorsuch was possibly a mistake for Democrats? I think so. It was a mistake attributable to a form of politics done for short-term emotional highs rather than a form of politics done for long-term power.

Regardless of whether you are convinced that this protest was savvy or shortsighted, or you aren't sure, it's important to see an underlying tension in protests generally. Angela Aldous, and the Voice of Westmoreland, help us understand the tension. Protests can be strategic and also cathartic. To recruit new members to her organization in Trump country, Angela and her group protest so that potential allies in hiding can find them. But from her anti–Scott Walker protests on, Angela has looked skeptically upon protests where the goal seems to be catharsis with no strategy.

Protests are a useful strategy not only for recruitment. Protests can also be a form of threat: after President Trump instituted a ban on Muslim travelers to the United States, protesters flooded airports, raising the threat that thousands of people across US cities were willing to shut down airports in response to the ban. Protests can also raise attention to an issue, such as Black Lives Matter protests targeting police brutality. When the protest's goal is to tell Chuck Schumer to "give a fuck," which Schumer could demonstrate to the protesters by denying the president all his cabinet nominations, the protest seems to me to be more about feelings than strategy.

Protests organized by groups with long-term visions, such as labor unions, will tend to be more strategic than cathartic. Even in a protest that feels like merely a cathartic exercise to outsiders, organizers will be weaving through the crowd with clipboards looking to recruit volunteers into more sustained actions. These organizers have a strategy even if participants do not realize it. In contrast, protests hastily organized by a lone citizen who wrote a viral social media post will likely be more cathartic than strategic.

On the far cathartic-only end of the spectrum are virtual "protests" that are strictly on social media. After all, the strategic organizers fomenting outrage online are largely not organizers at all; they are companies whose goal is to keep us on their platforms and for whom our feelings of outrage are merely a means to achieving that goal. If your goal is political power, putting feelings ahead of strategy is a problem. But if your goal is a shallow, leisure-time hobby activity, prioritizing short-term feelings of catharsis is the whole point.

CHAPTER 14

Outrage and Compromise

For decades now, political scientists have been studying polarization. The history of polarization is complicated, but the hobbyist
base of a political party, pushing politicians to dig in their heels and
fight, is a key part of that story.

In Congress, polarization usually means that Democrats and
Republicans don't work together, that they have moved into ideological camps that are far away from each other. Since the 1970s,
members of Congress have stopped crossing party lines to pass bills
on issues important to different regional interests or based on the
expertise of individual representatives. Members of Congress tend
to stick to their side and vote a party line.

The mass public hasn't become particularly polarized since the
1970s. In fact, more now than fifty years ago, voters tend to identify as
political independents rather than as partisans. Even on hot-button
issues such as abortion or guns, voters' policy positions are more
moderate than politicians' positions. On abortion, for instance, voters tend to favor more restrictions than Democratic politicians and
fewer restrictions than Republican politicians.[1]

But a certain segment of the mass public has become quite polarized, especially since the 1990s: voters who are well educated and
follow political news. In other words, probably you. You are probably more ideologically consistent, extreme on the issues, and partisan than a version of you from thirty years ago. In the 1970s, about
4 percent of Americans who didn't regularly follow news considered
themselves very liberal or very conservative. In 2016, 5 percent of
them considered themselves very ideological. No big change. But

117

among those very interested in politics, they have become almost twice as likely to identify as extremely ideological.[2] (If that describes you, you might reason that your polarization is a response to the polarized politicians, which has a lot of truth to it. But we'll also consider whether your move to a political pole reinforces the behavior of those politicians.)

Beyond polarization, a well-documented pattern of *partisan sorting* has been going on.[3] Fifty years ago, for instance, social conservatives and social liberals were found in both parties. Today, the social liberals are mostly Democrats and the social conservatives Republican. That's sorting. Racial groups have also sorted. Racial minority groups that were split between the parties in the 2000s, namely Latinos and Asians, have, in a short time, become mostly Democratic. In 2004, for instance, about 55 percent of Latinos and Asians voted for John Kerry, the Democratic candidate for president. In 2016, about 65 percent of these groups voted for Hillary Clinton.[4]

Democratic politicians look at their voters and see a group that is liberal and racially diverse and younger; Republicans see their voters as conservative and white and older. And while most of these voters have moderate—or just vague and ill-formed—policy positions,[5] the vocal core supporters who vote in primaries, follow the news, and fund campaigns are not moderate at all. By 2015, about 90 percent of Americans who called themselves strong Democrats or strong Republicans reported feeling well represented by their political parties. For independents, even those who say they lean toward a party, fewer than half say their views are well represented.[6]

Experts on polarization don't have one definitive explanation for why Congress and this pool of super-engaged voters got so extreme. Is it because members of Congress of both parties used to live in DC, send their kids to schools together, socialize together, but now they mostly commute back and forth to their home districts? That's one explanation as to why Democrats and Republicans in Congress don't work well together. The politicians polarized first, and the voters followed their lead.

Did polarization happen because Southern conservatives used to be Democrats and now they are Republicans? That's the biggest explanation. For much of the twentieth century, whites in the South were overwhelmingly Democratic. They were conservative, particularly in their views on race. By the end of the twentieth century, they became predominantly Republican. Their shift made the Democratic Party mostly liberal and the Republican Party mostly conservative. But the shift isn't sufficient to explain polarization because polarization has occurred outside the South as well. It isn't just that conservative Southern Democrats were replaced (in Congress and in the mass public) by conservative Southern Republicans. Non-Southern Republicans in particular have shifted starkly to the right.

Did polarization also happen because of changes in election laws over the last few decades, such as in redistricting or partisan primaries? These explanations are commonly brought up in conversations about polarization, but experts look at the data and largely dismiss them. Redistricting, also referred to as gerrymandering, is not a likely explanation for polarization. The same increase in polarization we have witnessed in the House of Representatives is just as visible in the Senate, which cannot be gerrymandered. It's also visible in states that only have one representative, which are also not gerrymander-able.[7]

As for primaries, advocates have long thought that closed primaries—elections in which only registered members of each party are eligible to participate—lead to polarization. The logic goes that moderate voters are registered as independent, and when a state political party forbids their participation in primaries, we get extreme voters and extreme representatives. But it isn't so. States have experimented with a wide range of rules for eligibility to vote in primaries, and the rules don't at all affect the level of polarization in those states.[8]

Regardless of who is allowed to participate in primaries, only certain voters wish to participate in them. Most voters take little interest in primaries. They don't follow politics closely enough to have an opinion. The voters who do participate, in states with open or closed rules, tend to have strong ideological preferences.

The candidates who emerge to run in those primaries—the kinds of people who want to be in Congress—are also strongly ideological. Why? One possibility is that if the primary voters have extreme views and want their politicians to represent those views, moderate candidates stay away. They don't even bother to run.[9]

Another possibility relates to the group other than politicians that has polarized most clearly in the last few decades: donors. Campaign funders have become noticeably more ideological. Twenty or thirty years ago, the typical congressional race was funded by corporate political action committees (PACs), committees that often give to members of both parties.[10] The wealthy individual donors who supported congressional campaigns on their own (not via PACs) typically resided in the state where the race was taking place. In 1990, for instance, 69 percent of individual congressional donations came from in-state.

By 2012, 68 percent of donations were from *out of state*, and most money now comes from these individual donors, not from PACs.[11] The individual donors, particularly the out-of-state ones, are ideologically motivated.[12] They are not the local business owners supporting whoever is in office so that the donors can keep an ear out for issues that affect the business community. The donors are purists, in politics for the ideology and spoiling for a fight. They don't want dealmakers in Congress; they want big ideas and clear differentiation between their team and the other team.[13]

Sorted liberals and conservatives, sorted whites and minorities, and polarized donors and primary voters; politicians in Congress are now constrained by their partisan camps. They may feel the way those Senate Democrats felt during the short-lived, failed negotiations over the Gorsuch nomination. As Princeton's Nolan McCarty puts it in his outstanding 2019 book, *Polarization*, "No longer do elected officials face the diverse partisan constituencies that might give them leeway to make important cross-party concessions and compromises. Ideologically sorted partisan activists, donors, and primary voters stand ready to sanction any such transgressions."[14]

Why did engaged voters and donors become like this? Changes to the media environment since the 1970s is the most obvious explanation. In 1979, for instance, C-SPAN began offering a live video feed of congressional proceedings. Then-representative Al Gore Jr. of Tennessee made the first ever live-televised floor speech. "Television will change this institution," he said, "but the good will far outweigh the bad."

Maybe.

The year C-SPAN came to Congress was also the year Newt Gingrich came to Congress. As recounted by the historian Julian Zelizer, Gingrich mastered using C-SPAN to take his unfiltered, purist message directly to the people, with regular floor speeches in the House not intended for his colleagues or even for reporters, but for the base who might catch clips on TV news.[15] Gingrich's no-compromise style rubbed off on other Republicans in the House who rose with him, many of whom eventually joined the Senate, such as Rick Santorum in Pennsylvania and Tom Coburn in Oklahoma. They took a media-savvy, noncompromising approach that presaged today's era of heightened congressional polarization.[16]

Changes to the media environment are obviously much bigger than the coming of C-SPAN. On cable and on social media, ideologues call out politicians who veer toward compromise. They one-up each other in taking more extreme positions.[17] A politician presents a proposal, and a news network can instantly find someone who is outraged that the proposal doesn't go far enough to please his or her side. To an audience, the outraged hot takes are more interesting than commentators praising compromises or deals that cede an inch to the opposition.

Scholars have long noted that Americans don't like slow stages of drafting laws and seeing bills go through so many iterations before anything gets done. We don't like hearing about compromises and brokered deals. We don't like committees. We don't like all the amendments along the way as the House and the Senate craft separate legislation and then negotiate to resolve their differences. "Much of what the public dislikes about Congress," two experts conclude, "is endemic to what a legislature is."[18] If we approach politics as a path to power, we can appreciate slow and steady progress and compromise. But if we approach politics as a form of entertainment, we are absolutely repelled by slow and steady compromise.

According to Morris Fiorina, one of the foremost political scholars in the country, members of Congress are pushed by the base—the donors and activists and primary voters—to take extreme positions and not compromise with the minority.[19] The majority tries to pass policy that the base wants. Meanwhile, the minority party tries not to cooperate but rather confronts and waits for the next election for the chance to get control themselves. Control of Congress keeps shifting back and forth between the two parties because most voters (everyone except those attentive, uncompromising base supporters) don't like this kind of governing.

Voters see the majority party as overreaching. Less engaged voters either sit out the next election or shift their vote from one party to the other, effectively switching out the party in the majority. The shifting of power is self-reinforcing. Both parties focus on scoring electoral points instead of legislating. Rather than negotiate, they taunt and wait for their turn to run the show.

Congressional scholar Frances Lee noticed that ever since 1980, when power in the Senate started shifting back and forth regularly between the two parties, senators started behaving differently from how they behaved before. In the Senate, senators can come to the floor of the chamber and offer amendments to bills after committees have already considered the bills. Before 1980, amendments from the floor tended to come from members of the majority and minority parties at the same rate. The party of the senator proposing the amendment wasn't a predictor of whether the amendment passed or failed. Moderate senators of both parties had the most success passing amendments.

After 1980, the pattern changed. The minority party started proposing many more amendments than the majority party. These amendments were no longer intended to persuade a majority of senators to adopt changes to bills. They were intended as part of a partisan public-relations strategy. Pretty quickly, amendments coming from senators in the minority party stopped passing at the same rate as those coming from the majority party. Amendments stopped serving as an opportunity to build coalitions around changes to laws. Amendments became a form of protest, a strategic disagreement with an eye toward the next election.[20]

Treating the legislative process as an opportunity to dig in one's heels and score electoral points has serious downsides. One is that Congress is able to get a lot less done. The least polarized Congresses have passed, on average, 111 percent more bills than the most polarized ones.[21] If you think gridlock is bad and Congress has a lot of work to do in lawmaking, then polarization is a problem. If politicians are always making a PR point to feed red meat to their respective bases, they can't pass compromise policies on issues of broad popular consensus. The bills that majorities pass without consensus are often rushed, ill-conceived, and unstable.

When we approach politics as hobbyists, on the sidelines rooting, on the phone lines demanding, on social media emoting, we are the ones who are pushing those in Congress to dig in their heels rather than legislate. We are the ones encouraging them not to compromise, calling out any attempts at compromise as a violation of our fundamental moral values. We want them to hold the line and wait for the next election when maybe we can get enough power to ram something through without talking to the other side.

When we do politics this way, politicians respond by making strategic choices that are bad in the long run in favor of the short-term emotional demands of the base. They pass quick, shaky policies or refuse to participate in negotiations at all. They are paralyzed from lawmaking or they overreach. Those of us engaged in politics as hobbyists hold some blame for all that. Our appetite for political hobbyism, combined with technologies that prioritize knee-jerk hot takes and with laws placing congressional deliberations on live stream and giving members of Congress the ability to raise millions in response to viral-video grandstanding, does not serve us well.

What in our psyches pushes us to push politicians to dig in their heels? The answer is more interesting than just our fascination with drama as well as changes to laws and media technology that accentuate our fascination with drama. Tim Ryan, a political scientist at the University of North Carolina in Chapel Hill, helps us understand why we act like this. It has to do with moral outrage.

Take any policy issue, say Social Security as an example. Suppose I asked you, "Is your position on Social Security a reflection of your core moral beliefs and convictions and is it connected to your beliefs about fundamental rights and wrongs?"

Think about it. What would you say? Is your view on Social Security very much connected to your fundamental values? Is it just a little connected? Which issues would you say this for and which ones wouldn't you? Would you say it about climate change? Health care? Immigration? Transportation infrastructure?

Hold on to those answers.

For any given policy area, Ryan asks how the issue relates to your moral values and also how important the issue is to you, how much the policy affects your life, and what your actual views are on any changes to the policy. To keep Social Security afloat in the next few decades, for instance, would you rather raise taxes, or would you rather cut benefits to future retirees?

How you answer the initial question I posed about moral conviction, Ryan shows, is not strongly related to how relevant the policy is to your life or how important you think the issue is. It is very much related to the extremeness of your views on the issue and the strength of your feelings of partisanship. If you feel you know, with certainty, the right answer to the benefit-cut/tax-cut question, or if you are a strong Democrat or a strong Republican, you are more likely to see the issue as tied to your fundamental moral values.

If you connect issues to fundamental moral values, you are distinct from most other people in some important ways: Namely, you don't want to compromise on the issue. You don't like politicians who compromise on the issue. That's true even if the issue is not that important to you personally.

Is that so bad? We'll see.

Ryan gives voters hypotheticals, such as this one: Suppose two liberal Democrats are running in a primary for Congress. They both think we need to increase taxes on the wealthy to keep Social Security afloat. They both say they would vote against any congressional bill raising the retirement age for eligibility for Social Security. One of these candidates, though, says that to maintain a healthy Social Security system, he'd be willing to negotiate on decreasing monthly Social Security payments. The other says he'd oppose that change and wouldn't negotiate on it.

Whether you think Social Security is important and whether Social Security is relevant to your life have no bearing on your choice of candidates in this hypothetical. But if you report having this feeling of moral conviction, you don't want compromises and wouldn't support candidates willing to compromise.

Not only do you not want compromise, you are also not open to learning new relevant information that might change your mind. You become obstinate. For instance, Ryan asks about positions on nuclear energy, and on how much one's views on nuclear energy are tied to deep moral convictions. He then asks about one's views on the issue—do you want the government to build more reactors? Do you want fewer reactors? Finally, he asks, would you change your view if the world's leading experts updated their evaluation of the safety of nuclear reactors? In experiments, Ryan has given hypotheticals where the experts deem reactors extremely safe (chance of an incident is one in ten million) or quite dangerous (chance of an incident is one in ten thousand).

Americans who really like the idea or really hate the idea of nuclear energy were willing to shift their views in light of updated expert opinion. But those respondents who connected nuclear energy to their fundamental values were the least likely to change their minds.[22]

Psychologists and political scientists look to both our genes and dispositions as well as our environment to explain the origins of moral conviction. What kind of person sees in each issue a fundamental moral choice? Looking at the data myself, I see one clear pattern that is tied to media use. Even back in 2012, when a nationally representative survey asked questions both about moral conviction and news consumption, individuals who obtained news from Facebook and Twitter were significantly more likely to tie issues to moral values. Beyond that, for Democrats (but not for independents or Republicans), how much you follow the news predicts your feelings of moral conviction. Democrats who follow the news closely were far more likely to say that they tied even random issues to moral values than those who follow the news less frequently.

Moral conviction seems like a good thing. What is wrong about making a connection between policy issues and moral values? Indeed, such convictions can help build energy around a cause. Marshall Ganz, a renowned political organizer and liberal intellectual, emphasizes that emotion and righteous anger are a means to an end. If you care about empowering a set of ideas, moral outrage is a way to energize yourself and others to translate values into concrete actions.

The problem arises when emotion and anger are the end rather than the means to the end. The problem is also if outrage leads to digging in our heels so much that we forgo compromise. When that happens, not only is outrage unproductive, it can tear causes apart, burn everything down, as Ganz is quoted at the opening of this section.[23] Political engagement characterized by reacting to news events, feeling upset, drifting from one event to the next, passively looking on, endlessly bickering about what can be done and what injustices have been done—these are the qualities exactly opposite to what it takes to organize for a cause, Ganz argues.[24] Political hobbyism isn't just a distinct activity from the pursuit of political power; it hinders the pursuit of political power.

But for many of us, anyway, isn't this precisely our diagnosis? Even when we think our motivations are higher, hobbyists are looking for entertainment, and so emotion—righteous anger—is an end rather than a means to an end. It's the same diagnosis that James Q. Wilson saw among club Democrats of the 1950s who "[see] each battle as a 'crisis' and each victory as a triumph and each loss as a defeat for a cause." We turn every political debate into a moral showdown because it makes us feel connected to political events without having to dirty our hands with power-seeking initiatives. Moral outrage is a shortcut to feeling engaged.

Thus concludes the first problem with political hobbyism. We are attracted to forms of politics that are entertaining and provocative and that elicit our moral outrage. New media technologies and laws elevate our emotional reactions and reward politicians who cater to them. In the halls of Congress and on the campaign trail, politicians behave badly, even act against their own side's policy goals and long-term political interests, because the people who pay the most attention to them demand that they behave like stubborn, outraged children.

CHAPTER 15

Bringing Out the Worst in Us

If I'm driving down the highway, my three kids strapped into car seats in the back of our minivan, and I see a car swerving in and out of lanes, accelerating past me at ninety miles an hour, I get upset. I tense up, clutch the steering wheel. Maybe I'll blurt out something just barely left of R-rated, mindful of the children. I honk an extended honk into the expanding distance between the speeding driver and my minivan to demonstrate how annoyed I am.

But do you know what my brother-in-law does in this situation, when he sees someone speed past him? He thinks to himself, or maybe he says to those in the car with him with a smile, "Driving that fast, I bet that guy really needs to use the bathroom."[1]

I don't naturally have that level of goodwill in me. I wish I did. A dangerous driver is being dangerous; what empathy does he deserve? I don't think my brother-in-law actually believes the driver is likely to be rushing to the bathroom. But my brother-in-law is able to not let his own blood boil about it. He shrugs it off and smiles, extending to this stranger, even just in his own mind, generosity almost certainly undeserved.

We often refer to social media sites, venues for shallow forms of political hobbyism where we offer our hot takes but where no one is depending on us, as "toxic environments." People who are "friends"— half strangers to one another—can read each other's language in the least generous light to find weaknesses instead of strengths in their arguments. They try to score points with their responses. On social media, we are not quite as anonymous as we are in our cars, but as with driving, we don't always act our best. Maybe more like me and less like my brother-in-law.

Does shallow political hobbyism bring out the worst in us? That's the second concern I want to raise about why this form of politics is harmful. It doesn't just incentivize politicians to behave badly. It incentivizes us to behave badly. And acting badly hurts our own political causes.

One reason I think so is that the organizers I have met while researching this book are some of the most empathetic people I've ever encountered. When it comes to being respectful to those who disagree with them politically, they draw a stark contrast to the ways many of us behave on social media or in front of the news. And, ironically, unlike most of us infatuated with news or lurking on social media, they are actually regularly interacting with the other side. If they can do it, how come we can't?

Here's the reason. They cultivate empathy because they want power for their views. Getting power means convincing people to take actions they wouldn't otherwise take. Power-seeking organizers can't do that by yelling or whining. They need to show empathy.

Dave Fleischer, the organizer from the LA LGBT Center who has pioneered the strategy of deep canvassing, tells it like this. In 2008, he was working with LGBT advocates to oppose Proposition 8 in California, which called for a state constitutional ban on gay marriage. Thousands of volunteers worked in favor of the gay rights position. But, Dave says, the consultants who were running the pro-gay-marriage side of the campaign went about it all wrong. They didn't have volunteers talk to voters who opposed gay marriage. The consultants just had volunteers talk to supporters of gay marriage and encourage them to vote. The problem was, gay marriage didn't have enough supporters. On the same day as Democrat Barack Obama won the presidency handily, gay marriage was constitutionally banned in California.

After the loss, in January 2009, Dave gathered with a group at a Methodist church in Los Angeles to talk about their next steps. Some activists had been protesting, including outside Mormon churches, since the Mormon Church had helped to fund the opponents of gay marriage. Dave thought that rather than just confronting people in protests, his side needed to talk to more people who voted against them. They needed to understand them. Dave needed to figure out a way to reach people who'd voted against gay marriage and convey how important gay rights are to him. He felt that if he could help them appreciate the personal stakes for people affected by the ban, opponents might see things his way.[2]

Oftentimes, debates that ordinary people have about politics are heated not because they have strong opposing views to one another, but because they perceive stakes differently. Some of Dave's antagonists on gay marriage had firmly held beliefs. But many others voted against gay marriage because they had never met someone like Dave and empathized with the person. That's Dave's running hypothesis.

Political discussions on social media (or at a Thanksgiving table) can feel toxic when an issue that affects you deeply is discussed flippantly by others, where your views seem to be summarily dismissed without regard to your feelings. How many of us are guilty of discussing political issues differently in the company of people who are deeply affected by them from how we would discuss those issues in their absence? We can discuss issues flippantly when the discussions are merely for fun, a hobby. The stakes are low. We're not talking about real people's lives.

The idea of political hobbyism helps me better understand political friction for precisely this reason. In an earlier chapter, we asked whether partisan feelings are deeply felt or more like sports fandom. They are more like fandom when we fail to see the connection between our issue positions and real lives. Sometimes, partisan animosity between us and our antagonists is really masking differently felt stakes.

Dave believed that he could connect to voters who opposed gay marriage by showing them that this issue, which might be low stakes for them, was high stakes for him. That is the origin story of deep canvassing. When opponents of gay rights talk about gay rights with their friends, Dave Fleischer wants them not to think of some abstract policy that affects some abstract other; Dave Fleischer wants them to think about Dave Fleischer, a nice person they met at their door.

Dave compares his approach to saving for retirement. Retirement savings is high-stakes stuff: without enough savings, our quality of life will be severely compromised in retirement. So what do we do? We don't sit on the sidelines and hope for a magical solution. We save, slowly and steadily, each month socking away a few dollars that eventually add up. For retirement savings, this is the only responsible path, and it's also the only responsible path for getting political power. One voter at a time. In the back of our heads, we know that our investments might not pay off. The stock market might crash unrecoverably just as political institutions might. Nevertheless, we proceed with slow and steady investments because the alternative, maybe playing the lottery, is far worse. Each voter Dave talks to and shows kindness to, that might be one more person in this country who respects his right to live freely.

So Dave goes to houses and tells skeptical strangers about the people he loves. He says he tries to treat the person at the door more like a friend than a stranger, and he opens up to them. He shows them vulnerability. He is not an automaton canvasser reciting a script crafted by a consultant. And he's not treating the voter at the door like an automaton nemesis, either.

At first, as Dave shares something personal at the door, usually a story about someone he loves, the person at the door probably thinks, "Why the hell is this person telling me about his personal life?" That's what Dave imagines the person thinking. But then, if Dave is lucky, the person thinks, "This is not the conversation I was expecting to have from someone canvassing my door about politics. I'm not being condescended to." Then maybe the person opens up about where he or she is coming from. Dave listens back intently. He's not there to argue. He's there for mutual understanding.[3]

I have already discussed the evidence showing that Dave's methods seem to have long-lasting persuasive effects on voters. Less quantitative evidence is available on the effects on volunteers. Anecdotally, volunteers say they become better listeners, that they see the humanity in people who are so unlike them. "Every door knock, we meet another human being. That keeps me coming back," said one of those Staten Island canvassers I met in Brooklyn. Cultivating empathy for citizens who don't vote or for citizens who do vote but not the way you like turns out to be a pretty hopeful way to spend your time, makes you a better listener, gives you a more generous heart.

Organizers such as Dave are not just generous to the voters who oppose them. They are more compassionate than you might expect to people on their own side who don't show up to help. Sure, the organizers wish more people would join them in the political trenches, and, sure, they are frustrated by so much energy wasted on social media. But they know everyone is busy. They know their friends dillydallying online must be going through a lot. These forgiving organizers have lives that are as complicated and busy as everyone else's, but they think of us on our couches the way my brother-in-law thinks of the jerk who cut him off on the road: maybe he's acting that way because he just has to go to the bathroom. Everyone gets the benefit of the doubt.

Dave is also generous to people who he thinks are doing politics the wrong way. After Trump's 2016 election, Dave had to get a roomful of volunteers to stop talking about a protest banner they wanted to hang over the Los Angeles freeway, which Dave didn't think would be impactful, and get them to refocus on reaching out to voters in person. He was frustrated that they would obsess over a highway banner, but patiently, slowly, he moves them toward his goals. Another organizer, in Kansas, reflected on all the bumps in the road that all activists inevitably experience. "People don't know what they're doing, but they are trying. Thousands of people are trying. And there's going to be a lot of failure." Organizers tend to develop generous hearts for those who are trying to engage because they themselves know how hard it is to have real impact.

Volunteering the way Dave Fleischer does may bring out the best in us, making us more patient and empathetic. I believe that. But it's worth pointing out that Dave's form of civic engagement is not typical. If you've ever gone canvassing yourself, you were probably sent to doors with a short script. One typical canvassing director told sociologist Dana Fisher, "We have a standard [script], so it's like everything is just written out for you, and we actually require that people say *exactly* what's there and memorize it, and it's really not that hard to memorize 'cause it's not that long. It's less than two minutes . . . [and] it basically has the main points that we want to get across so . . . [canvassers are] sending out the same message."[4] If you have ever been the recipient of a canvass, it probably was more like this script than like a genuine conversation.

Fisher, along with political scientist Hahrie Han and other intellectual leaders on organizing, criticize these consultant-led, top-down approaches to mobilization where volunteers must rush to meet a quota of phone calls or door knocks. In successful organizations, leaders build trust with volunteers, empathize with their path of active engagement, encourage them to extend that same empathy to those they encounter at doors along the way.[5] They build genuine communities, as with the organizations that Lisa, Naakh, Angela, and Drew are all part of.

Most campaigns don't think that what Dave Fleischer does is worth their time and money. For one thing, deep canvassing doesn't scale quickly, which makes it unappetizing. Foundations, presidential campaigns, and national parties typically want to say they did something big. They will hand over money to consultants who can reach millions of people in a short time. After an election, they can say, "We impacted millions of people." And they may care less that the impact they had was tiny or short-lived.

Campaigns may also not like deep canvassing because it requires delegating power to others. If an expert gives a volunteer a script and says to stay on message, the expert retains control of the message. In deep canvassing, control has to trickle down to volunteers because the personal connections at the heart of organizing are just that, *personal*. Someone in a national campaign office has to give up some control for that to work.

Most important, big national campaigns and organizations don't do what Dave Fleischer does because, to bring us full circle, they perceive the stakes differently from Dave. To wealthy funders or to consultants, the stakes in politics are lower than for Dave. If they lose—they invested in a strategy that didn't work well—they are not personally much worse off. The same consultants will probably be hired again for the next campaign. They may throw money at a get-out-the-vote drive that reaches a lot of people but with an ineffective message. They may pay a lot of money for a flashy video ad, hoping it will go viral. They may take a one-in-a-million bet that some quick fix can fundamentally change politics. In short, they'll play the lottery. If they felt the stakes the way Dave did, the way organizers do, they might realize that politics isn't something you gamble with.

Instead, you take the retirement-savings approach, slowly and steadily acquiring power, one tiny contribution at a time, one voter at a time, for your whole life. It's grueling and requires patience, but if you're not rich and comfortable, what other choice do you have?

If we do politics the way Dave wants, will it make us more empathetic, which will in turn help us convince more people to act in politics the way we want them to? The quantitative empirical evidence on this question is nonexistent. So, for now, let's just each put the question to ourselves. For those of us doing politics as a hobby instead of politics for power, could we see ourselves being better people and more effective citizens if we did what Dave does? I know my own answer, and in a few chapters I'll tell you how I found that answer by taking politics more seriously in my own life.

CHAPTER 16

Gateway Slacktivism

The college Democrats at my university host campus events, such as an annual West Wing and Wings event that draws a few dozen students. They also work hard to try to get students to leave campus to canvass. They have had trouble with that. In 2018, when anti-Trump energy on campus was high, the Democratic group's best showing was to get seven students to go up to Londonderry, New Hampshire, for a few hours of canvassing. The students whom the Democratic leaders tried to recruit tell the leaders that it was hard to find the time to drive all the way up to New Hampshire and canvass there; they were too busy. In response, the student leaders tried organizing canvasses for competitive local races near campus. When they tried that, they recruited no more students than they got up to New Hampshire.

In spring of 2019, at the beginning of the 2020 presidential primary race, the college Democrats announced that they'd be going back up to New Hampshire, but this time not to canvass. They'd be going to the Currier Museum of Art in Manchester to attend an event featuring South Bend, Indiana, mayor Pete Buttigieg, who had announced his bid for the presidency. This time, the student group could not find enough cars to meet the demand of everyone who wanted to go. Students who were way too busy to canvass locally or canvass in New Hampshire would drop everything to drive to Manchester and post a picture with Pete Buttigieg on their Instagram.

Not every citizen is expected to knock on doors or make a serious commitment to political engagement. But the person who gets in a car and drives to New Hampshire for a selfie with Pete Buttigieg or

134

who spends two hours a day following news on Twitter or cable, that *is* the kind of person who could be engaging seriously in politics. But mostly these people do not.

The third critique of political hobbyism is that our time spent on leisure is replacing time that we would—or could—spend on politics for power. Leisure time is finite. Only so many hours of our day can be dedicated to activities other than work and family obligations. The typical person who is spending two hours following political news is unlikely to have another hour to spend on actual civic participation.

The argument that hobbyism replaces real politics is trickier than it may seem. If we suddenly stopped consuming news, for example, would we actually spend our time effectively engaging in politics? Maybe instead of checking polling stats, we'd just check sports standings. Maybe instead of watching cable news, we'd watch endless reruns of *Diners, Drive-Ins and Dives.* Maybe instead of taking a selfie in New Hampshire, we wouldn't dutifully knock on doors and talk to voters; we would just take a selfie somewhere else.

More important, maybe the hobbyist behaviors that we are doing right now are exactly the behaviors that will inspire us to one day take deeper actions. That is the objective of the words you are reading, after all, words that you are likely reading in your leisure time because you like politics, but which are written deliberately to motivate you to consider doing politics not as a leisure activity. Whoa, this is so meta. We have to consider the possibility that hobbyism is not a distraction at all, but an inspiration!

The US Bureau of Labor Statistics asks random samples of Americans how they spent their previous day. From this survey, we can summarize how we allocate our free hours. The typical American spends about five hours and fifteen minutes each day in leisure time. Retirees and young adults in their teens and twenties have a bit more leisure time. The age group I just entered, ages thirty-five to forty-four, sadly has the least free time.[1]

The biggest use of our leisure hours, by far, is watching TV shows. On weekdays, Americans spend about two and a half hours watching TV. On weekends, it's even more. Little of our leisure time is spent in in-person socializing. Apart from TV, most is spent "relaxing and thinking," playing games, using a computer, reading, or exercise. Maybe three-quarters of our leisure time is spent solitarily or in front of a screen.

In contrast to the hours we spend on media consumption, the Bureau of Labor Statistics reports that on average we spend twenty minutes a day, total, on any kind of religious, civic, or volunteer activity. Most of that is religious activity, such as prayer. The civic or volunteer activity collectively takes up about nine minutes a day if averaged across Americans. This average masks that some people spend a lot of time volunteering and most people spend zero time on it. On a typical day, about 6 percent of the US population is volunteering for some cause or organization.[2]

If you cannot imagine finding time in the day to join a political organization but can find time to binge-watch an endless queue of TV series, you are, so the survey shows, in good company.

The time-use statistics are about the general US population. What about the behaviors of the politically informed and engaged Americans, that subset of people you are probably part of? The subset of the population that consumes political news every day and cares a lot about politics isn't particularly active in community life, either. Consider the American National Election Study, the flagship political science survey of American attitudes since the 1940s. Among daily news consumers in 2016, less than 4 percent reported doing any work whatsoever on behalf of a campaign or party that election year. Even among those who reported they were afraid of Donald Trump, only 5 percent reported that they did any work to support their side.

Of Americans who consume news every day, most report belonging to zero organizations. Sixty-five percent report that in the last year they have done no work with other people to solve a community problem. Sixty-eight percent say they have attended zero meetings in the last year about a community issue. The population that is informed enough and cares enough about politics to follow the daily news is mostly disengaged from participation in political and community endeavors.

All of these numbers, by the way, *exaggerate* the rates of participation because some people feel they ought to have done these things, leading to what's called overreporting bias, a fancy way of saying that people inflate their political involvement when taking surveys. We encountered that phenomenon earlier, in a discussion about voting: on surveys, lots of people, but especially those who are well educated and follow political news, say they voted even when they didn't. It's harder to validate the rate of lying about organizational participation. (Unlike with voting, organized participation cannot be validated against government records.) But the principle holds. Many people, maybe most of them, who say on surveys that they are part of organizations or attend meetings are lying.

The lack of organizational engagement in America is puzzling because over the last fifty years the country has become much better educated. Political scientists have long thought that education confers on voters skills and knowledge to understand politics and participate in sophisticated political discussions, plus a social network where political participation is expected.[3] With so many educated Americans, we should be living in a golden age of participation.

Yet, while the proportion of people who *say* they are interested in elections reached a record high in 2016, the rate at which people report volunteering or participating has sharply declined. In the 1960, 1964, and 1968 election seasons, respectively, 13, 17, and 9 percent of college-educated respondents said they did some work for a campaign or candidate. In the 2012 and 2016 elections, when the college-educated population was three times larger, the rate of those saying they worked for a campaign was a third as large as it had been in the 1960s. Only 5 percent reported doing any work in the 2012 or 2016 elections. Asked if they attended any kind of political meeting or rally in the 1960, 1964, and 1968 elections, 11, 24, and 18 percent of college-educated respondents, respectively, said yes. In 2012 and 2016, 8 and 9 percent, respectively, said so. Education may have conferred on the country a growing sophistication in talking about elections or consuming news about elections or proclaiming interest in elections, but not in attending a meeting of a political organization or working on its behalf.[4]

But put the history aside. For any person *now*, is shallow hobbyism replacing time that otherwise would be spent on real politics? Is hobbyism inspiring deeper engagement? To answer these questions, it's useful to distinguish hobbyist actions that are focused on news consumption from those focused on token behaviors such as signing an online petition or changing your social media profile picture to a rainbow flag. The latter represents a class of behaviors that has been labeled slacktivism—a kind of activity, usually done online, that is merely symbolic.

One of the cleverest studies of slacktivism was conducted a few years ago in Canada. In honor of a Canadian holiday memorializing soldiers, the custom is to wear a poppy, a red flower, pinned to one's shirt. At the University of British Columbia, a team of researchers offered a poppy to students as they walked by on campus. Some of these students were asked if they would wear the poppy, and the researchers helped affix the poppy to the students' shirts or coats. Other students were handed a poppy in an envelope. A third group, the control group, was given no poppy.

The research team handing out the red flowers positioned themselves so that afterward the students had to walk down a public concourse. At the end of the concourse, other members of the research team (though not known as such to the students) asked the students if they would donate money to help military veterans. The students who were given a poppy on their shirt (in public display) gave an amount indistinguishable from those who had not received a poppy at all. But the group that was given a poppy in an envelope—a private token action—gave significantly more.[5]

The poppy in the envelope may remind you of a strategy often deployed by charitable organizations, such as when they send free pens or notepads or return-address labels in the mail. These organizations hope the small gift makes you feel indebted to them, makes you feel that you are the kind of person who supports their cause. So in return for taking the private gift, you will respond with a donation or other form of support. That's the idea. And that's the theory of why those who took a poppy in an envelope donated more.

When the token action is done in public, however, you have already done something for the cause, sort of. You have broadcast your commitment to it. Having made this moral statement, you are now of free conscience to focus on more selfish stuff. In your mind, you want to do a balance of selfish and selfless things in your life, and the public display of support filled up your selfless basket for the day. You don't give money to help the veterans because your commitment to them was fulfilled by your pubic show of support. This basic insight has been replicated with "cause-marketed products" (similar to those VOTE VOTE VOTE EVERYONE IS DOING IT Urban Outfitters T-shirts).[6] Public token actions, slacktivism, may take time and money away from serious actions without inspiring serious action.

There's a wrinkle to the theory. The slacktivism effect is found among people who are *less* enthusiastic about the causes being targeted. If you are very committed to something, a public token action may actually inspire further action.

The Canadian team studied this nuance through hockey. They offered students either private or public displays of support for the Vancouver Canucks, a hockey team. The students were given either pins that were placed directly on their shirts or magnets that they could take home with them. The researchers gauged each student's level of fandom for the Canucks. Later on, a separate group of researchers asked if the students would take a time-consuming survey "on behalf of the Vancouver Canucks." Lukewarm fans who were given the magnet (a private token) were more likely to take the survey, similar to the result in the poppy study. However, intense fans of the Canucks who were given the pin on their shirt (a public token) also were more likely to take the survey.

To put this result in context, consider, for one last time, the Urban Outfitters T-shirt declaring VOTE VOTE VOTE EVERYONE IS DOING IT. It's important to remember that voting is genuinely challenging for people who don't love politics. Oftentimes, ballots have lots of offices on them and complex initiative questions. Voters can feel inadequate to the task of voting. For these people, particularly if they are in a social network where voting is socially desirable, such as on a college campus, a token action such as wearing a T-shirt conveys an image of support and fulfills a desire to be altruistic. And it is much easier than learning how to vote for a whole bunch of offices that seem completely foreign to their experience. Conditions are ripe for a slacktivism effect.

For individuals who are deeply engaged in organizations or advocacy, a similar token action may contribute to a feeling of shared purpose and inspire action. Soon after Angela Aldous and her group in Westmoreland County, Pennsylvania, got together and formed the Voice of Westmoreland (VOW), a labor union paid for a few hundred purple VOW T-shirts. The shirts were a big hit among the volunteers. For a group of committed activists, the shirt didn't likely replace hard work; this small thing helped build community around the new organization.

Social media use, in general, probably operates differently for those committed to organizing than for those who tepidly support the efforts of organizers. For volunteers who are embedded in real-life political communities, social media may reinforce their commitments—they share pictures, reflections, or relevant news for their community. But for hobbyists, social media is a token form of involvement that makes them feel connected to those doing hard work and may replace the desire to actually do the hard work.

Slacktivism is difficult to measure. My best guess is that token actions, when taken in public such as on a Facebook page or on a T-shirt, may have positive reinforcing effects for those who are most committed but not for those who are more tentatively committed. But scholars still have a lot to learn about this phenomenon.

Setting aside the issue of slacktivism, is our time spent on news replacing real politics in our lives? In late 2017, a group of researchers recruited experimental subjects who said they were active on social media every day. The subjects agreed, for the benefit of scientific research, to abstain from social media for a time. Researchers would monitor their online behavior to make sure they weren't logging on. Participants were randomly assigned to give up social media for either one, two, three, or four weeks.[7] During the study, the participants filled out a diary that described what activities they did each day. The question was, what happens when you take a break from social media? What would you spend your time doing instead?

When the experimental subjects abstained from social media, they filled their time with Internet browsing, working, sleeping, and household chores such as meal preparation and childcare. The idea behind these findings is that social media replaces activities that are similar to social media (such as Internet browsing) or that are unstructured allotments of time (when you are bored at work, or when you don't want to prepare your children's lunch boxes). Because these activities don't tend to be enjoyable, participants who abstain from social media don't report higher levels of happiness when they take a break.[8] And they certainly don't report a surge in civic volunteerism.

Is the upshot that social media (and news consumption) are taking up time we would otherwise spend on work, chores, sleep, and mindless Internet browsing and therefore they're not taking us away from *real* politics?

Not quite. As with slacktivism, studying media displacement is difficult. Taking a few weeks off social media doesn't replicate how we would behave if we truly cut down on social media, as the authors of the study fully acknowledge. It isn't realistic to think that taking a short break from social media would cause you to start joining political organizations or volunteering. Political participation as it is exemplified by Lisa, Naakh, Angela, and Drew doesn't emerge out of thin air. It takes time to develop. Active volunteers usually take a gradual path, with several false starts, that leads them to power-seeking political engagement. That a person could find that path just from avoiding social media for a couple of weeks is unlikely.

Just before the November 2018 election, I asked a random sample of a thousand Americans if they thought the Democratic Party or Republican Party had the right ideas for improving the United States and the lives of its citizens. About 30 percent said Republicans, 30 percent said Democrats, 30 percent said neither, and 10 percent said both.

For those who thought one of the two parties had the right ideas, I asked if they were involved in any kind of volunteer work to help advance those ideas. In this intense political moment of 2018, which had seen a doubling of viewership on MSNBC, 83 percent of the Democratic supporters said no, they didn't participate in any volunteering. Ninety percent on the Republican side said no.

Of those volunteering, some said they helped advance political ideas by watching speeches and signing petitions. Others said they canvassed or made calls or donated. But this kind of question is rife with misreporting. People who canvassed one time in 2008 might well have answered this question in 2018 by saying that they volunteer for the Democratic Party by canvassing. After all, they do canvass, or at least they did once a decade ago! Which is to say, when 10 to 15 percent of people say they volunteer, it is an overestimate.

What can we learn from the people who favor one of the parties but do not themselves volunteer? I asked them why they didn't. About 15 percent cited a physical disability. Another 20 percent said they weren't interested. Another 20 percent felt demoralized about volunteering. Some were afraid of reprisals for their views if they participated. A woman wrote, "Frankly, where I live is on the dangerously radical side of the Republican spectrum and it's rather unsafe for a woman like me to express such contradictory views in public so long as I live here." A Republican respondent said he doesn't participate "because liberals can be the meanest most vile people there are. They are a violent mob that have verbally and physically attacked people with opposing views."

Some people say they hadn't volunteered because they'd never been asked, or they felt that their one voice wouldn't have a real impact. Some felt they didn't know enough to be involved. Some felt they didn't have the right personality for it: "I prefer to be on the sidelines. I am too passionate about what I believe, so I think that type of view is not helpful." "I'm old and very opinionated and don't like to work with people."

Several respondents said they aren't involved because they are not fully on board with any party or organization. (I suppose they think that those who are involved in organizational life are 100 percent in agreement with the organizations they support.) A Republican who felt this way wrote, "There are still Republicans that don't support President Trump and until the Republican Party stands firmly behind the President I will not be involved." A Democratic respondent wrote, "The entire message of the Democratic Party is way off. They have the best views and ideas to really help people but their messaging is horrible. They need a clear message on how they are going to help. . . . I don't volunteer because it is frustrating to see this lack of messaging and marketing. You have some of the best marketing people out there on your side and you don't reach out to anyone. I know many marketing people that would help if asked. If you get better messaging and stayed on message then maybe I would consider volunteering."

By far, the most common answer people give for why they don't volunteer is not disability or lack of interest or feeling demoralized or anything like that. It's time. Just about half of all the people who say they support a side but don't volunteer cite time as the reason why not. They don't have enough time. College graduates, by the way, are less likely to cite disability or lack of interest than noncollege grads, and more likely to cite time constraints.

After the 2018 election, this representative sample of Americans was again surveyed. I asked them details about their leisure time. How much time do they spend on politics? What do they do with that time?

Fifty-six percent of all respondents said they spend an hour or more each day on politics. Those who said they aren't particularly interested in politics report spending about twenty minutes a day in leisure time connected somehow to politics. For those who are interested, the median respondent spends ninety minutes. Among those individuals who said, on the earlier survey, that they didn't engage in volunteering because they didn't have time, they typically spend over an hour a day on politics.

I asked the respondents how they allocate the time they spend on politics. How much time do they spend on news? How much discussing and sharing on social media? How much communicating with friends and family not on social media? How much thinking about politics by themselves? How much volunteering? How much in some other way?

Among those Americans who spend an hour or more a day on politics, 83 percent of them say that 0 percent of that time is spent in organized political activity. For most of the others, volunteering makes up a tiny fraction of the time they say they spend on politics.

Those who are college educated or report being interested in politics spend more time on politics than other Americans, but they just spend more time thinking about politics, reading about it, and talking about it. The average college-educated respondent says that 41 percent of the time he or she spends on politics is news consumption, 26 percent is discussing with friends and family either on social media or off-line, 21 percent is spent thinking about politics by themselves, 10 percent is in some way unclassifiable, and under 2 percent is in volunteering.

So, is hobbyism useful because, by soaking in so much information or by arguing on social media, we are inspired to take further action? One critic of my theory of political hobbyism wrote that reading and discussing news "offers us both practice and moral clarity. It gives us a chance to place ourselves on the spectrum and determine our values so that when the time comes to act, we can."[9]

For Democrats especially, the 2018 election cycle was a pretty good time to act. The base was energized. Elections all over the country, from state legislatures to the US Senate, were at stake. Indeed, the Democratic Party's computer system showed volunteers knocked on 155 million doors, well more than they did even in the previous presidential election.[10] Even so, the overwhelming majority of those who spend hundreds of hours every year on politics claimed to not be involved in any form of politics other than consuming information and talking and thinking about it. We say we don't volunteer because we don't have time to volunteer. But we leave plenty of time for political consumption. Sure, Americans who are most engaged in political volunteerism tend to also spend a lot of our time consuming politics. But the opposite just is not true. The vast majority of those who spend a lot time consuming politics are not participating actively in politics at all.

If our friends and family were engaged in organizations and not online, we'd probably feel some pressure to do the same. But since it's easy enough to pay attention to a social network online or to watch TV news alone at home, we don't feel the pressure to get into deep forms of political engagement. It's hard to know whether average political hobbyists are spending time on a game that they would otherwise spend on effectively advocating for their community. Certainly, average political hobbyists are spending time on a game that they *could* otherwise spend on their community.

So why don't they?

PART IV

What headway can the notion of civic purity, of honesty of
administration, make against [the ward boss's] big manifestation of human friendliness, this stalking survival of village
kindness? The notions of the civic reformer are negative and
impotent before it. The reformers give themselves over largely
to criticisms of the present state of affairs, to writing and talking of what the future must be; but their goodness is not dramatic; it is not even concrete and human.

—Jane Addams, "Why the Ward
Boss Rules," 1898[1]

CHAPTER 17

The Dukakis Buffet

From the time of the American founding, the United States has consistently seen obsessive intrigue about political celebrities and scandals, and plenty of shallow partisan fights. Our baser motivations in politics are probably a historical constant. Is anything about this new? Is political hobbyism a bigger problem today than in the past?

Three sets of changes have emerged that are worth our attention because they explain why political hobbyism is indeed more prominent now. The first is a set of phenomena I explored already: changes in leisure time, media, and technology. The second and third elements that have changed are the topics of the next few chapters: institutions and a culture of privilege. Institutions—specifically political parties, but also others such as religious organizations and labor unions—can channel citizen energy into productive, power-seeking forms of collective action. They can, but mostly they don't. We do politics as a hobby because such organizations as local party committees do not typically have a serious vision or resources to help ordinary, concerned citizens act any differently. We are also in a culture that encourages us to treat politics as a pastime; one reason why organizations are so weak is that they are operating in a culture of privilege that, in spite of our serious national problems, fails to treat politics as if lives are on the line. We'll take the institutional argument and cultural argument in turn.

In the early 2000s, the Democratic Party organization in Washington County, Oregon, was on life support. Washington County is a large county in suburban Portland. It was once fairly Republican. Now, it's Democratic. In the early years of the George W. Bush administration, the party committee could barely get a quorum of thirteen members at its monthly meetings, in a county with a population of a half million.

Then, in 2006, things began to change. A growing number of active Democrats started investing in the county party. They chipped in with monthly contributions and hired a field director. The field director recruited volunteers and staffed a permanent office that could be a home base for a range of projects. Washington County was the first in the state to have a paid, permanent Democratic Party staffer.

With the help of the field director, the group initiated a "neighborhood leader" program.[1] Neighborhood leaders in Washington County were, and still are, responsible for turning out the vote for thirty-five households in their own neighborhood. They report to one of the three or four volunteer coordinators who split responsibility for the area of a statehouse district. The county has about ten statehouse districts.

Carol Greenough, now age seventy-one, a retired psychologist, a widow, is one of those coordinators whom the neighborhood leaders report to. She is also a neighborhood leader herself. Carol was part of the group that barely made a quorum in the early 2000s but then started investing in the party. In Carol's assigned area of the statehouse district, she has recruited eighty leaders, sixty-five of whom are active. She recruits them at the library, on Facebook, on the website Nextdoor, at the local crawfish festival, and anywhere else she can find them.

Carol's volunteerism—managing eighty other volunteers—is a big commitment, but being a neighborhood leader within Carol's turf is not too burdensome. That's the beauty of the neighborhood leader program. It's only thirty-five doors. In the first step, a potential leader meets with Carol, maybe over coffee. This meeting isn't strictly necessary, but Carol wants to gauge the depth of the person's interest. Sometimes, in the heat of a national crisis, people will sign up to participate in some form of politics but soon after they lose interest and back out. Carol is looking for people who are more committed than that. If they sign up at the crawfish festival but then don't return her note to talk or meet, she knows they're not for real.

A neighborhood leader, when she signs on with Carol, is asked to go around and introduce herself to her thirty-five assigned households and find out what issues, if any, the voters care about or what questions, if any, they have. Then, right before each election, the leader goes around again and encourages the neighbors to vote. She passes out a slate card, which recommends how neighbors ought to cast their votes for all the offices and initiatives on the ballot. The county party's endorsement committee determines who gets the nod on the slate card. Carol is on that committee, too.

Carol says that by the third election a volunteer does this, the experience has evolved from awkward and forced to a more pleasant ritual. The voters start to know the neighborhood leader and expect the leader's visit. In Oregon, where every voter receives a mail-in ballot, some of Carol's own neighbors wait for her to visit their homes so they can talk through the ballot together before the voter fills it out.

Some of the people whom Carol tries to recruit will question the value of organizing their own neighborhoods, especially now that their county and state are reliably Democratic. Carol sets them straight. The state legislature, she says, considers bills about rent control, green jobs, cap and trade, school funding, gun safety, Medicaid expansion, and many other issues that Carol cares about. The county needs to elect legislators who support all of those things. "Washington, DC, is out of my hands," Carol says, "but a lot is happening here in Oregon." Plus, she points out, frequent use of the ballot initiative in Oregon means that, at any moment, but particularly when the chips are down for Democrats, progressive policies passed by the legislature can be undone by a popular vote. Democrats need to be on guard and not take any policy victory for granted.

The neighborhood leader program has strengthened the county party. Those monthly meetings, where it was previously hard to get thirteen people to show up, are now attended by 100 to 150 people, and the group struggles to find a space big enough to accommodate them all.

Challenges still abound. Lots of people who sign up to be neighborhood leaders fail to follow through. Tensions also arise between the old guard (people such as Carol who have been involved in the area for a long time) and the new guard, who in her area tend to be Bernie Sanders devotees, she says. The county party has responded to their voices by electing younger and more progressive leaders to its governing committee. Carol sees it as part of her responsibility to show newcomers how the county party can be a vehicle for empowering their values rather than an obstacle to those values.

Another challenge: the group can't always control the neighborhood leaders. Sometimes, neighborhood leaders disagree with the endorsements made by the county party. They pass out the county party's slate card, as they are asked to do, but then they also tell the voters that they should vote a different way, particularly in the nonpartisan local elections.

Top-down leaders would bristle at this kind of insubordination. Indeed, it's the main reason why an organization wouldn't want to empower an army of local neighborhood leaders. As one of Barack Obama's policy advisers once said, lamenting how little grassroots organizing the Democrats did during Obama's tenure, "If you're not really that committed, as a matter of principle, to a bottom-up theory of change, then you will find it nonsensical to cede some control in order to gain more power."[2] Carol, who is committed to the bottom-up theory of change, laughs off the stories of neighborhood leaders who go a little rogue. The party is so much stronger by being the home of a large, diverse pool of volunteers. She's happy to tolerate a few of them telling voters that the endorsement committee got it wrong on a race here or there.

If there's a local political party committee in your area, it probably looks nothing like the organization I just described. In most of the country, the state and local parties are *hollow*, to use the term of political scientists Sam Rosenfeld and Daniel Schlozman. As another political scientist, Julia Azari, has put it, politics in the United States is defined by the strange combination of strong partisanship but weak party organizations. In many states, the *state* Democratic and Republican Party offices, let alone the county ones, are barely staffed except during election seasons.[3]

The typical local party doesn't look like Carol's party.[4] Does it look like mine? I wanted to find out.

I live in Brookline, Massachusetts, a town of about sixty thousand people, a dense enclave right next door to Boston. It's 73 percent white and filled with the kind of urban professionals who can afford expensive real estate but would prefer to live in a third-floor walk-up near public transit than in a big house in suburbia.

Brookline is a very Democratic town. In 2016, Hillary Clinton received almost 90 percent of the vote here. The only places in Massachusetts where she earned a higher vote were across the Charles River in Cambridge, home of Harvard and MIT, and in Province-town, down on Cape Cod, the gayest city in America, according to Census data.[5] Brookline is also fewer than thirty miles from the border with New Hampshire, a state that Hillary Clinton won by less than half a percentage point in 2016, which makes Brookline a useful place to recruit Democratic volunteers for national elections.

Curiously, in 2016, the biggest expenditure of the Brookline Democratic Town Committee wasn't for organizers, office space, or transportation to New Hampshire, but a $1,300 payment to Sichuan Garden for the committee's annual Chinese buffet dinner. Like other local Democratic committees across the state and country, the Brookline Democratic committee has little money, and what it has it mostly spends on its own social events. According to public data on the committee's expenditures, at least 60 percent of its budget in 2016 was spent on the Chinese buffet, a fall garden party, and an election night party. In 2018, with newfound volunteer energy, the committee spent about $10,000 on short-term organizers.

In a town where half of the adults are younger than forty-five, no one in the committee's leadership is in their teens, twenties, thirties, or forties. There are no monthly meetings for members. There is no permanent staff. There is no office (commercial rents in town are high and the committee's revenue is low). Some events draw crowds—impressively, over a hundred people attended a question-and-answer session with state representatives in 2019. Others not so much—an event I attended featuring a vigorous debate among primary candidates for statewide office in 2018 drew about fifteen people, with a median age maybe around eighty. No events compare with those in

Drew's precinct in Davidson, North Carolina, which has a fraction of the population of Brookline but could draw a crowd of seven hundred.

After the 2016 presidential election, I did what many concerned citizens did: tried to find ways to get involved in politics. I hadn't yet learned the stories of Drew in Davidson or Angela in Westmoreland County or Carol in Oregon, but I knew I wanted to do something along the lines of what they were doing.

I got in touch with the chairwoman of the Brookline Democrats. She is in her midfifties and has dedicated her career and volunteer time to political and civic causes. She is a kind and patient leader. After the Trump victory in 2016, many community members who were upset about the election sought the chair's advice about how they could get involved. She brought all the emerging local anti-Trump groups together and started a new umbrella organization to support House races in 2018. Drawing from Brookline and several neighboring towns, the group raised $700,000 from thirteen hundred donors supporting a slate of fifteen candidates whom the group had strategically selected.

When the chairwoman and I first met, at night at the Athan's Bakery café in Brookline's Washington Square, I was a little nervous. While I have always actively participated in religious and civic volunteerism, I had shied away from political engagement for a lot of the same reasons brought up by survey respondents in the last chapter. I have a pretty good claim to being busy. I have three small kids and a wife who has a demanding job. As a professor, I have flexibility in my schedule, but my mornings are completely taken by childcare from six to eight thirty, and I usually have to stop working and rush to get a kid off the bus at four forty-five in the afternoon. At eight at night, when the kids are sleeping, I often go back to work.

A better reason for not being involved is that I've never considered myself particularly ideological or partisan. I am more aligned with Democrats on issues, and I was alarmed by the election of Donald Trump, which is what inspired me to reach out to the party committee, but I have plenty of policy disagreements with Democrats, too, and I have never felt a strong emotional connection to party labels.

An even better reason not to be involved is that my professional life depends on my being able to weigh evidence about politics and form independent judgments. When I teach students about such polarizing issues as *Citizens United* or voting rights legislation, I have a professional duty to convey the evidence about the effects of these laws as a scholar, not as some partisan pushing an agenda. I also conduct my own research on sensitive political questions, and I regularly serve as an expert witness in court cases, helping judges understand empirical questions, such as how many noncitizens are voting in US elections or how many racial minorities are affected by voter ID laws. I would never want my assessments based on careful research to be clouded by the appearance of a partisan bias. And indeed, in some cases, I have reached conclusions at odds with the Democratic Party line. I haven't been shy about saying so, which has gotten me into public disputes with partisan hacks in academia and in the press.

Which brings me to the final reason I shouldn't be involved in a political organization: temperament. When I conjure up a caricature of a political organizer, I see someone very different from me. It's not just because I think of my views as moderate, but because I am too often impatient and insensitive. I get antsy at the pace of meetings. When an organizer stands in the front of a room and asks thirty new volunteers what brought them in today, all I can think about is how long it's going to take for everyone to be done talking. Half the time that I say anything at any meeting, I end up wishing afterward that I had kept quieter.

Nevertheless, after 2016, I suppressed all those good excuses and started meeting with the chairwoman of the Brookline Democrats, and I started looking for ways to be involved. At one of our one-on-one meetings, I brought up local elections. Important issues happen at the local level, yet even in this highly educated town we have low participation in local elections, especially in my precinct. Could I help by working on a voter engagement plan for local elections? Maybe we could help the town better engage in affordable housing, transportation, environmental regulation, racial tensions, and other issues that affect this and so many other cities and towns, issues I take to be Democratic priorities.

A hard no. Local elections are nonpartisan in Brookline. Unlike Carol's Democratic Party in Oregon or Drew's in North Carolina, my town's Democratic committee does not get involved in nonpartisan elections. The committee sees its lane as races involving Democrats versus Republicans, and it stays in that lane. The chairwoman's rationale is understandable. Since nearly the whole town is Democratic, the big fights in local politics are within the Democratic Party. The local party committee wants to be a big tent where Democrats who differ on local issues can come together to get out the vote for Democratic candidates in state elections. The chairwoman doesn't want her committee to enter the thicket of local intraparty fights.

Still, I suggested, even without endorsing candidates or weighing in on local issues, the Democratic committee could focus on increasing participation in municipal elections. Maybe that would at least raise public attention on local issues. I told the chair that I'd love to help with that. Surely, I thought, the local Democratic committee supports higher turnout in local elections. She told me that working to increase turnout in local elections is outside the purview of the Democratic committee. Some members of the local Democratic Party may not want higher turnout. After all, incumbent officials were elected under the conditions of severely low turnout. Higher turnout might not be good for them.[6] The chairwoman herself supports higher participation in elections, she tells me, but some of her group may disagree and so the party stays out.

I tried another tack. I thought I might help by organizing my own neighborhood. My precinct is almost all apartment buildings and multifamily houses. From expensive condos to low-income public housing for elderly residents to small rental apartments, eighteen hundred households in all, lots of kids, packed within 0.4 square miles. The precinct is fairly young and transient, and probably because of that it has had among the lowest rates of electoral participation in the town.

In the way that Carol's volunteers in Oregon go around introducing themselves, seeing if voters have questions, hearing what they care about, that's how I wanted to be involved. I thought the Democratic Party could have a bigger presence, hosting picnics like those Drew hosted with his precinct committee in Davidson. I imagined going further, using the party committee to provide social services to people with unmet needs. I thought about how Brian Golden and Naakh Vysoky helped address mobility issues of the elderly. I thought about the regulars who staffed party machines in the old days of Boston, handing out free vaccines and turkeys. Maybe we could find some modern ways to help those in need through the party organization today.

Over coffee at a busy chain restaurant in the neighborhood, I told the chair what I had in mind, to organize a precinct and try to build rapport with neighbors who are mostly disengaged from politics. She told me that the Democratic committee focuses on mobilizing voters in the days preceding a state election. The committee gets volunteers to knock on doors or make calls in October and November of even-numbered years. She loves the idea of civic engagement and neighborliness, but that's not what a political party is for.

I responded that I thought the way to increase participation is not by strangers knocking on doors with scripts but by neighbors knowing one another. I said, most people don't care much about public policy. If you show them that the Democratic Party cares about them—by meeting them, by hosting a picnic, by doing social service work—then maybe they'll vote for your side when you need them. They'll know that people from this party care about them.

I mentioned that special Senate election that had taken place in Massachusetts about a decade earlier, when the Democratic candidate to replace Ted Kennedy lost in a close upset—a hundred-thousand-vote margin statewide—denying Democrats a crucial sixtieth vote in the US Senate. In Brookline, voter turnout dropped over fifteen percentage points between the landslide presidential election and the close Senate election. For the Democrats to get their vote out even when their candidates are weak but when the stakes are high, such as in that 2010 special election, communities such as Brookline need robust, long-term party engagement. That's what they lack in communities all around the state and country.

She said she was uncomfortable with this vision of mixing civic engagement with political mobilization. She said it didn't feel natural to her.

I later sent her an email, pointing out that the Massachusetts Democratic Party has published a "field guide," with instructions about what local party committees are supposed to do.[7] The field guide, I quoted to her, says that community service is an important part of what party committees ought to do. Community service, the document reads, "creates goodwill, publicity, and image projection, a development of contacts . . . skills and experience for the member-ship." The field guide recommends that local Democratic commit-tees reach out to new residents when they move in, host community events, develop civics opportunities for schools, and support charita-ble causes. That's exactly the kind of stuff I wanted to do! Right there in writing, the party is plainly stating what local committees ought to do, and I'm here eager to help do it!

The chair wrote back, "I read the paragraph you cited in the field manual, and it really doesn't feel like what the Brookline Dems are all about." But, she continued, "how can we adapt this to make it accom-plish what you want in terms of long-term engagement but in a way that feels right for our town?" She was generous with her time with me and she did allow me to try out some new ideas, as I'll describe later. But her vision for what a local political party should do is more focused on one-off, get-out-the-vote drives than deep organizing or civic engagement.

I don't blame the chairwoman for her disagreements with my suggestions. Compared to many other communities where the local party committees do literally nothing, the Brookline committee is a real organization that puts on events and recruits volunteers for canvassing. It sends dozens of volunteers to New Hampshire every four years to knock on doors for the Democratic presidential campaign. The chairwoman is also working within the rules and norms of her organization, rules and norms that she herself isn't responsible for. And she is a volunteer with limited time. Even if she wanted to make her organization more like Carol's in Oregon, she is busy with other work. In her day job, she runs an advocacy group in Boston, fighting for immigrant rights, gun control, and other progressive issues.

Nevertheless, as of now, the Democratic committee in Brookline plays a marginal role in politics. A few weeks before a statewide elec-tion, it will run phone banks and canvasses with strangers using a script to talk to strangers. It will host occasional forums for residents to ask questions of politicians and learn about national policy. It will connect activists to national races, such as House contests in other states to which they can donate.

And it will run its social programs. A hundred supporters will attend the annual buffet at the Sichuan Garden. There, they will commiserate over how long they have to wait for the sesame chicken on the buffet line. They may hear a speech from beloved Brookline resident and onetime presidential candidate Michael Dukakis, who shows up and rallies the crowd. The chairwoman will appeal for people to attend not just the buffet but also "activist Wednesdays" in the weeks leading up to the next statewide election, where volunteers can participate in a phone bank hosted at a local realtor's office. After the 2018 buffet, I visited a couple of those phone banks. They were sparsely attended. The buffet-to-volunteer pipeline is, I learned, not as robust as you would expect from a town chock-full of highly educated liberals who have plenty of leisure time to spend on political consumption. Many of these liberals are engaged in charitable causes, advocacy organizations, and even candidate campaigns, but the party committee itself is not central to their engagement.

In case it isn't obvious, party organizations—not just individuals with partisan attitudes—are essential to building political power. We can see this most clearly outside the United States. Consider the Arab Spring.[8] The Arab Spring is the name of a series of revolutionary movements that started as antigovernment protests in 2010. The Arab Spring started in Tunisia and spread through Egypt, Libya, Yemen, Syria, and Bahrain, and to a lesser extent in other countries. By all accounts, social media played an important role in coordinating the protests, telling activists where and when to gather, transmitting information about where and when to send medical supplies and food.

The Arab Spring failed nearly everywhere. The aftermath has been called the Arab Winter, a wake of death, destruction, and capsized rickety boats that carried now-drowned refugee children. The Arab Spring was a tragedy.

The movement failed, according to several scholars, because it lacked durable party organizations. In Egypt, for instance, protests in Cairo's Tahrir Square spurred elections, which was a major victory—after a mere eighteen days of protest, the country's leader of almost thirty years stepped down. But the secular movement in Tahrir Square had no leaders, no ability to organize, and no capacity to mobilize voters. The liberal energy that spurred change lost the elections to an organized party, the right-wing Muslim Brotherhood, which was eventually forced out of power by a military coup. Activists with an Internet connection could crumble a government but could not build one in its place.[9] To do that, you need a hierarchy of leaders from low-level people willing to knock on thirty-five doors to middle-level organizers to higher-level leaders with a plan. In short, you need an organization. In Egypt, the protesters never had that.

In the contemporary United States, robust party organizations such as Carol's in Oregon are rare. One of the reasons why so many pop-up "resistance" groups emerged after the 2016 election is because traditional institutions, such as local Democratic Party committees, do not have on-ramps to incorporate new volunteers. After 2016, when concerned citizens wanted to get involved, maybe they googled around for local Democratic committees, but in most towns Democratic Party committees barely exist. If they exist, they often have a small elected group of party veterans who mostly just wait for a sleepy county convention or state party convention that they can attend. The organizations have structure—a chair, a treasurer—but, as Drew told us about in Mecklenburg County, North Carolina, the committees seek and deploy "a comical amount of power." They don't do anything. The existence of so many post-Trump pop-up groups is a symptom of the Democratic Party's hollowness.

Why are local party organizations today so weak in the United States? In large part, it's because, over the course of decades, political leaders chose to weaken them. Responding to the problems of corruption, secrecy, election tampering, and racist party committees, political leaders have weakened local organizations. They have done so through changes to party regulations, federal and state legislation, and court rulings. In the process, they have strengthened non-organizational forms of political engagement. Those non-organizational forms tend to be the shallow, one-off efforts that characterize contemporary political hobbyism. As in Tahrir Square, political energy can be channeled into hastily planned protests but, without organizations, cannot be channeled into long-term power.

When politicians make well-meaning changes to the status quo, they focus more on the problems they want to solve and less on the problems that change will create.[10] When, for instance, Congress decided to broadcast its proceedings on C-SPAN, it was responding to a broad-based movement, spurred, in part, by the Watergate scandal, for more transparency in government. In addition to C-SPAN, the 1970s saw the passage of open-records laws and open-meetings laws in the states and in the federal government. In opening up government for all to see, lawmakers might not have thought through the negative consequences, for instance that legislative hearings can now be hijacked by politicians hoping to make a statement that can be turned into a viral video.[11]

As we'll now examine, the changes that leaders made in response to serious issues such as racism and corruption in local party organizations diminished the role of local party committees altogether. Today, you will see national parties and affiliated groups spend millions of dollars on TV or Internet ads, but they won't spend much on staffing permanent organizer positions across the country. They don't typically do what Carol is doing in Oregon. In part, Americans interested in politics today *do* politics as a hobby because most of us don't have a Carol to show us another way.

Why did political parties let their durable grassroots organizations wither? It's an interesting story.

CHAPTER 18

Rage Against the Machine

Richard J. Daley was elected to six terms as mayor of Chicago between 1955 and 1976. Concurrently, he served as one of eighty members of the Cook County Democratic Central Committee. On the committee, he represented the working-class Irish ward where he was born and lived out his life. The committee elected Daley its chairman, and that's what made him, in addition to being mayor, the party boss of the last powerful political machine in the United States.

According to Milton Rakove, author of *Don't Make No Waves . . . Don't Back No Losers*, a classic account of Daley's operation, the machine, situated in the Cook County Democratic Committee, handpicked the candidates to stand for office, and it got the vote out to make sure those candidates were elected.[1] Precinct captains turned out the vote in their neighborhoods for the candidates who were endorsed by Daley's committee. The captains were told that they should not pay attention at all to how the machine's candidates performed overall in an election year. All that mattered was how they did in the one little precinct they were personally responsible for.

Daley was laser-focused on the idea that the power ultimately rested with the voters. If a Democratic candidate in Chicago lost an election and Daley was asked for his analysis of why the candidate lost, he would famously respond, "He didn't get enough votes!"[2] That's all there was to it.

The captains earned votes in the neighborhoods by serving the needs of the voters. The hierarchy of leaders from precinct captains to the mayor himself was focused not on national issues, but exclusively on Cook County and Chicago. They would get residents new garbage cans or legal aid, they would address rodent issues, even offer cash assistance to a neighbor who was struggling to pay bills. They would get to know the people in the precinct and do them favors. One precinct captain whom Rakove talked with kept track of the 125 favors the captain did for his constituents over a year.

The machine rewarded the precinct captains in return. Many were employed in patronage positions for the city, serving at the mayor's discretion, fired if they failed to get out their votes. Others worked in legal or insurance industries and the city sent them its business. A hundred of Daley's own family members and even more of his neighbors held patronage positions and worked on behalf of the machine. Daley did not think of patronage as corrupt.

It should not be mistaken that Daley earned power merely through an innocuous hierarchy of neighborly lieutenants; some of the lieutenants were unambiguously corrupt[3] and the Daley machine was racist.[4] To appease the growing white middle class in the city, the machine shifted its focus over time from social services geared to the poor to meeting the demands of homeowners. Some of those demands were to keep the trees trimmed and property taxes low. Demands also included keeping black students out of white schools and black residents out of white neighborhoods.[5] As in other Irish American machines, the leaders themselves went to Catholic parochial schools and sent their children to these schools as well. They not only satisfied white demands for segregated schools, but underfunded the school system at least in part because they didn't use the schools. Similarly, to keep the white supporters happy, the mayor's housing authority "became a veritable model of ghetto building, enforcing segregation, poverty and racism," as one scholar put it; the mayor's police force perpetrated violence against blacks; the mayor's hiring practices favored whites over blacks.[6]

Daley's machine is a historical curiosity because it thrived at a time when local political committees in the rest of the country were already dead. Political historians consider the "party era" of American politics to have run from the 1830s through the 1880s. Parties, in that era, were a regular part of Americans' "social and recreational lives."[7] Local party organizations offered their members jobs or money in return for securing votes. That was the basis of their power. Securing votes often meant providing entertainment and liquor to the public and addressing voters' personal needs, the way Daley's machine continued to do through much of the twentieth century.[8] As with Daley's machine, ordinary citizens felt attachment to local political parties even though (or more likely, because) the party didn't focus on taking positions in national ideological disputes.

Importantly, during the party era and into the first decades of the twentieth centuries, parties, as well as civic organizations, were providing for people's basic needs because people were poorer and governments played a minimal role in a social safety net. As Theda Skocpol notes, one of the functions of fraternal organizations in the early twentieth century was to provide for its members in times of hardship. If a member of a fraternity died, his fellows would support his widow and children.[9] That's a pretty practical reason to join a fraternity. Similarly, parties had loyal followings when they saw their function as taking care of people's basic needs. In return, the people gave to parties their loyalty.

Local political party organizations started to die off toward the end of the nineteenth century. Population growth and urbanization presented the parties with new challenges they were ill-equipped to overcome. Party machines could govern small cities, but they did not adjust well to massive overcrowded ones.

For example, before 1888, political parties, not governments, printed and distributed paper ballots in elections. The ballots, called tickets, listed the names of the candidates running for office under the party's label. A voter would take a ticket from their party of choice and drop it in the ballot box.[10] These party-printed ballots functioned well enough in face-to-face pre-industrial towns where everyone knew everyone else. But in the rapidly growing cities, party-printed ballots became a problem. They led to corruption—vote buying, where local party representatives would pay people on the streets to vote with the party's ticket. They led to trickery—a nonparty group printing ballots made to look like a traditional party's ballots but with different candidates' names listed. They were an administrative hassle—sometimes voters would take a party ticket but then paste over part of it with a slip of paper from a nonparty slate of candidates running for some of the offices.

In a remarkably short time, between 1888 and 1893, all states moved to a government-printed ballot. According to political historian Alan Ware, political parties willingly gave up printing their own ballots even though this meant giving up power over the electoral process. They were similarly complicit in new voter-registration laws in this era, which were being enacted in cities as a way to make Election Day more orderly. Both of these changes made party mobilization more difficult.[11] But in the bigger cities, the parties' involvement in election administrative functions was drawing negative attention to them. Elections were clouded by fraud and mismanagement. So the parties ceded control to government.

All of a sudden, the parties' roles became different. They started to have to educate and convince voters about the candidates who were running for each office rather than exchanging liquor and/or social services for loyalty to the party itself. The parties had to begin persuading voters about the importance of registering to vote.

A few years later, between 1896 and 1915, the parties largely ceded control of yet another of their important functions: nominations. In the party era, each party's candidates for the general election were selected by local party committees in the way that the Daley machine continued to select them through the mid-twentieth century. Through a series of local and state conventions, party committees would vote among themselves to decide who would stand for each office under the party's label. Ordinary voters were not involved. Ordinary voters only cast ballots in general elections.

Around the turn of the twentieth century, most states replaced the convention system with popular primaries, where ordinary voters could participate in choosing nominees through a government-run election, at least for all offices other than the presidency. By 1917, all but four states used primaries to choose candidates for statewide offices such as governor.[12]

Why would the parties agree to give up insider control over nominations? Remember, the parties selected the candidates serving in the state legislatures. Presumably, they wouldn't choose legislators who would vote for laws that took away power from the parties. Part of the answer is that a number of states then, like today, did not have much Democratic versus Republican competition. All the competition, particularly in the white-only electorate in the South, was within one party. In those states, people pressed to allow for popular participation in the selection of nominees because this was the only opportunity for voters to weigh in.[13]

A bigger part of the answer to why parties adopted primaries is, as with the printing of ballots, that the parties became overwhelmed with the responsibility of managing nominations. According to the famed political scientist V. O. Key, "Bribery, disorder, boss domination, and picturesque manipulations occurred with great frequency and were believed to be inherent in the convention system."[14] Fraud, such as stuffing ballot boxes used in convention halls, was tolerated because party-run nominations weren't seen as real elections. Party leaders, who were concerned that their brand was being tarnished, were relieved that the government took over this process. Elections are hard to run, and the parties largely did not want to be in that business any longer.[15]

Almost immediately, leaders were disagreeing about the consequences of switching from convention systems to primaries for state and local offices. Robert La Follette, who served as representative, then governor, then senator for Wisconsin from 1885 to 1925, and who was one of the leading proponents of primaries, claimed, "Under a primary election law, men of the highest talent and especial fitness for public life will readily consent to become candidates for public office—men who can scarcely be tempted to stand as candidates under the present system."[16] Political scientists have measured no noticeable change in the quality of candidates. And to the surprise of reformers, most voters didn't take any interest in primaries. They would vote in general elections but didn't care to weigh in on the party nominations.[17] That's true even today; only a fraction of general-election voters participate in primaries for state and local offices.

Critics of primaries were also uneasy that high-profile candidates who hadn't proven themselves as stewards of a party's values could swoop in and dominate. In his Pulitzer Prize–winning account of this era, Richard Hofstadter argued that by creating two campaigns (a primary and a general) instead of one, primary reform increased the influence of money and celebrity without many benefits in terms of candidate quality or citizen participation.[18]

Parties ceded control not merely because their role got too big for them to handle. Change was also pushed forward because of the antiparty Progressive movement, which gained popularity in the last years of the nineteenth century. Progressives lashed out at the corruption of party machines. The machines were serving the poor immigrant populations then crowding in cities, offering social services and jobs in exchange for votes. Transactional politics of this sort was distasteful to the growing American urban middle class (as was the liquor freely flowing in poor neighborhoods and in party politics, leading to Progressive support for prohibition). Patronage, bossism, and raucous political parties were an affront to middle-class tastes. Progressive reformers wanted to break down the parties—the intermediaries between voters and governance—and let voters participate in politics without that corrupt influence.[19]

The Progressive worldview held that citizens should participate in politics not by thinking of their own self-interest or the interest of their religious, racial, or ethnic group, but by considering their duty to the common good. Uneducated citizens must be educated to have this enlightened worldview.[20] A citizen did not need party machines to vote for the common good.

The party bosses obviously disagreed. From their working-class perspective, the machines were focused on their constituents' basic human needs. Tending to those needs was the basis of the parties' power. Voters should cast ballots for the party that took care of them, not the party or candidate with some grand vision of the common good.

This brings us back to the Ukrainian boss, Naakh Vysoky, leader of the Russians of Brighton. Naakh, if you remember, tended to his neighbors' needs. He helped three hundred of them naturalize as citizens to make sure they would keep their food stamps and Social Security benefits. He served his community and in return controlled a thousand of their votes. When you think back to the story of Naakh, you might think of him fondly. I know I do. But he's exactly the kind of person who rubbed the Progressives at the turn of the twentieth century the wrong way. Those thousand votes that Naakh controlled—those are people who aren't thinking through politics themselves, according to his critics. They are being controlled by the boss, it seems.

In 2002, when Naakh helped Brian Golden win a state legislative seat by three hundred votes in a closely fought primary, somebody asked the US Department of Justice to investigate Naakh. His precinct was such an outlier—a precinct with unusually high voter turnout and all the votes going to the same candidate. That's the kind of thing that triggers an investigation.

Was Naakh somehow communicating with the Russian interpreters stationed in the polling place and coercing his neighbors to vote the way he wanted? Was state representative Golden somehow benefiting financially from his relationship with Naakh? Was anything amiss? In 2005, during a special election to replace Golden, who had a few months before announced he was stepping down, the federal government descended on the precinct.[21]

On Election Day, an assistant US attorney (AUSA) stood with Naakh and Golden observing their behavior, Golden tells me. As was their routine, the two of them were positioned in the lobby of the housing complex, distant enough from the polling place where they could legally urge residents to vote and to support their preferred candidate as Golden's replacement. The AUSA held a clipboard, took notes. Another AUSA was stationed in the polling place itself, as voters, accompanied by their Russian- and Chinese-speaking translators, cast ballots.

The election monitoring was funny in Golden's telling. First of all, nothing was amiss. Obviously Naakh's precinct was an outlier. If you took a few minutes to learn how Naakh built trust with his neighbors and helped them with their needs, you could see the source of Naakh's power. What made the scene funny, though, was that the AUSAs, who weren't Russian speakers, were at a complete loss. Almost no English was being spoken by the translators in the polling station or by Naakh in the lobby. If some kind of coordinated coercion was going on, the federal officials would never have picked up on it. The scene was also funny because Naakh, doing nothing wrong, relished in the oversight, was emboldened by it, Golden tells me. This man had been tortured by Hitler and by Stalin and had now amassed hard-won democratic power in his little precinct in Brighton. Golden thinks Naakh loved the idea that the federal government was checking him out. Nothing ever came of the inquiry.

Suppose I never told you the story of Naakh, an elderly, white refugee from Europe, but instead I told you an equivalent story of a young, brown immigrant from Mexico. It may have been more obvious to you, if it wasn't obvious before, that the ward boss is a polarizing figure, that some people would praise him for empowering his community while many others would find him threatening to their democratic values. It's important to see these two sides. The typical reader of this book probably identifies with the spirit of the Progressives against the machines. But I hope you also see Naakh as a sympathetic character.

To take control away from the machines, and from leaders such as Naakh, turn-of-the-twentieth-century Progressives favored primaries over conventions run by insiders. They favored city managers and nonpartisan municipal elections rather than entrenched party bosses running cities and towns. Progressives had a vision that these kinds of changes would depoliticize American politics, ending the party era by removing the powers that parties possessed.[22]

Probably the biggest blow that the Progressives levied against the parties was civil service reform. In 1883, Congress passed the Pendleton Act, moving the federal government away from patronage positions filled by the presidential administration to a merit system in which bureaucrats could not be fired just because they didn't support the campaign efforts of a political party or candidate. After the Pendleton Act, states and cities followed suit. A few states required municipal governments to move to a merit system right away.[23] Most other states instituted reform by the mid-twentieth century. In Chicago and a few other places, patronage continued through the Daley years and beyond.

The Supreme Court has since weighed in and ruled that most public servants—everyone except the top-level political appointees—cannot be fired from their positions because of their lack of loyalty to the mayor's or governor's political party. The court now considers this a free speech issue; that is, government workers have the right to affiliate or not affiliate with a party of their choosing, and they shouldn't be fired for having a different affiliation from a newly elected executive's. Some justices have dissented from the court rulings, and their dissents merit attention. In a famous case from 1990, Justice Antonin Scalia argued that patronage serves an important role in society. The government may function better when party organizations are strong, he reasoned. Strong parties need to incentivize people through jobs and economic benefits "to perform such tasks as organizing precincts, registering new voters, and providing constituent services."[24] Most of the justices did not agree with Scalia.

Progressive-era reforms such as the secret ballot and primaries took specific roles away from parties, making the parties less important; civil service reform took away the source of their power. When parties could no longer offer government jobs and contracts in return for campaign labor, the precinct-captain model of local organizing became unsustainable.[25] Parties could not recruit rank-and-file supporters to knock on doors and offer favors to neighbors. Other factors also contributed to the demise of this system. Federal, state, and local government started providing more social services, replacing a core party function. Additionally, once immigrants settled in and had better employment opportunities, few would choose to be a precinct captain and hold a low-level patronage job.[26]

The overall effect was something like what the Progressives envisioned. Parties have little power, so they are not particularly vulnerable to corruption. To get out the vote, parties do not offer inducements to precinct captains. They don't manage a hierarchy of local leaders, except in rare cases such as Carol's group in Oregon. Parties take a back seat to candidates. Candidates staff short-term campaigns when they need votes. Because neither party is active year-round, the candidates get away with shallow forms of engagement—broadcasting glossy advertisements, searching for short-term attention right before an election, and then going away.

Political parties were not able to weather population growth, urbanization, and Progressive opposition. Political party *affiliations*—Democratic and Republican—retained important roles in organizing congressional factions and in the hearts of voters. Partisanship remained. But, as two leading scholars of political parties note, the Progressive reformers "killed positive party spirit," with an impact lasting even till today.[27] From then on, party labels have commanded loyalty but the party organizations have had a bad name. Even today, few people would probably think favorably of local ward bosses. Few would think of someone such as Naakh and see the benefits of organization in addition to some potential for abuse. The idea that a leader can do good deeds for a community in exchange for political power still feels to many people, in the Progressive tradition, like an affront to civic virtue.

CHAPTER 19

The Verbalist Elite

There's a story from the summer of 1968, in Missouri.[1] An activist wanted to attend a local precinct meeting of a Democratic committee. He was there to support a presidential candidate who opposed the Vietnam War. The meeting was taking place at a private home. The entrance was through a garage and a back door. At this meeting, the attendees were going to elect a list of delegates to a county convention. The county convention would then elect delegates to a state convention. And the state convention would elect delegates to the 1968 Democratic National Convention, to take place in Chicago. At the Chicago convention, delegates would select the Democratic nominee for president. This activist wanted to do his part in the political process. He took the most concrete step he could: show up to the local precinct meeting, the lowest-level rung in choosing the next president.

Though local political parties had lost much of their power and resources beginning in the 1880s, they retained one major power through 1968: the power to select delegates in a system of conventions, culminating in the national convention. For one final time in 1968, it wasn't mainly voters in primaries but insiders in so-called smoke-filled rooms who selected the party nominee for president.

The Missouri activist could not get any information from the local party insiders about the time and date of the meeting until the day before it was to take place. That's a classic tactic employed by the committee leaders to suppress participation of your opponents. Most likely, the committee chairman was moderate or conservative and a supporter of the Vietnam War. At the county, state, and national conventions, he would back insider candidates who shared his views. He didn't want young antiwar activists stirring up trouble at the meetings.

The activist arrived fifteen minutes early to the local meeting so he could give directions to his allies who were also going to show up that night. When he arrived, he learned that the committee chairman started the meeting even earlier than that, another classic suppression tactic. In front of the assembled group, the chairman held in his hand a list of delegates he wished to see elected to the county convention. He asked for votes to support the names on his list. Curiously, he didn't ask for votes of those who opposed his slate of delegates, even though fewer than half the people present apparently signaled they were in favor of the chairman's list. Immediately after this sort-of vote, as recounted by the activist, "[the chairman] struck me in the jaw and knocked me down, escaping with the list and, I presume, having ended the meeting."

The insiders' candidate and eventual nominee was Hubert Humphrey. Humphrey was vice president under Lyndon Johnson and stood behind Johnson's war policy in Vietnam. Activists who supported Humphrey's opponents faced a number of challenges in working their way through the Democratic Party's convention system. To avoid opposition, local parties selected meeting times without public disclosure. They failed to follow any kind of standard procedures. They also allowed for proxy voting, whereby insiders not present at meetings could delegate their votes to the committee's chairman.[2] At least in this one case, they also resorted to violence.

The growing cohort of liberal, educated, anti–Vietnam War voters in the Democratic Party detested these procedural shenanigans. They followed in the antiparty footsteps of the Progressives from decades earlier. They also followed in the footsteps of those "club Democrats," the amateurs from the 1950s whom we encountered at the beginning of the book. By 1968, the club Democrats, middle-class professionals who opposed party machines, were already a shell of their 1950s selves. The clubs died off quickly in part because they largely opposed the Vietnam War and didn't want to be associated with the pro-war Democratic Party. The demise of the amateur-club Democrats also coincided with the rise of television. In the 1950s, before most households had TVs, activists socialized in person, chatting about politics in clubhouses and living rooms. As soon as TV became a dominant part of life, their desire to leave their own living rooms waned. So the organized antimachine Democratic clubs ceased to be popular.[3]

As political historian Sam Rosenfeld notes in his book *The Polarizers*, and as he notes with Daniel Schlozman in *The Hollow Parties*, the club Democrats of the fifties and the antiwar liberal middle class of the sixties bristled at party loyalty.[4] Even though the power of state and local parties was much diminished from their heyday, the character of the party boss, which still was alive in men such as Richard Daley in Chicago, irked them. The midcentury liberals believed that parties "should mobilize voters and organize governance on the basis of issues and programs—not patronage, personality, or ties of geography and demography."[5] Said Ed Muskie, the Democrats' vice-presidential candidate in 1968, "Vast numbers of intelligent and energetic Americans today . . . do not respond to the traditional inducements of party loyalty or patronage. They are issue-oriented citizens."[6]

The middle-class wing of the Democratic Party pushed for antiparty candidates, such as Eugene McCarthy in 1968 and then George McGovern in 1972, men who repelled the remnants of working-class party machines. Those machines practiced an old-fashioned, distasteful, corrupt form of politics, the kind of undemocratic insider game on display in that Missouri town, the kind that the Progressives had worked hard to purge decades before. Nineteen sixty-eight was the year to hammer the last nails in the coffin.

The reformers had a point. The story in Missouri was one of many stories in 1968 where newly engaged activists faced hostile local committees who tried hard to prevent the newcomers from being elected as convention delegates. The convention system was also mired in racism. African Americans were underrepresented in the delegate system, and in the South they were excluded altogether. In the previous presidential election, in 1964, the Mississippi Freedom Democratic Party elected its own slate of delegates to the Democratic National Convention because the white-only party in Mississippi refused to allow African Americans to participate. The Freedom Democratic Party went to the National Convention and demanded that they be seated instead of the white delegates. Only their delegates, after all, were democratically elected according to the Democratic Party's own rules. Nevertheless, the convention seated the white delegates. Attempting to retain white support in the South for the general election, President Lyndon Johnson himself sided with the racist wing of the party.[7]

In addition to the malpractice leading up to the 1968 convention and the racism rampant in local party committees, the '68 convention was, as scholars might call it, a shitshow. The convention took place in Mayor Daley's Chicago, and Daley was exactly the kind of old-school insider who favored strong local committees of party regulars over newly engaged, highly educated, policy-focused liberals. In response to protests in and around the convention, Daley directed the Chicago police to suppress opposition with overwhelming force and violence, which was broadcast on TVs across the country.

Whatever value we might find in working-class party machines and local ward bosses such as Naakh Vysoky, opponents of the machines had a lot of evidence on their side in 1968. In response to their complaints, the '68 convention voted to study the issues they raised. A commission would propose a set of recommendations to be used for the next convention.

The McGovern-Fraser Commission, named for its chairmen, was put on the case. From the beginning of its process, the deck was stacked in favor of transformational reform between the 1968 and 1972 conventions. The committee was composed primarily of reform advocates, and the young committee staff was overwhelmingly gunning for change.[8] Between April and August of 1969, the commission held public hearings in seventeen cities. At the public hearing in St. Louis, the activist who got punched in the jaw testified about his experience. Across the country, the commission heard about all the ways the party insiders made a mockery of democratic procedures.

The commission adopted guidelines requiring that delegates be elected under transparent and fair rules. No more no-shows casting ballots by proxy. No more meetings called without proper notice of time and place. States would have to use either government-run primaries to choose nominees or a caucus system open to all eligible voters. The system of presidential primaries as we now know it came into being.

Within a few election cycles, most states began using primaries. Because primaries are government-run, state legislatures had to shift control of nominations from party organizations to election administrators. Once the government was already running primaries to accommodate new Democratic rules, Republicans began mirroring some of the Democrats' procedures.

The reforms in the Democratic Party were passed over the objections of opponents, including the remaining machine bosses such as Daley, some powerful labor unions such as the AFL-CIO, and white Southern Democrats, groups that benefited from insider politics and local control. Because the opponents of reform were, in the case of machines, weakened by the decades of antiparty reform, and in the case of Southerners, weakened by being on the wrong side of morality, the new rules were adopted without much of a fight.[9]

The years following the reform weren't so hot for Democrats. The first candidate nominated under the modern primary system was one of the reform leaders, George McGovern. He lost in an epic landslide. The second Democratic candidate under the new system, a relative outsider, Jimmy Carter, won the presidency but had a rocky single four-year term in office.

The Democrats began worrying about problems that the reforms created and not just the problems that reform solved. What were the new problems? For one, the Democrats worried about the continuing decline of local party committees. Without a real role in presidential nominations or any other major area of politics, why would anyone participate in local committees? How could local parties recruit new active volunteers when they had so little power? And if the Democrats couldn't get volunteers to care about parties, how was the party going to maintain power through the sleepier downtimes of political cycles, in state and local elections or in times when the Democratic Party wasn't popular but still needed to get out the vote? Seeing the nominations of McGovern and then Carter, Democrats also worried that primaries weren't well equipped to select viable candidates who could be trusted to govern effectively. As political scientist Nelson Polsby warned in the 1980s, the primary reform made the entire political system vulnerable to an unvetted celebrity outsider swooping in and standing for election.[10]

The old-guard "party regulars" of the Democratic Party were also taken aback just by the quick pace of change. Following rules that promoted diversity, the 1972 convention had almost three times as many African American delegates (16 percent) as the 1968 convention (6 percent). Women and young people were also well represented for the first time. Long-haired, über-liberal delegates were walking the convention halls in 1972, and it rubbed the old guard the wrong way. Remarked one labor leader, "There is too much hair and not enough cigars at this convention."[11]

The counterreformation began.

One proposal to dial back the reforms was to encourage states to adopt caucuses instead of primaries and to only allow participation if citizens registered as Democrats at least a month in advance.[12] Caucuses, like today's Iowa caucuses, operate more like the convention system of old. They focus on building local grassroots support and can be places to recruit volunteers who can help sustain the weakened parties when the presidential season is over. Requiring advance party registration would weed out some of the fair-weather activists who do not care about the party except when an exciting candidate suddenly appears.

This idea never took hold. Since nominations for all the other offices in American politics are decided by primaries, with easy ballot-casting, presidential caucuses seemed (and still seem to many people today) like a bygone method of political participation.[13]

The one counterreformation idea that did gain traction, at least for a while, was superdelegates. Superdelegates, on the Democratic side, were the insiders, such as members of Congress and governors. Starting in 1980, they have been given votes at the party's National Convention alongside the delegates elected through primaries and caucuses. The idea behind superdelegates is that these insiders have a deeper well of knowledge about the presidential candidates, and so, in a close contest, they could help push the convention toward better candidates. Some early supporters of superdelegates, however, thought that they wouldn't be useful additions to nominations unless they composed a large share of all delegates.[14] If they were a small share of delegates, then the insiders wouldn't be willing to overrule the winner of the primaries and caucuses. Indeed, superdelegates have never overruled the elected winner. In any case, for 2020, the Democrats minimized the role of superdelegates. Beginning in 2020, superdelegates only get a vote if the regular system for choosing delegates (primaries and caucuses) fails to produce majority support for one of the candidates. Thus, the one concession to the counterreformation has partially been rescinded.

Local political parties have been gutted of their powers.[15] No control over nominations for president or most state and local offices, no control over Election Day functions such as balloting, no control over patronage positions in city governments. As we saw, these changes were responses to urbanization, population growth, corruption, undemocratic procedures, and racism.

From the Progressive era to the McGovern-Fraser Commission, the antiparty reforms were also the handiwork of educated elites exerting their tastes over party politics, molding the historically blue-collar Democratic Party into a party "increasingly bourgeois in orientation."[16] Much of the friction between the party regulars and the college-educated liberals probably comes down to class. The middle class who cared about politics cared about big ideas. The working class who cared about politics cared about serving their own communities.

The perception that party reforms have given preference to professionals over the working class has always cast a shadow over the changes. As one anti-reform group put it in 1977, the Democratic Party was being overrun by "a politics of celebrities, of excessive media influence, of political fad-of-the-month clubs . . . of heightened interest in 'personalities.' "[17] In primaries, for instance, candidates who don't have long-run ties to a party can nevertheless form a campaign, raise money, and broadcast ads without forming relationships to the people on the ground or attending to their interests. They can keep the campaign shallow. To the party regulars, who toiled year in and year out as precinct captains in the trenches with the poor, these well-financed newcomers seemed more interested in debating national political ideas than addressing everyday concerns of American workers.

Jeane Kirkpatrick was a Democrat who turned Republican during the Reagan years due to disillusionment with the Democratic Party's direction. She served under Reagan as United Nations ambassador. Kirkpatrick, still a high-profile Democrat in the 1970s, testified about her concern with how the McGovern-Fraser changes were impacting the party: suddenly, working-class Democrats were harder to find in the Democratic Party's convention halls. The party, she argued, was being overtaken by a "verbalist elite," people who loved talking endlessly about "style and symbolic issues . . . and [held] much less interest in the bread and butter questions."[18] Half the delegates to the 1976 Democratic National Convention were professionals, Kirkpatrick found, lawyers and teachers and writers "skilled in the persuasive arts." The former precinct captains stopped coming to conventions because they weren't interested in or good at arguing about big issues. "They don't do so good at that, if you will," Kirkpatrick said.[19] Another Democrat, Daniel Patrick Moynihan, was famously quoted after Jimmy Carter's loss to Ronald Reagan as saying, "A party of the working class cannot be dominated by former editors of the *Harvard Crimson*."[20]

This may sound like a familiar trope of conservative rhetoric. Critiques of the Democratic Party as having abandoned the interests of the working class and become bourgeois and Hollywood are not unfamiliar to Fox News audiences, especially in recent years as the working class has lost more and more economic clout as well as political clout. Even back in the 1970s, Republicans such as Spiro Agnew were alleging that the Democratic Party had become a party of "exotics, elitists, and philosophical abstractionists."[21] Is the critique merely meant to dismiss the serious concerns of racism and undemocratic bossism that the Democratic reforms were trying to address?

The critique that educated Democrats have molded their party to their professional tastes and interests has been levied from all sides, not just from conservatives. Recall the research by Theda Skocpol, who tracked the midcentury decline of membership organizations to the changing tastes of the middle class. Rather than participating in local committees to engage in social service and advocacy, in the decades after World War II liberal professionals tended to embrace a detached form of civic engagement. Advocacy organizations in Washington would solicit donations from "members" or ask them to sign petitions but would expect little more. The hands-off relationship suited the staff of the organizations and the busy lives of their supporters.

Left-leaning advocacy organizations that grew up beginning in the 1970s tended to focus on "postmaterialist" issues, issues related to the environment and tolerance. They placed much less emphasis on bread-and-butter economic issues facing the working class, on economic inequality, on job training. When the time came for actions on issues that liberals cared about, such as the environment, the organizations felt hollow. As one John Kerry staffer told the sociologist Dana Fisher in 2004, in reference to national advocacy groups, "None of these organizations can actually produce two bodies . . . when they need to."[22]

In 2012, when Skocpol, joined by Vanessa Williamson, assessed the growing Tea Party movement, they were struck by the well-organized meetings and volunteers willing to roll up their sleeves and take on all the logistical headaches of running local groups. This felt different from their experience on the left. "Opinionated, educated liberals," they write, "often have no idea what happens in state legislatures, local government boards, or political party committees. Grassroots Tea Partiers, by contrast, know the rules and procedures for passing bills and advancing regulations in detail—for local, state, and national government."[23] Tea Party groups were often short-lived local organizations that withered away by the end of the Obama era. For some activists, participation was surely motivated more by short-term hobbyism, news obsession, and conspiracy theories than by a commitment to long-term power. Nevertheless, when the groups were strong, they were committed to the logistics and rules of power acquisition. They got off their couches and into the weeds of bottom-up leadership.[24]

The obvious reason why the professional class in the Democratic Party would focus more on environmental and social issues instead of economic ones is that their class interests aren't aligned with those of working-class Democrats on economic issues.[25] Even so, why has the college-educated middle class generally failed to participate in concrete local committees where they might work to address issues such as environmental policy or civil rights? The answer is also, of course, self-interest, in the form of NIMBYism (Not In My BackYard). For someone who cares about environmental protection or racial justice, it's easier to sign a petition or send in a donation to an organization in Washington supporting liberal positions than to face one's neighbors and deal with the issue in one's own backyard.[26] It's easier for parents to let their children skip school to march in support of national and international climate action than to let them skip school to demand serious and immediate changes from their own cities and towns.

Carol's county Democratic committee in Oregon takes positions in municipal races because it wants to push the agenda its members care about at the local level. But other local party committees don't do that because the professional class of liberals who dominate local Democratic groups either aren't themselves on board with economic, environmental, and racial policy priorities when it comes to local politics or else they do not want to face their immediate neighbors on those issues.

In Brookline, a public opinion survey would no doubt show widespread support for environmental regulation and racial equality. But when proposals come up, for example, to build high-density housing in town, housing that would be partially reserved for low-income residents, the liberal attitudes quickly melt away and yield to strongly felt concerns about the risk of a neighborhood "changing its character." The local Democratic committee in Brookline claims it is fully committed to supporting the Democratic Party's platform, which has a lot to say about environmental priorities and racial equality, but the committee doesn't want to weigh in on those issues locally, such as through candidate endorsements or advocacy, because it doesn't want to alienate local Democrats who oppose such measures in their own neighborhoods.

When a local political party has no influence in national politics because of the reforms that gutted its power, and when it seeks no influence in local politics because it wants to stay above the fray, it is no wonder that it's a tough sell to get volunteers to support it. The organization is hollow. In many communities, the organization is dead.

Let's return to our search for answers about why political hobbyism is an acute problem today. The answer of these last couple of chapters is a change in political institutions. And no one helps us understand the change as well as Naakh.

I find Naakh's activism admirable, but local ward bosses such as him are hard to control. They can be corrupt. They can be racist. They can suppress newcomers trying to have a voice. That's what they did in lots of places when local parties had more power. For those good reasons, Naakh's model has largely been discontinued. He operated outside any formal political committee and organized effectively only because his voters shared a common ethnicity, a common immigrant experience, and they all lived in the same housing development. Because they had real material needs, they were organized to meet those needs, not for chatting about divisive political issues. It also doesn't hurt that Naakh's group of immigrants, though poor, were mostly educated professionals in their countries of origin. They were savvy enough to know how to mobilize and get the power they needed to serve their material needs. Finally, Naakh's role as boss isn't tied to any power of office, which means it would have been hard for someone in his position to be corrupt if he wanted to, in comparison to a boss who also served in elective office.

Naakh's model of leadership has been discontinued not only in party politics, but also in other domains where local leaders once dominated communities. Over the last few decades, for instance, labor unions have shifted their focus away from providing services to laborers or organizing local affiliates. Instead, they focus on consultants and donations to national political candidates.[27] Why centralize power instead of empower the locals? Because ceding control risks soiling the organization's name. Top-down leadership retains control so that no local can go rogue and embarrass the national organization. Top-down unions, according to labor scholar and activist Jane McAlevey, recruit leaders based on "likability and charisma . . . [the] ability to speak with the media and chair meetings," characteristics that aren't particularly meaningful to trust-building with workers. McAlevey argues that unions have collapsed in part because they've lost sight of local workers' potential for grassroots leadership.[28]

There are plenty of exceptions to this trend, such as unions that support "worker centers" that combine social services to members with political organizing,[29] just as strong and innovative local political committees occasionally emerge and thrive. But the trend has been toward political and labor organizations that expect little of ordinary participants, that ask them to defer to the experts, and that have let local affiliated committees decay.

The story of disempowering local leaders is not so different from the story of religious decline. Organized religion empowers local bosses—the clergy. Clergy have been put in positions of trust and power. But enough members of the clergy have taken such unconscionable advantage of their power and have been so abusive to their followers that Americans are demanding more oversight and abandoning religious institutions altogether. For many people, particularly on the political left, the local pastor, no matter what good he or she could do for building community, is just not worth the downsides. So the people seek alternative ways to plug into religion that are deliberately powerless: without a local leader, there is no power to harness for good but also no power to abuse. The spiritual-but-not-religious identifier and the political hobbyist share a mentality that rejects the power of community and thereby avoids getting burned.

Within a political party, a union, or a church, a character such as Naakh comes with too great a risk to the brand, or so organizations have learned. Over time, the risks have led to serious shifts in how organizations encourage individuals to participate. Party organizations want you to come around to them during elections, give some money, knock on some doors with a canned script, follow a procedure that keeps you from embarrassing them. Because those forms of engagement feel so shallow, because they lack all the substance that we saw in the stories of Angela, Naakh, Lisa, and Drew, not many of us want to do that. To get our political fix, we can't go to the local committee because the local committee doesn't do anything interesting. Hobbyism fills the vacuum. Our taste for not dirtying our hands with actual politics combined with organizations' desire to maintain top-down control results in many of us having a hard time learning how to channel our political energy in useful ways.

CHAPTER 20

Fear and Fate

Even if we mostly spend our leisure time in five-minute stints, and even if political organizations are disempowered, at times we set aside our normal rationales and feel called to action by our fears. Thinking back to Lisa from Brooklyn, who started knocking on doors every weekend on Staten Island even though she would rather be at her sons' soccer games, or to Angela from Pennsylvania, who was so affected by Trump's election that she committed to taking a political action every day of his presidency and logging it in her journal, we see how fear of the Trump presidency has spurred political engagement among those who weren't previously engaged.

Whereas the 2014 midterm election featured the lowest levels of voter participation in decades (36 percent), the 2018 election featured the highest midterm turnout in over a century (50 percent). Fear may help us explain the change. In psychology, the theory of "loss aversion" describes a human tendency to feel more strongly about losing something than winning something. Rationally, we should care the same about the chance that someone will hand us $100 as the chance that someone will take away from us $100. But we don't tend to consider these to be the same. We will put in significantly more effort to avoid the chance of losing than we'd put in for the chance at a gain.

When, in 2008, Barack Obama won the White House and the Democrats controlled the Senate and House, the Tea Party movement suddenly emerged. Republicans feared that their interests or values were at risk. Many got off their couches and took to the streets or to Tea Party meetings. One explanation of Trump's election in 2016 is that America's dominant group, white men, witnessed the growing population of racial minorities and immigrants and the growing interdependency of the international economy, and they felt their dominant status in society was under threat. In the future, it won't be as straightforward as it once was for white men to achieve economic comfort because they face competition from other members of society who were previously excluded from competing for good jobs. Under this theory, white men support the Republican Party because it offers rhetoric and public policies to help white men avert their losses, such as restrictions on immigration, opposition to affirmative action, and protectionist trade policies.[1]

Loss aversion may help explain, too, why Democrats, energized by the Trump presidency, had disengaged from political activity during the Obama years, sitting at home while Tea Party activists dominated town hall meetings, sitting at home during midterm elections in which Democratic candidates were crushed. When their party was in control of the White House, Democrats weren't willing to work for the chance to advance policy they cared about. Activists reemerged *after* Trump was elected and not before, the fear of loss having suddenly set in.

Fear waxes and wanes in history. When we think of voting out of fear, the first thing that comes to mind, at least for the older generations, may be fear of war. Most Americans alive today have never personally known war. While we have in recent memory the lengthy and expensive wars in Afghanistan and Iraq, no American has been drafted into military service in almost fifty years.[2] Those of us who do not feel the burden of war may take for granted the ways that a stable government helps protect economic and social freedom.[3] It is difficult to fear the loss of stability if you've never known instability. For those of us who haven't volunteered for military service, or whose children haven't volunteered, the long peace may have the consequence of shielding us from fear, which in turn demobilizes us from political activity.

In his study of civic decline over the twentieth century, Robert Putnam posed the question of why the World War II generation, the "greatest generation," participated actively in civil society, and why subsequent generations stopped participating like that. Part of Putnam's answer is technology. Television replaced active civic participation. But another key to Putnam's study is the common experience of war and military conscription among World War II veterans.

War put Americans into small army units. In these groups, soldiers got to know Americans from other walks of life and learned to rely on them for their survival. This experience led the veterans to seek out small-group camaraderie when they returned home. They sought opportunities to engage with neighbors in political and social activism. In local units, they continued to build communities alongside one another.[4]

Feeling threatened by foreign aggressors and learning to collaborate in a conscripted military may inspire political activity. But what about when threats emanate not from other countries but from our own economic hardships, from personal dangers, from discrimination, health insecurity, or domestic political concerns? How do those threats translate into action?

Feeling personally threatened sometimes mobilizes us into action. Victims of terrorism, for example, tend to participate more actively in politics after they've been attacked.[5] Feeling threatened, though, can also lead us to hunker down, shy away from politics, and keep to ourselves.[6] In one recent study, voters were prompted to think about their economic insecurities. They were reminded of how much work they have to do to deal with their personal situation. They ended up saying they wanted to disengage from activism so they could focus on their own needs.

Maybe feeling threatened is what got some conservative activists off their couches during the Obama years and some liberal ones off their couches in the Trump years. But it doesn't work like that for everyone. If an election gives you reminders that you may lose your health care, you may focus on what you can do to get yourself away from insecurity as quickly as possible, such as job hunting, rather than do your part in a political organization.[7] Or, because policy issues that affect you personally are a bummer to think about, maybe instead of pitching in on those issues in politics, you retreat: you fantasize about how a magical solution to political woes, such as a Robert Mueller investigation or an impeachment inquiry, could instantly fix everything that is wrong.

• • •

Fear and insecurity are an important part of the story of hobbyism. They help us understand why political hobbyism may be particularly prevalent not just for college-educated professionals, who live pretty comfortable lives in America, free of most fears, but for white people specifically.

To this point in the book, I have written little about race. In the introduction, I wrote that political hobbyism describes the behavior of whites more than other Americans, but I did not dive into why. Throughout the book, I have deliberately focused on white people. In the stories I have shared with you, I have shown you Americans who are young and old, rich and poor, men and women, but all whites and all with professional backgrounds. I wanted to show you how the kind of person who might have been just another hobbyist ended up not being one. In choosing deep actions, they bucked the trend of whites, who are so overrepresented in hobbyist forms of politics.

A certain detachment from feelings of fear and insecurity is needed to experience politics as a leisure-time activity. While non-white Americans, particularly those in the middle and upper classes, can engage in political hobbyism as much as anyone else, research on racial politics suggests some important differences in minority communities that should limit the phenomenon. Namely, no matter how economically or professionally successful, black voters tend to see their own fate, and the fate of their families, as tied to the fate of the racial group as a whole. To a lesser extent this pattern is visible among Latinos as well.[8] The idea of *linked fate* may be the best explanation for why racial minorities, blacks especially, tend to be unified politically even though they exhibit internal diversity in wealth or religiosity or other traits that are predictive of political divisions among whites. Linked fate also rationalizes political action as a form of self-preservation and self-interest. Supporting the group, empowering the group, also helps empower oneself and one's family.

If you are reasonably well-off and white, and if you mostly live among other people like you, then you may have trouble seeing how your fate is linked to the fate of those less fortunate. Maybe you understand it intellectually but don't feel it day to day. You may not *fear* that your personal security is tied up with politics in a way that inspires you to treat politics less like a hobby and more like a necessary path to power. You may engage in political hobbyism because, as much as you dislike the state of affairs in America for one reason or another, you aren't afraid. On a personal level, you implicitly perceive the stakes to be low.

According to the 2018 survey, when I asked about how people use their time on politics, whites said they spend more time on politics than nonwhites, but that's only because they spend more time consuming the news. Blacks and Latinos dedicated a significantly larger portion of their political time to actual volunteerism than whites reported. Blacks and Latinos were *twice* as likely as whites to report that part of the time they spent on politics was spent on volunteering. Among respondents who were not college educated, or among those who were not interested in politics, minorities were three times more likely to say they engage in political volunteerism.[9]

To help us understand the relationship between race and hobbyism, I want to tell you just two more short stories about two more nonhobbyists. The first is the story of Querys Matias. Querys is sixty-three, an immigrant from the Dominican Republic, who lives in Haverhill, Massachusetts, a city of about sixty thousand people, forty-five minutes north of Boston on the New Hampshire border. She lives in a multifamily house, a block from the 7-Eleven on Main Street. I met her at her home on a warm spring day. She works as a school bus monitor for a special-needs school, and between her early-morning to-school shift and the afternoon from-school shift, she made a couple of hours for me. We sat at her kitchen table.

Querys and I were joined at the table by Kathy Rurak. Kathy at times translated and filled in some of the details of Querys's remarkable story. Kathy's own story is pretty remarkable. Early in her career, Kathy was a nun, and she spent time as a missionary in Mexico, where she became fluent in Spanish. After she returned to the United States from Mexico, she left the convent and married her husband, Jim. They spent a few years in Texas. There, they learned about political organizing, but soon they moved to Haverhill, which was Jim's hometown. Kathy worked at the local Catholic church in Haverhill as a coordinator for the Spanish speakers. She also was the campaign manager for Jim's campaigns for mayor. Jim came from a political family, his father a state senator in the 1970s. With Kathy as campaign manager, Jim won four terms as mayor from 1994 to 2002.[10] Kathy is now retired but spends a lot of time working with the Latino community, which is her connection to Querys.

Twenty percent of Haverhill residents are Latino. Roughly four thousand Dominicans, four thousand Puerto Ricans, and four thousand from other, mostly Central American, countries. Querys tells me that many in the Dominican community of Haverhill were professionals in their home country, and they were politically engaged there. They have made Haverhill a permanent home. The Puerto Rican community, by contrast, according to Querys and Kathy, tends to be more working class and more transient. The communities also have a church divide. The Puerto Ricans tend to go to evangelical churches, whereas the Dominicans attend the Catholic church.

Querys, and her late husband, who died young just a couple of years ago, is part of a well-respected family in the local Dominican community. Her husband's brother came to Haverhill before the area had a large Dominican population. Many in the family followed him. I asked Querys and Kathy how many Matias family members are in Haverhill and the surrounding area. Twenty to forty, they said. It depends if you count the children. Querys's brother-in-law, Ismael, the first to arrive, now runs a Spanish-language radio station in Lawrence, the next town over.

In the jobs Querys has held—working at Central Metal Finishing as a precision finisher, running a money-transfer business, on the school bus—people have always come to her for help. They need help translating government or school forms. They need help dealing with an immigration issue. Newcomers from Latin America come to her for help, and because she is kind and because she has a strong network of family and community, Querys has always made it her business to help others.

The Latino community was never particularly organized or integrated into the politics of the town, nor was the Dominican community particularly integrated with the other Latino communities. Over the years, Querys occasionally knocked on doors or held signs for local candidates she believed in, but the community as a whole was not organized. That changed in 2016, but not, as you might expect, because of Donald Trump. It changed because of Querys's daughter, Juana.

Juana Matias is in her thirties. She came to the United States from the Dominican Republic when she was five. Her father was already there. Querys was the last to come. Juana was educated in the Haverhill public schools, then paid her way through college at UMass Boston and then through Suffolk Law School. In 2016, she won in an upset in a race for a state representative seat in the neighboring city of Lawrence. In 2018, instead of seeking reelection to the statehouse, Juana ran for an open US congressional seat. Ten Democrats contested the primary for Congress. Juana was vastly outspent by several of the other candidates but got 15 percent of the vote. The winner, Lori Trahan, got 22 percent. When Juana was on the ballot, Querys says she was out every night after work till ten o'clock knocking on doors. She put everything into her daughter's races.

After Juana lost, Querys wanted to keep the Latino community together. They had come together, Dominicans and Puerto Ricans and others, and stood behind Juana. They got voters registered and to the polls. Querys didn't want everyone to recede after Juana's election was over. A member of the community told Querys, "We were in the shadows before. Now [after Juana's election], we're out." Querys wanted it to stay that way. The community has a lot of needs. Political power could help address those needs.

After Lori Trahan won the congressional primary against Juana, Querys told Trahan that the Latino community in Haverhill would get out the vote for her in the general election, but under one condition: that she meet with them after the election was over. Trahan agreed. And Querys got out the vote.

Querys and Kathy imagine that Trahan expected five or six people would attend the promised meeting. Instead, forty showed up. At Querys's kitchen table, Kathy showed me the picture of the meeting attendees. She also showed me a copy of the meeting's agenda. The group had concrete requests. They wanted the congresswoman-elect to hold regular office hours for the community, and they wanted Spanish speakers available in Trahan's office for constituent service calls. They also talked policy: immigration reform, particularly for Dreamers, federal help with affordable housing, federal money for local initiatives.

The Haverhill mayor saw that forty people attended a meeting with Trahan. He realized this community was getting well organized, and he asked them for his own meeting with them, Kathy tells me. Sixty-four people showed up to that one. The group keeps careful track of the exact numbers who show up. Sitting at the kitchen table, I look through another detailed meeting agenda, another set of concrete requests. They want more Latinos filling city jobs and serving on boards. They want more Latinos hired by the schools, in some of which Latino students are a majority. They want to know how the city is interacting with US Immigration and Customs Enforcement. They want to know what the mayor can do about affordable housing. They also had simpler requests: the city website was only in English. Within a week of the meeting, the website was available in Spanish.

The Latino Coalition, as they call themselves, meets weekly at Querys's home. About ten members of the community form the leadership committee. Kathy attends but rarely talks. She is a veteran of community organizing from her days in Texas and knows that members of the Latino community need to be driving every part of this work. Querys has organized meetings with the police department and with the school superintendent. Within months after the 2018 election, the city's leadership realized that the Latino community is organized and has specific goals, and that the coalition understands clearly the relationship between voting power and serving the community's needs.

Though Latinos are 20 percent of the city's population, no Latino serves on the city council or on the school board. One of the elementary schools, attended by a large number of Latinos, has no Spanish speakers available in the office to answer parents' questions. There are tensions between the white community and the Latino community. Forty-one percent of the town voted for Trump, which might have been close to half of the white voters.

Immigrant parents have lots of questions, especially newcomers who are trying to navigate the school system, legal system, health system, and employment. Querys has always been there trying to help these friends and neighbors, trying to get them answers and solutions. She started much the same way as Naakh Vysoky started with his immigrant community: doing favors, helping wherever he could, building trust. Now Querys is taking the next logical step, the same one Naakh took: bringing together the people whom she has helped and who know her values, and organizing them to serve their needs not just by mutual aid and favors but by flexing political muscle.

Reading Querys's story, it is obvious, isn't it, how distant her political activity is from shallow political hobbyism. If you are a political hobbyist, it might be hard to see yourself in her position. She is in a community that has needs and that is deeply affected by state and local policy choices. She is not messing around on social media, throwing $5 at a long-shot presidential candidate, or signing an online petition into the void. She wants power.

Back in Boston, I talk to a different kind of political activist: Alicia Payne. She just graduated from college at Northeastern and started a job at Boston City Hall. Alicia grew up in the only black family in Oxford, Connecticut, one of the most Republican towns in that state, one town over from Sandy Hook. She describes the area she was raised as "meth and cows . . . no sidewalks, a few small schools, a church, and a few traffic lights here and there." Alicia's parents wanted her to avoid the local public schools in Oxford and got her a scholarship to a nearby elite prep school. She was educated there from kindergarten through twelfth grade. The prep school, like her town, was overwhelmingly Republican.

To the disappointment of Alicia's liberal black parents, Alicia emerged from her private school education as a die-hard Republican. "I thought, if you're on welfare, you're lazy; if you're an immigrant, you're probably illegal; that all my friends' parents were rich because of hard work." In 2012, then in high school, she remembers watching the presidential election returns on TV and seeing her parents delighted by the outcome. "I was weeping that Romney lost."

Her worldview changed quickly once she left home for Boston. For the first time, she met people whose parents were undocumented immigrants. She met people who wore hijabs. On a whim, she found her way to a student organization called Strong Women Strong Girls, SWSG for short, which they pronounce "swidge." SWSG is a mentoring program, with locations in Boston and Pittsburgh. College women in SWSG are placed in Boston public schools and they mentor girls in the third, fourth, and fifth grades. Alicia's SWSG friends welcomed her when she was conservative, and they also welcomed her as she went through an identity crisis and became liberal. SWSG became an important part of Alicia's college life.

In the program, the SWSG professional office sends a curriculum to the college students each week. The curriculum focuses on stories of women. Some weeks it features biographies of politicians such as current members of the Boston City Council, six of whom are women of color. But more often, the curriculum is about girls closer to the age of the elementary school students.

One week, they talked about twin fifteen-year-old sisters who received multiple detentions and were banned from attending their prom at nearby Mystic Valley Regional Charter School, in Malden, Massachusetts. The girls were disciplined because they wore braided hair extensions. They and their supporters complained that the school policy was racist. The school argued that its dress code is meant to promote equality in the school. Hair extensions are expensive, and allowing them to be worn showcases differences in wealth among the students in a way the school wants to avoid.[11] The SWSG curriculum described the decisions of the school and the students that led to the conflict and helped the girls in SWSG think through the issues.

Before they visit with the girls, the college mentors meet and talk through the curriculum. They make notes and edits. Then, once a week, they head to their placements, which change every semester. When I talk to Alicia, she, along with five other Northeastern students, is placed at the Everett School in Dorchester. The school is 4 percent white. Two-thirds of the students are considered by the state to be economically disadvantaged.

The mentors start their session by asking each of the girls in this after-school program about their peaks and valleys, the high point and low point of their week. The mentors share their peaks and valleys, too, though they are coached to never talk about their own schoolwork as a valley. They make sure to show the girls they are actively listening to each of girls' stories. Then they start digging into the curriculum of the week.

SWSG is an all-encompassing activity for the mentors. "It's sort of like a sorority, but I don't like that comparison," Alicia tells me. "But it's my whole life. . . . The work we do encompasses a big part of [our] daily lives. If you're not mentoring, you're talking about the girls [or planning] events." SWSG is also one of most competitive activities on campus. Each year, according to Alicia, some five hundred students at Northeastern apply to be part of it. From this pool the group's volunteer board selects eight new members each year.

In her last year on campus, Alicia was elected director of the Northeastern chapter. She wanted to run the organization largely because of the racial dynamics. The college women are mostly white. The children they work with in primary schools are mostly not white. Alicia, a black woman, wanted to help SWSG do a better job recruiting minority mentors. She also wanted to help the group confront the inherent tension of mostly privileged white women mentoring poor girls of color. "We need to make deliberate space for [discussing] white savior complex," she says, referencing the delicate dynamic of well-to-do whites giving advice about how to handle life experiences to poor girls of color. The thing to do, Alicia says, is to confront that dynamic head-on. "It's not a place for hostility. It needs to be out in the open. No one is going to join SWSG and never feel uncomfortable."

Most of us would classify Alicia's SWSG activity as community service. Alicia's leadership in SWSG may seem like a cheerful, but unremarkable, college community service project. What's remarkable is that Alicia sees it clearly as something more than that. She sees it as politics.[12]

"When you join a women's organization that's not a sorority," she says, "there's already a frame of empowerment to it. We're a feminist club. It's very hard to join SWSG and not care about empowering women. That's what the curriculum is focused on."

When the schoolgirls talk about their peaks and valleys, racism is bound to come up. For instance, Alicia has heard from girls whose parents won't let them play with one another because they are of different races. "When racism comes up," Alicia goes on, "it's always political." They talk through it.

Alicia also sees her role in shaping the other mentors as political. White people doing service such as SWSG, "[we're] not gonna coddle you. You go because you want to better yourself, [because you want to] start working in communities that isn't tokenizing . . . [because you want to start] getting to know people." Some people find it hard to do that—to find their way to an organization such as SWSG and work in communities that are different from their personal comfort zone. Alicia knows it's hard. "Suck it up," she says.

Through the stories in this book, I have tried to show both that politics is a form of service we do for our communities and that political power is earned through service to the community. But the person I take to be the typical reader of this book—a college-educated white person—might think of politics as a separate category from community service. To the hobbyists, the amateurs, to the verbalist elite, politics is about ideas and it's national. The local version of politics they can envision is supporting candidates for state and national offices. But to Alicia Payne and to Querys Matias, and to Lisa Mann and Dave Fleischer, and to Angela Aldous and Drew Kromer and Naakh Vysoky, politics *is* service. They are one and the same.[13]

Group empowerment is the connection between service and politics. In communities with real needs, where stakes are high, where fears are palpable, politics and service are not different things. We saw that with Naakh and Querys most clearly. Naakh helped three hundred people pass citizenship tests, helped immigrants obtain government benefits in their new country, helped them demand constituent services from their local politicians. Querys is organizing neighbors whose trust she has gained and is persuading the city's leadership to take the needs of the Latino community more seriously. With Querys and Naakh and Alicia, there is no daylight between community service and political organizing.

The meshing of politics and service happens in minority communities and immigrant communities not only because of clear needs but because group members feel mutual obligation to serve those needs. They feel a linked fate. In immigrant communities, political mobilization happens not through the lethargic political parties, which generally no longer see their role as serving those in need, but in local community organizations, which help families facing legal issues, health issues, and work issues. These organizations know that part of the way they help is through political empowerment.[14]

In black communities, the church has historically played a role both in providing social services and in organizing politically.[15] So have community organizations. And so have radical black movements throughout history. Political scientist Michael Dawson argues that radical black movements in the 1930s and in the 1970s were most successful in recruiting supporters to their causes when they focused on such issues as working conditions, discrimination by employers and unions, and police brutality.[16] Black power groups in the 1970s, Dawson recounts, engaged in "service programs such as drug rehab, breakfast, education, and medical care." They met needs, responded to their communities' fears, and sought power. The source of their power was the ordinary people who might not have cared much about theories of empowerment but who saw community organizations who paid attention to them and their day-to-day struggles.

What's special about Alicia Payne isn't that she is a college student who does community service, but that she consciously does a form of community service that empowers her political values. When Alicia is mentoring third-grade girls, teaching them about feminism and their own agency, and when she selects and mentors her mostly white peers at Northeastern, she is doing politics and she knows it, because she wants power for her views.

The tight relationship between community service and political power is nothing new. It's obvious to everyone except the political hobbyists. Your community has needs. You meet those needs directly by providing service and indirectly by amassing political power. To amass power in a democracy, you meet the needs of people and show them you care so they will give you their votes and their voices when you call upon them to act.

This cause and effect is obvious to the National Rifle Association, which supports local clubs across the country, building community and training local leaders, offering services such as gun-safety classes and insurance. It is also obvious to politically engaged churches on the left and the right.[17] It is obvious to the new crop of Democratic Socialist chapters, such as one in Pennsylvania that hosts all-day childcare events when public schools are closed, free lunches, and runs free car-repair clinics.[18] It was obvious to one of the most famous middle-class reform advocates in American history, Jane Addams, who, as quoted in the start of this section, recognized the power of the political boss, that "big manifestation of human friendliness, this stalking survival of village kindness," compared to the impotent reformer who is all talk of big ideas but offers nothing concrete.

It is certainly obvious to powerful political groups outside the United States, such as Hamas, Hezbollah, and the Muslim Brotherhood, all of which provide health and education services in addition to a political agenda. To ordinary people who don't care much about politics, these groups say, "We care about you. We support you. When the time comes for a vote or a protest, be there for us." In the story from Egypt and the Arab Spring, the leaderless resistance groups stood no chance in an election against the Muslim Brotherhood, which built a brand not just based on an ideology but on a commitment to community service.

White nationalists are figuring this out, too. As I mentioned in the book's introduction, the Ku Klux Klan in North Carolina was out in 2018 offering assistance to opioid addicts.[19] When your ideology is as noxious as the KKK's, you won't win many supporters on your policy views alone. But you may win supporters if you show people you care about them. And if you show voters empathy and take care of people and the mainstream parties aren't doing the same, maybe you'll get some converts to your cause.

The only political entities that haven't figured out the relationship between community service and political power are those that are comfortable enough with the status quo that they don't act as if they need more power than they already have.

Finally, then, we have come to the culture of privilege as an explanation for why we treat politics more as a leisure activity than a path to power. The explanation is that college-educated white people are not motivated by fears, either fears of foreign countries, or fears of domestic social unrest, or fears of personal discrimination or poverty or safety. And, so goes the theory, they fail to internalize how their own fates are linked to those who live with these fears. If they did internalize those fears, they would not spend close to 100 percent of the many hours each week they dedicate to politics on news consumption and political debate. Indeed, such use of free time would be embarrassing excess.

In 1967, Kwame Ture, the civil rights leader formerly known as Stokely Carmichael, along with political scientist Charles Hamilton, authored a famous book, *Black Power*. They argued that African Americans had tried for too long to work in coalitions with white liberals. African Americans needed to focus more on amassing power on their own. The authors cited the amateur club Democrats from the 1950s as an example of white liberal coalition partners who failed to be good partners to blacks. Too often, the authors say, white liberal groups didn't genuinely share the value of long-term black empowerment and, in fact, tried to impede progress and failed to treat blacks as equal partners in coalitions. "Let black people organize themselves *first*," the authors argued, "define their interests and goals, and then see what kinds of allies are available."[20]

Ture and Hamilton accused the white liberals not just of being disingenuous in their support of black empowerment. They accused them of being hobbyists, of participating in politics from their perch of middle-class comfort and failing to come to grips with the true life-and-death stakes of political power in America. Being white and financially comfortable makes it hard to understand a sense of fear that would push people to want power. Being white and comfortable means already having enough power. Only if you don't need more power than you already have could politics be for fun. It's when you don't have as much as you need—that's when politics is for power.

196

PART V

And when you lift up your hands,
I will turn My eyes away from you;
Though you pray at length, I will not listen.
Your hands are stained with crime. . . .

Learn to do good.
Devote yourselves to justice;
Aid the wronged.
Uphold the rights of the orphan;
Defend the cause of the widow.

Come, let us reach an understanding.
                    —Isaiah 1:15–18[1]

CHAPTER 21

Learning to Want Power

As I started to dip my toes into local politics, I got skeptical reactions from friends. They understood why I wanted to do some volunteering, but they had a hard time understanding why I wanted to pay attention to my well-off, Democratic town in an over-whelmingly Democratic state. My friends follow the national news and know about the important things going on elsewhere. It feels important to follow the latest investigations into the president, to watch Senate confirmation hearings of Supreme Court justices, and to check the polls for Democratic presidential candidates. How can anything happening locally compare in terms of importance? If I am to volunteer at all—and what impact could I possible have?—why not at least focus my time on a competitive congressional race or a swing state somewhere else? Activism here feels both uninteresting and unimportant, a huge waste of time.

Their reaction reminded me of something I had read about Ella Baker.[1] Baker is largely unknown to the public, but she was one of the most important figures in the American civil rights movement. Before she formed the Mississippi Freedom Democratic Party, which demanded participation in the 1964 Democratic National Convention; before she led students to create the Student Nonviolent Coordinating Committee (SNCC) in 1960; before she ran the operations of Martin Luther King's Southern Christian Leadership Conference (SCLC); Baker was the lead organizer for the National Association for the Advancement of Colored People (NAACP).

During World War II, a surge of civic engagement across the country drew many new black Americans to NAACP chapters. Baker wanted to take advantage of the moment and help local chapters grow into durable organizations that could be leveraged for future civil rights work. She wanted the local organizations to take concrete political action in their communities. The chapters wouldn't be strong if all they did was raise money for the national organization. They needed to have a plan that they, not some national committee, were in charge of.

In 1941 and 1942, then in her late thirties, Baker spoke at over a hundred chapters around the country, and even more church groups and other organizations. She kept a grueling pace, speaking about the value of organizing, patiently answering questions, and recruiting volunteers.

The story goes that when she was visiting Albany, New York, Baker learned something that unsettled her about the schools in Albany. The schools used a tiered tracking system. The highest level was for college preparation. The middle level was for vocational training. And the third tier, according to one of Baker's biographers, "did little more than mark attendance." Most of Albany's black students were placed by the school district into that third tier.[2]

When Baker spoke at a meeting with the Albany NAACP branch, all that anyone wanted to talk about was the Deep South, where the racial violence was most intense. Whenever Baker traveled outside the Deep South, it seemed as if the middle-class attendees who dominated chapter meetings mainly wanted to hear from Baker about how things were going in the Deep South. Baker was outraged. "They were always talking about the poor people down South," she said. "And so the question was, what do you do about the poor children right here?" When she heard people talking endlessly about the South, "[that] meant to them that's where the problem was and they had not identified the problem in their own area."[3]

I wanted to focus on my own area, and the neighboring communities of Boston, because I wanted to be able to identify problems that I could get my hands on and fix. I thought of Baker and I thought of Carol Greenough out in Oregon, who has a list of state legislative bills she wants to see supported by her local elected officials. I thought of all the organizers I've told you about, all building local political power.

Still, if I am to get involved, why would I focus on my well-to-do town and not volunteer in neighboring areas of Boston that have more serious issues than Brookline has: more poverty, worse schools. I think back to that book by Kwame Ture and Charles Hamilton arguing that whites could not be trusted as allies, which is why, they said, the black civil rights movement needed to turn toward black power.

Ture and Hamilton write, "One of the most disturbing things about almost all white supporters has been that they are reluctant to go into their own communities—which is where the racism exists—and work to get rid of it." Fast-forward fifty years from that book, when I sit and read through public comments arguing against low-income housing development in well-to-do communities, saying that new developments will "change the character of the town," and when I see little or no organized effort in privileged white communities to support lower-income housing, I know what Ture and Hamilton were talking about.

Another reason to get involved locally: I am not on a six-month plan, trying to think strategically about how I can make the biggest difference in the Democratic-versus-Republican battle for control of the national government in the next election. Instead, I'm thinking about a ten-year plan, a thirty-year plan, how can I make a difference in a lifetime of elections, how I can help build up community so that one day I will have some power to deploy. That doesn't mean I ignore what is happening now. It just means I want a time horizon that is more than a series of short election seasons and cycles. I want to figure out how to turn the one vote I am entitled to into a thousand votes as Naakh has earned. That takes time. To me, it seemed as if the right first step was to get involved where I am, to learn about people and organizations here, to learn who has power and why, to learn where the gaps are. That won't be everyone's first step. There are lots of paths. But this was mine.

As I think more about it, I realize that I also wanted to get involved locally because, and this is a strange thing to say, I wanted to become an adult in the community. That's strange because I am thirty-six years old. I have three children. I own an apartment and a minivan. In certain realms of my life, I feel like an adult. At a parent-teacher conference when I hear a preschool teacher tell me about *my* child, then I feel like an adult.

Do I feel like an adult of my town, of my neighborhood, of my state? Do I feel ownership, that I am a steward of the community? Mostly, I have felt like a passive observer. Since graduating from college, my wife and I have moved homes six times, which is normal for people our age. We finally were able to buy an apartment a few years ago, but we might not live in this increasingly cramped space forever. If we aren't going to live in this apartment forever, is it still too early to feel of sense of ownership for a community?

Also, we aren't rich. Rich people can feel responsible for a community because they are solicited to serve on governing boards of civic organizations. They are asked to attend meetings and give their advice, mostly as a pretext for a solicitation of money. Serving on those boards, I imagine, makes them feel responsible for the community, as if they are wealthy benefactors tasked with keeping a community running smoothly. If you're not rich, how do you come to assume responsibility for your community, see that you are a steward, too, that you have power to deploy to solve pressing needs?

Maybe you do what Naakh and Querys did: help people and earn influence over their votes. If you do that, you get power. Maybe you work with a nonprofit service organization like Alicia does in Boston. Maybe you do politics like Drew, Angela, Lisa, or Carol. Whatever you do, you start to insert yourself into the community. You build rapport. If you don't have money, you put in time.

I started to put in time. I wanted to learn more about the local Democratic Party. In addition to meetings with the chair of the committee, I also ended up, by a fluke, attending the state Democratic convention as a delegate. At a house party in Brookline months before the 2018 state convention, I learned that a group of insiders was organizing a slate of local delegates. The longtime Democratic activist at the house party told me that if I agreed to support the gubernatorial candidate that the insiders liked, I could join their slate. I agreed and joined. It seemed like a good chance to see a state convention and vote as a delegate. Delegates vote for the candidates who wish to participate in primaries. If a candidate doesn't get 15 percent of the delegate votes at the convention, they don't get to appear on the primary ballot. Attending the convention, I thought, would afford me an opportunity to meet people and learn about a political process that I had never seen firsthand.

To be elected delegate, I attended the local caucus, which took place in the local high school cafeteria. People on the slate were handed a list of the names of delegates to vote for. A number of other people, particularly people my age and younger, attended and hoped to be elected delegate but not as part of the slate. They hadn't been tipped off about the slate and so didn't bring enough of their own supporters to outvote the slate. So they lost. I imagine they felt disappointed about there being an insider's game and not knowing about it. Because by chance I learned about the slate, I was among the insiders.

Per Democratic Party rules, male delegates and female delegates were elected separately in the cafeteria, to ensure equal gender representation at the convention. A one-gendered group goes up and makes speeches about why they should be delegates. A paper ballot and a tally follow. Then the other gender goes. After the delegates are elected, separate elections are held, tediously, for male and then female alternate delegates, who attend the convention in case the regular delegates can't make it or in case a delegate needs to use the bathroom when a vote is called. The candidates for alternate delegates, male and then female, make speeches, too, about why they should be elected as alternate delegates. Then, if the town has been granted an odd number of delegates to the convention, the caucus holds an entirely separate election for a single delegate who could be male *or* female. They also hold a vote for a male-or-female alternate. That last one was me. After hours of these speeches and paper-ballot counting, I was elected on the slate as the male-or-female alternate delegate from Brookline to attend the state Democratic convention to be held in Worcester.

In Worcester for about thirty hours, I learned about the party rules and met some interesting people. Was it otherwise a waste of time? My snarky first reaction is that, well, it wasn't not a waste of time. But as I learned from the organizers I have interviewed, the path to power is filled with wasted time and false starts. When I tell their stories to you, I hope to convey how profound their work is.

I gloss over the wasted time. You never know when spending a few hours with other engaged citizens will turn into something big. A lot of times it doesn't.

After attending the convention, attending a couple of events that were sponsored by the local Democratic committee, and getting to know the local chair, I am embarked on my first project. I wanted to talk to voters the way Dave Fleischer and Lisa Mann did, focusing on making a personal connection, listening, being empathetic. As a modest first step, I eventually settled on a series of phone banks to voters in the congressional district. The plan was to recruit volunteers, particularly volunteers with a background in counseling—social workers, psychologists—and have them to talk to voters on behalf of the Democratic town committee. Volunteers would introduce themselves and say the following:

> Political parties usually call people to ask them for something, like their vote. But it's important to the local Democrats that we listen. We want to make sure that Democratic committees like ours are doing a good job understanding our neighbors. We're trying to get a sense of issues folks are facing day to day, whether big or small. So, I would love to hear about you, about things you think are going well or not so well, whether in the country, community, or in your own life.

After this prompt, the volunteer was instructed to focus on listening respectfully to the voter.

Getting this project off the ground wasn't easy. I needed to get the approval of the local Democratic committee, the state party, and the congressional campaign in the district. I needed to get the phone system to do the calls and the voter files to get the phone numbers. Mostly, I needed to get volunteers. A couple of people helped me recruit. We advertised around the community. We recruited a couple of activist groups. In the end, about twenty people made calls.

Like many others in our trainings, I was at first afraid to talk to strangers. But once I got going, I enjoyed it. I enjoyed it for the reasons that Dave Fleischer, the guru of deep canvassing, anticipated: we weren't trying to score points and rush through an awkward script.

We were listening. As soon as the person on the other end realized we were there to listen rather than to talk, they often opened up.

I learned from a swing voter that her kids' school was underfunded by the state. She lives in a working-class town, Attleboro, with dwindling industry, and she resented how little the state was willing to invest in the local school system.

I spoke for a long time with a Latino immigrant who said he doesn't like Trump but likes the Democrats less than Trump. Though an immigrant himself, he shares President Trump's views on immigration and protectionism. He kept telling me that more recent immigrants were taking advantage of the system and getting free health care. He thinks the state and national Democrats are selfish. I didn't argue with him. I reiterated in different ways that his views were valuable for us to hear and that the local Democratic committee is listening. At the end, he said he was grateful that we cared about what he had to say.

A phone call focused on listening is, I think, the mildest possible form of transactional politics. That is, we were giving voters a simple form of service, a listening ear, a nonjudgmental sounding board for what's on their mind about politics. In exchange, we didn't explicitly ask for anything, but implicitly we asked them to think well of a party's brand name. A less mild version of transactional politics is the stuff Naakh did: decades of favors and good deeds in return for which he earned votes.

Even my mild form, though, bothered some of the volunteers I tried to recruit. A few weeks before the training, I was talking to a prospective volunteer, a retired social worker, urging him to participate. He said he didn't like that the "empathetic canvassing" strategy could be used by any side. Any side can recruit counselors or train volunteers to connect personally with voters. If the Republicans do this, too, he explained, "then what's the point?" He never participated.

His reaction was rather common. Politically engaged citizens know the basics about public policy and even more about the drama in Washington. If they were to get off their couches and talk to voters, they imagine they would want to talk to voters about the benefits of their side's policies and the drawbacks of their opponents' policies. Or maybe they would just want to talk to voters about how awful the other side is behaving. They may imagine that if two canvassers, one from each political side, were to come to a voter's door and give the policy rationale for voting for their side or tell their perspective on the latest DC drama, the best argument would win.

The idea of approaching a citizen who is not knowledgeable or interested in politics and focusing on listening rather than talking, or focusing on serving the material needs of the voter, feels dirty, in part, because any side can do it. We saw that in the previous chapter: the most pernicious political organizations offer services in exchange for political support. It feels dirty because politics, to hobbyists, is about ideas more than it is about power. Even if hobbyists think their side has the best ideas and ought to be in power, the thought of approaching people who don't know anything about politics and saying, "Vote for my party because we are going to take care of you in these concrete ways," is exactly like the kind of dirty transactional politics that they want to avoid. To the retired social worker I failed to recruit, even offering voters an empathetic ear felt dirty and transactional.

The phone banks we ran were a positive experience for me and the other volunteers, a first step. We learned how difficult it is to recruit volunteers and how hard it is to connect with voters on the telephone today. Few people are willing to answer the phone. We were calling people in an expansive congressional district, and I realized I wanted the chance to instead talk to my neighbors. Maybe when neighbors brought up problems they were facing, I could help them more directly than in the phone bank. I wanted to ratchet up the transactional politics a little more. I wanted to be a little more like Naakh.

In the fall of 2018, I started a precinct organization. After back-and-forths with the chair of the local Democratic Party, she consented to let me start a precinct organization within the party. I wrote a letter to a thousand households in my precinct. I had to raise money to pay for printing and postage because the local Democratic Party doesn't have a budget for this kind of thing. For several evenings after I put my kids to bed, I sat with two huge boxes of envelopes, and I hand-addressed a thousand letters. Is hand-addressing a thousand envelopes hard? Not when you do it an hour or two at a time, late at night, a beer or two by your side, while listening to music or talking with a spouse. It's actually kind of nice.

In the letter, after I introduced myself and told the neighbors that we live in a small area that makes up Precinct 7, I noted:

> Our precinct is small, and I think we would benefit from more connections within it. My goal is to help facilitate those connections. I'd like to get to know you and listen to any ideas, interests, or concerns you have in our neighborhood. I'd like to help address concerns and to connect you to people who care about the same things you do. If you have ideas for political, social, or civic activities for the neighborhood (or are looking to get more involved), I can help.

I asked the neighbors to send me an email and introduce themselves. I shared my email address. A couple dozen responded, some young and some old, some who have lived here for decades and some who just recently moved in. I invited them to form a precinct committee with me. We've been meeting monthly and planning civic and political activities for our neighborhood.

One thing I noticed almost immediately was an idea I raised earlier in the book: that political organizing cultivates, and demands, empathy. A few days after I sent the letter out to neighbors, a time when neighbors would just be receiving it, I drove into the supermarket parking lot with two of my children. The supermarket is in the precinct. Next to the handicapped-parking spots, a couple of parking spaces are reserved for shoppers with infants. When you have to walk through a parking lot with bags of groceries and multiple kids, it's a small but nice gesture that the store reserves spots near the door.

That day, I approached the reserved area with my car just as a couple of women in their twenties, no kids, were returning to their car, which was parked in the spot. As I waited for them to vacate the spot, they sat in their car and conversed, oblivious of me waiting and oblivious that they weren't supposed to be in that spot. I was annoyed, especially once my baby in the back started getting antsy.

Though it annoyed me, I had an immediate reaction that I hadn't anticipated. "These people might have just received my letter. Maybe they will come to one of my meetings." How could I ever ask anything of them if I didn't see past minor errors, if I responded with a honk or an aggressive gesture rather than with eye contact and a smile? So instead of being annoyed, I rolled down my window and introduced myself. I talked to them, the way Dave Fleischer might have, more like a friend than a stranger.

A woman responded to my letter with a handwritten note. She told me she didn't use a computer so she couldn't email me. She said she had an idea she wanted to share, a five-question civics questionnaire that she thought all good citizens should be able to answer; she thought the country would be better off if we could all answer this quiz. I wrote to her asking her to share it, and we carried on a mail-only conversation back and forth a few times.

If a stranger had contacted me on social media and told me she thought the country would be better off if people could answer a five-question quiz she herself had written, I am sorry to say that I might have rolled my eyes. I'm not proud of that, but because I don't think a five-question quiz is a particularly helpful response to what's ailing our country, I wouldn't have taken it seriously. But when I reached out to neighbors asking to connect with them, and this is the way someone connected back, I reacted differently. Behind the quiz, I saw an idea about citizens talking to each other and realizing their own political agency, an idea I agree with. I responded the way I ought to have responded online: by dignifying the person and her ideas.

When you reach out to neighbors and make yourself available as a listener, you also learn about people's needs. Sending my initial letter, assuming a community-oriented stance, I opened my eyes more to those needs. A person wrote to me saying she was anxious about her evacuation plan in the case of an emergency. I connected her to the town office responsible for evacuation plans. An elderly woman who lives a block from me responded by saying that she was too old to get involved in a precinct committee but she appreciated the letter. She also mentioned she was increasingly immobile and had just given up driving. I wrote her back that my kids and I walk by her apartment almost every day, and it would be no trouble if she ever needed help with a run to the grocery store or pharmacy. I gave her my number. She hasn't called on me yet, but I hope she will. We are trying to teach our children that what makes us proud of them is that they serve others. To do that, we need to be showing them that we're on the lookout for ways we can help.

What have I accomplished so far in my political work? Compared to the stories I have told you about other people, very little. I have formed a modest precinct committee starting off with some modest political projects, focused mainly on voter engagement in local elections. The group started off as part of the Democratic town committee, but because after several meetings we decided that we could have the most impact in local elections, we had to cut ties with the Democrats. Remember, the Brookline Democrats don't want to engage in local politics and did not want a precinct committee doing so in their name. So we're on our own (though we recently partnered on a project with the local League of Women Voters). Beyond this group, I have met people and learned about the organizations and individuals in my area. I have learned about the political and policy dynamics on issues I care about.

I have also learned that I am on a long-term path. That path starts with inserting myself. I don't insert myself because I'm an expert. In spite of being a political scientist, I'm a non-expert in 95 percent of politics. I have no more claim to political power than any other citizen. I insert myself under no authority except the realization that I can acquire power if I want it. I can build knowledge and relationships that will enable me to have an impact in some small way.

I have learned that the way to think about my own power as a citizen is not that I'm one out of 130 million votes, but that I can get more than one vote if I convince other people how they should vote or advocate. I have learned that some people out there have a thousand times the voting power that I have not because they are rich or perpetrators of fraud, but because they have earned the respect of their neighbors. I am in awe of that power. I think that I crave that power. If I care about my political values, how could I not crave that power?

CHAPTER 22

To-Do Lists

I mplicit in this book is a hierarchy. At the bottom of the hierarchy is the majority of Americans who are mostly disengaged from elections and political discourse. If they vote, it's only in the presidential elections, and many don't vote in those. They don't think much about public policy. Because many voters are like this, and because their decisions to vote and how they will vote are not set firm, they represent the core of political power. Whoever can motivate more of them to cast ballots gets power. Naakh influenced a thousand of them.

In the middle of the hierarchy of political engagement are a small number of organizers who try to move votes and a large number of hobbyists who do not: all those millions of people who spend an hour or more a day consuming political news but not acting in ways that bring their views political power. The hobbyists have strongly held beliefs. They are more likely to vote than ordinary citizens, though they still largely abstain from local elections. A campaign ad or organizer from the other side has little chance of persuading the hobbyists to change their views, since their views are generally well-formed. Can a campaign from their own side convince them to spend less time on the news and dedicate some time to supporting a party or candidate? Typically, so far, no, unless a celebrity candidate gets them to jump on a bandwagon.

At the top of the hierarchy are those who currently have political and economic power. Politicians, party leaders, big donors. Some of them are hobbyists and some actually want to empower their views. They have the ability to direct money and political resources. So far, they have mostly focused on shallow, one-off strategies, mostly ads. In 2016, campaigns and parties spent about $3 billion on media, way, way, way more than they spent on salaries of organizers. And they spent approximately zero dollars on direct forms of community service, helping neighbors in the ways of Naakh and Querys.[1]

How could a party organization invest in direct forms of community service? Take, for example, childcare and eldercare. My employer, Tufts University, has a contract with a firm, Care.com.[2] If I ever need backup childcare or eldercare, I can use the discounted service and pay $8 an hour for a sitter or an aide who can be at my home within a few hours. (Market rate for a care provider is over $20 an hour.) Every regular employee of the university can use this benefit for up to twenty days a year. I can use it last minute if I need to give a lecture and my regular childcare falls through. I can use it if I need to take my children on a work trip such as to a conference in another city. The sitter can meet me at the hotel. This benefit not only allows staff to come to work when there's a hiccup at home, it conveys to employees and potential employees that this workplace understands how hard it can be to care for family and that the university wants to do a small part to help.

Imagine if the Democratic Party did this. Or the Republican Party. Imagine if a political party in a city or state said, "We want to support working families. We know how hard it is when childcare or eldercare falls through. We have public policy ideas that support families, but we also want to convey in the most concrete way that we care about your daily struggles. We will get you providers when you need backup care." Political parties, super PACs, and businesses already spend hundreds of millions of dollars on politics, mostly on ads. Imagine if some of those millions of dollars were instead allocated to tie a party's brand name to actual service such as backup childcare or eldercare.

Backup childcare and eldercare speak to me as a way to signal that politicians are not just looking for a vote and then going away: they are there to serve the public. Anyone who is financially secure and who has a flexible job should be able to sympathize with how much harder childcare and eldercare are if your work life is more rigid or home life is more complicated.

Even better than a contract with a firm such as Care.com would be for a local or state party organization to develop a network of volunteers, including students and retirees, who helped with backup care as both a service to their political side and a service to their community. Developing this network would be better because in addition to serving the community, the parties would also be recruiting and training an army of potential political volunteers. Setting up a program such as this would require lawyers and disclaimers and lots of money, but you know what else costs lots of money? Pandering advertisements.

I would experiment with other forms of direct service, too: mental health counseling, religious pastoral care, financial clinics, clinics for those suffering from addiction or abuse—any way that a political party can convey its values in concrete terms to the majority of Americans who have a hard time seeing why a vote for a party affects their day-to-day lives. Voters shouldn't have to wait for a party to one day take power and implement a grand new national policy. A party or campaign, not just a government, can take care of people's needs right now. That's what the organizers in this book have done in different ways. They realized that power is derived from serving others.

Beyond direct service, if I were a wealthy donor or party leader, I would direct resources toward building a locally based network of organizers. I would prioritize paying for local offices staffed by fairly compensated organizers who are on the lookout for volunteers like Angela, Naakh, Drew, Lisa, Carol, Querys, and Alicia, and who can help support their work. If I had $50,000 that I could spend on politics and my options were helping pay for TV ads or paying a year's salary to an organizer who could spend every day recruiting volunteers and talking to voters, that would not be a difficult choice for me.

Would any of this work?

The experimental evidence we have in political science suggests it would. When campaigns and parties engage in more personalized, more genuine, more neighborhood-based electioneering, they get more votes. When they leverage personal relationships and social pressure, they get more votes.[3] Local organizers who don't just show up in the weeks preceding an election but who are in a community long-term are the logical conclusion of the experimental evidence that political scientists have amassed.

As far as I know, neither campaigns nor social scientists have yet experimented to learn about the effects of direct service on political participation. To me, direct service seems like an extension of deep canvassing, which has begun to be studied experimentally. In deep canvassing, canvassers build goodwill with strangers by listening to them, taking their personal stories seriously, and showing them they care. What is direct service, community service, family service, but an attempt to build goodwill and show you care? Beyond that, as I have already discussed, political organizations from the NRA to the Muslim Brotherhood to the Democratic Socialists of America to the KKK are already doing direct service. If I controlled the financial resources of a mainstream political party, I would test direct service as a means of building goodwill and support.

Would it be easy? For a political party or wealthy political bene-factor to do what I am suggesting—shifting resources to goods and services and hiring local organizers—requires them to empower local people, which means they will not maintain tight centralized con-trol. This is sometimes hard for them to stomach. Empowering local organizers comes with risk. Leaders who hire local organizers need to know how to find good people, how to train them, how to empower and monitor them. If done well, this can be much more effective than any top-down approach, as I have suggested in the stories of orga-nizers in this book. But do not confuse my endorsement with a claim that it is easy to pull off. If donors and parties want to do something more effective than silly campaigns ads, which have, at best, tiny effects on politics, they need to take some risks and do harder things.

But you still may believe that political parties should be convinc-ing voters on the issues not by offering babysitters, mental health services, or neighborly favors. This just doesn't feel natural to you, like something a party you would support ought to be doing.

Anyone, from any side, can use these strategies, that's true. They already do. The question is whether the verbalist elite, who from the Progressive Era to the Twitterati have looked down on trans-actional politics, are finally interested in getting in the trenches to amass durable political power. If they don't want to, they should at least recognize that political organizations they fear are doing it in their place.

POLITICS IS FOR POWER

Is it even legal for a political party or organization to offer direct goods and services to people? Good question. I'm glad you asked it. I asked it, too. Specifically, in 2019, with the help of a friend and local attorney, Jamie Hoag, I met in person and on the phone with attorneys from the Massachusetts Office of Campaign and Political Finance, which has jurisdiction in this area in my state. Every state has its own regulations for what political organizations can do. I figured I would start with Massachusetts.

I wrote to the regulators, "I want to understand the limits of party committees offering to citizens goods and services as a party-building activity. That is, I am not asking about parties providing goods and services in exchange for votes, which I understand to be illegal. I'm asking about parties providing, on an ongoing basis (i.e., NOT tied to any election), goods and services to voters in order to build rapport with voters, to convince voters that the party cares about them." I gave a bunch of examples, such as babysitting services and goods such as gift cards for groceries for members of the community struggling to get by.

I learned that, at least in Massachusetts, the regulatory office expressed no concern about volunteer services. If in building goodwill with the community, a local party wants to run a clinic (e.g., free babysitting, tax assistance, auto repair) and it recruits volunteers to do the work, the state regulator, which mostly concerns itself with financial matters, sees no problem.

Furthermore, if a local or state party committee wants to support the community in "an acute situation," such as after a natural disaster or during a government shutdown, by passing out gift cards for groceries, diapers, gas, or other goods, the state regulator sees no problem with that, either.

In the hypothetical scenarios I presented to the state regulators, the attorneys were uncomfortable with a committee *paying* for *ongoing* goods and services. For instance, they thought that a party committee could pass out gift cards during an "acute" situation but not ongoing. They thought a party could offer babysitting services with volunteers but not pay for babysitters ongoing, permanently.

What is the regulator's rationale? Though I emphasized that the services I am asking about are explicitly motivated to build goodwill for a political party, not to do charity, the regulators responded that these activities feel to them like charity. "The campaign finance law does not contemplate party committees engaging in on-going charitable activities," the lawyers wrote.

I checked in with a couple of attorneys on the officials' response, and they were baffled. That the law merely does not contemplate party committees paying for ongoing services is not an appropriate legal rationale, I was advised. Furthermore, the lines that the regulator is trying to draw are quite blurry. If a party committee can host a monthly pancake breakfast to foster community and political goodwill, which nobody doubts, can it not call that pancake breakfast a food pantry and welcome the hungry to partake?

The Massachusetts Office of Campaign and Political Finance soon lost patience with my academic questions. So long as the questions remain hypothetical, bureaucrats will avoid making decisions on potentially thorny issues. For now, they have assented in this state to the provision of ongoing voluntary services and goods such as gift cards in acute situations. To find the boundaries of the law beyond that, and the boundaries in other states, an actual political organization with its own lawyers will have to start asking the questions.

If political leaders and donors should invest in hiring local people and experimenting with building goodwill through goods and services, what should ordinary hobbyists do? Maybe you want to do more in politics than you've been doing but are not sure what to do. What are you supposed to do?

My first suggestion would be to do the bare minimum, which is to be a good voter. It's harder than it sounds. If you know a lot about the national news but know so little about state or local issues that you either abstain from voting in those elections or show up but cast random votes, make a change. Figure out how you can learn enough about local politics that you can cast an informed ballot in every election you are asked to vote in. You may need to find those in your neighborhood who know what's going on and learn from them. You may need to attend a candidate forum because it's the only venue in which to learn what the candidates think. You may find that simply redirecting your news consumption toward state and local affairs gives you information about how you could make a difference on issues you care about.

If you want to do more, you have to just start somewhere; there is no cookie-cutter path. In some places, the local Democratic and Republican Party committees are a good place to start. In other places, those committees are too decrepit and closed off to be a vehicle for power. You may be able to find a community organization that you can help support. You may not. Wherever you are, try to build a cell of a few friends or neighbors who can act together. Finding or forming a local group where you can meet in person every once in a while helps push you along. Try hard to work within an existing institution—an active party or group that you think more or less gets things right. Sometimes, these institutions don't exist and you'll have to reinvent the wheel, but patiently inserting yourself into existing organizations and learning from their leaders is often a better pathway.

If you are young and not yet settled into a more permanent phase of life, do not wait. Do not wait until you graduate from college, until after you find a job, a spouse, have children, buy a home, and raise your children to tell yourself that you can now take ownership of your community. Even in the more nomadic phases of life, you can still do a lot. Think back to the stories of organizers in this book. I focused on local leaders: Angela, Drew, Naakh, and Lisa, Carol, Querys, and Alicia. Behind all of these leaders are many more people who work with them in the background. Before you are settled, it may be hard to lead, but it's not hard to support leaders. So follow them, support them, and when you leave them—when you move homes to enter your next phase—you'll carry the skills and relationships with you.

Whether you are young or old, mobile or stationary, you have the power to turn your vote into more than one vote, to turn your voice into more than one voice. The organizers we have seen in this book earned the votes of others. Mostly, they did so by showing their neighbors that they cared about them. They didn't earn votes by talking to people who were already sure to vote and already sure to vote in the way that the organizer wanted. That's no path to power. Power is getting ten, fifty, a hundred, a thousand people to vote and to vote the way you want. That's the kind of power that a person who already spends hours every week on politics can amass if the hours on hobbyism are converted to hours on organizing. When people amass that power, they know they are doing it as part of an army of other people all over the country who are doing the same thing.

Anyone who wants power can do this. I hope the people who want power agree with me about what to do with power. But I know that many of them do not. At least I can step up myself to see how many votes and voices I can influence in my own small way.

Writing those sentences is a commitment strategy for me. Now that I've written them, can I live up to the task? Writing it down helps me hold myself accountable.

I think back to Angela Aldous, the young mom in her new home in Westmoreland County who, starting the first day of the Trump administration, kept a journal. Every night before bed, she logs what she did that day to help empower her views.

I picture Angela, after putting her children to bed, after cleaning up, after packing lunches, logging another day of accomplishments. I remember her telling me about one of those first logs, about how pathetic it felt when she hadn't done anything that day, so late at night she called her congressman's office and left a quiet message of resistance. And I think about the powerful local organization she has built in her county since that call. Her journal was her first commitment strategy, but now she has a whole organization of friends and neighbors who depend on her commitment and her leadership. Her power had modest beginnings.

Power often starts modestly, with writing down plans, making a to-do list. Do you have a to-do list? A plan to shift the time you are currently spending on political hobbyism to multiply the power of your vote? I would bet that if you did what Angela did, what all the volunteer leaders and followers we have encountered here have done, not only would you turn your vote into more votes, but you would turn the shallow pleasures and persistent melancholy that political hobbyism yields into the deep joys that community participation yields. So, what will you do?

Acknowledgments

The volunteers and organizers I interviewed—the ones whose names you know from the book and many others whose stories I could not fit into the book—were generous with their time and taught me more about politics than I ever expected. This book, and my general understanding of politics, is much richer because of them.

I thank my agent, Jill Kneerim, who believed in the project when it was no more than a draft of a proposal in an email. She guided me through this attempt at writing a work of political science for an audience beyond the academy. I am grateful she took a chance on me. I also thank my editor, Colin Harrison, for truly editing this book. Working with an editor such as Colin, who is so good at his craft and who so cares about making a manuscript strong, is a privilege. I thank him and the team at Scribner for their dedication to this project.

Before anyone else laid eyes on them, the first drafts of every chapter were read by Laurel Bliss, an undergraduate at Tufts who served as the primary research assistant for the writing. I asked Laurel to take on the difficult task of helping a professor see what is unpersuasive, unclear, boring, and otherwise bad in his writing. Laurel is a gifted editor who profoundly influenced the direction of the manuscript.

I began this project while on faculty at Yale, and I thank Yale's Department of Political Science and the Institution for Social and Policy Studies for research support. The project was completed at Tufts, and I thank the Department of Political Science and the Tisch College of Civic Life for support. My colleagues at both institutions have helped me grow as a scholar and have made this book possible.

ACKNOWLEDGMENTS

Much of the book was written at cafés and libraries around Boston, and I thank them all for their Wi-Fi, and when I really needed to focus, for their lack of Wi-Fi.

For the last four years, friends, family, and colleagues have been kind enough to talk to me, debate with me, and teach me about the ideas in this book. I thank my extended family and friends for all of their help. For detailed comments they gave along the way, I especially want to thank Stephen Ansolabehere, Perry Bacon, Jeffrey Berry, David Broockman, David Campbell, Jessica Fechtor, David Fleischer, Joshua Foer, Ned Foley, Anthony Fowler, Steven Gelber, Justin Grimmer, Leah and Kenneth Hersh, Jamie Hoag, Eva and Mel Hoffman, Liam Kerr, Yanna Krupnikov, Adam Levine, Peter Levine, Juana Matias, David Mayhew, Clayton Nall, Betsy Pattullo, Chloe Prendergast, Lara Putnam, Tim Ryan, Brian Schaffner, Debbie Schildkraut, Daniel Schlozman, Rebecca Sendor-Israel, Paul Sniderman, Lynn Vavreck, Emily Zhang, and Daniel Ziblatt.

Professor Lara Putnam deserves special recognition. I didn't know Lara before this project, but because of our shared research interests and her extraordinary generosity, Lara became a mentor to me. Her ideas shaped everything from the book's structure to the tone to the empirical evidence. In hindsight, I see that every suggestion Lara made was astute, even when it sometimes took me a while to realize it. Lara's footprint is all over this project, and any remaining faults and insensitivities may well be in places where I simply failed to follow Lara's advice closely enough.

I am thankful for my inspiring children, Levi, Jonah, and Margaret, the latter two of whom were born while I was working on this project. Right now, you are mostly interested in books and magazines about animals (Levi), truly excruciating books about superheroes (Jonah), and short, touch-and-feel board books that are read over and over and over (Margaret). One day, maybe you'll read this book. I hope you'll see that it conveys our family's core values of mutual obligation and community service. Our blessing for you is to feel in your bones both the burden and the opportunity to serve your neighbors, community, and country.

I dedicate this book to Julia, my wife. One time, when we were twenty-two and engaged, on a hot and stressful moving day from

Boston to Washington, in the front cab of a rental truck, we had one of our first arguments. It was about hobbies. I had hobbies; Julia didn't. I thought hobbies were important to have. Julia did not. That was basically the argument. We didn't yet know that on a self-packing, self-unpacking summer moving day, any discussion can turn into a heated argument for no reason at all. This one happened to be about hobbies. Also at the time, we didn't have children and hadn't chosen careers. We had lots of free time, which I filled with hobbies and Julia did not. One day, soon after the move to Washington, Julia saw me make a shopping list, which read, "Goggles. Harmonica." She smiled and pointed out that our shopping lists wouldn't always be so simple.

Since that argument, we have chosen our careers and built our family. Julia works hard every day in a career dedicated to politics. She helps candidates and causes she believes in. She wakes up and goes to bed thinking about how she can do more, do better. She also devotes herself to our family, not only thinking about what everyone else needs but also thinking about how to teach our children to think about what everyone else needs. Julia still doesn't have hobbies; her mind and heart and time are filled with a passion for the political work she believes in and for the family she loves. I am grateful that I get to be part of Julia's story, to raise our children with her, to support her in her career, to be her teammate and her spouse. One day, when life calms down a bit, even if we haven't yet solved every pressing political problem, maybe we can buy some new goggles and harmonicas and try some hobbies together.

Notes

Introduction

1 See Megan Brooker, "Indivisible: Invigorating and Redirecting the Grassroots," in *The Resistance*, ed. David S. Meyer and Sidney Tarrow (Oxford: Oxford University Press, 2018); Lara Putnam and Theda Skocpol, "Middle America Reboots Democracy," *Democracy*, February 20, 2018.

2 While survey responders may not accurately estimate how they spend their time, research suggests they may *underestimate* passive activities such as TV watching and *overestimate* socially desirable activities such as volunteerism. On overestimation of socially desirable political behaviors, see Stephen Ansolabehere and Eitan Hersh, "Validation: What Big Data Reveal about Survey Misreporting and the Real Electorate," *Political Analysis* 20 (4) (2012): 437–59. There's little research on accuracy of estimates of activities such as TV watching. One small study of overweight adults found an underestimation of time spent watching TV: see Jennifer J. Otten, Benjamin Littenberg, and Jean R. Harvey-Berino, "Relationship Between Self-Report and Objective Measure of Television-Viewing Time in Adults," *Obesity* 18 (6) (2010): 1273–75.

3 OLS regression analysis predicting time spent on politics (in nonvolunteer activities) by demographics.

4 Chris Hayes and George Goehl, "Why Is This Happening?: Organizing in Trump Country with George Goehl," NBC News, January 8, 2019, https://www.nbcnews.com/think/opinion/organizing-trump-country-george-goehl-podcast-transcript-ncna956386.

5 "Americans Know Surprisingly Little about Their Government, Survey Finds," Annenberg Public Policy Center, September 17, 2014, https://www.annenbergpublicpolicycenter.org/americans-know-surprisingly-little-about-their-government-survey-finds/. Observing voter ignorance back in the 1850s, John Stuart Mill suggested a college-educated person should have more votes than an unskilled laborer. Still today, theorists express concern about the uneducated masses, suggesting that we reduce the role of government altogether because we are too ignorant to make it work. See Ilya Somin, *Democracy and Political Ignorance: Why Smaller Government Is Smarter* (Palo Alto, CA: Stanford University

Press, 2013). See also Jason Brennan, *Against Democracy* (Princeton: Princeton University Press, 2016); Bryan Caplan, *The Myth of the Rational Voter* (Princeton: Princeton University Press, 2008); and Christopher Achen and Larry Bartels, *Democracy for Realists: Why Elections Do Not Produce Responsive Government* (Princeton: Princeton University Press, 2017).

6 Reid Wilson, "More Americans Have College Degrees Than Ever Before," Hill, April 3, 2017, https://thehill.com/homenews/state-watch/326995-census-more-americans-have-college-degrees-than-ever-before. Theda Skocpol, *Diminished Democracy: From Membership to Management in American Civic Life* (Norman: University of Oklahoma Press, 2003), 211–15. See also Alan Ware, *The Breakdown of Democratic Party Organization, 1940–1980* (Oxford: Oxford University Press, 1989); Lily Geismer, *Don't Blame Us: Suburban Liberals and the Transformation of the Democratic Party* (Princeton: Princeton University Press, 2014).

7 Samara Klar and Yanna Krupnikov, *Independent Politics: How American Disdain for Parties Leads to Political Inaction* (Cambridge: Cambridge University Press, 2016).

8 In the 2018 CCES (Tufts module), 57 percent of college-educated, news-following whites identified as Democratic or as Democratic leaners, compared to 36 percent who identified as Republican or Republican leaners.

Political hobbyism on the Democratic side may be more important, too, because the political vision of the left is, arguably, more aspirational than the vision of the right. Conservatism, as an idea of governance, is more interested in maintaining the status quo. The left envisions sweeping political changes: a Green New Deal, universal government health care, universal pre-K, and so on. That is why, for instance, thought leaders on the left see the Senate filibuster as a protector of the status quo that serves Republican interests over Democratic ones (see, e.g., Jamelle Bouie, "Let the Filibuster Burn!," *Slate*, April 6, 2017, https://slate.com/news-and-politics/2017/04/let-the-filibuster-burn-in-truth-democrats-are-better-off-without-it.html). Even though engaged citizens on the left and right are both largely abstaining from politics and failing to act in ways that bring them power, this phenomenon matters more for the left because the left actually seeks, in principle, to change the status quo. See Richard Rorty, *Achieving Our Nation: Leftist Thought in Twentieth Century America* (Cambridge, MA: Harvard University Press, 1999). On Republican changes to the status quo, see Matt Grossmann, *Red State Blues: How the Conservative Revolution Stalled in the States*, forthcoming.

9 Time spent volunteering by race will analyzed in chapter 20. In addition, in the last several presidential election years (2008, 2012, 2016), the American National Election Study survey shows African Americans reporting higher rates of campaign volunteering compared to whites.

10 See Theda Skocpol, "APSA Presidential Address: Voice and Inequality: The Transformation of American Civic Democracy," *Perspectives on Politics* 2 (1) (2004): 3–20; Ziad Munson, *The Making of Pro-Life Activists: How Social Movement Mobilization Works* (Chicago: University of Chicago Press, 2009); Hahrie Han, "Want Gun Control? Learn from the N.R.A.," *New York Times*, October 4, 2017; Jen Schradie, *The Revolution That Wasn't* (Cambridge, MA: Harvard University Press, 2019).

11 James Q. Wilson, *The Amateur Democrat: Club Politics in Three Cities* (Chicago: University of Chicago Press, 1962).

12 An extreme version of political hobbyism after the club era, in 1970, was "radical chic" parties put on by wealthy liberal New Yorkers, as described in Tom Wolfe's famous essay "Radical Chic: That Party at Lenny's," *New York*, June 8, 1970.

PART I

1 Quote given to Wilson, *Amateur Democrat*, 173, I have rewritten as poetic stanzas.
2 Political scientists and theorists have, for a long time, debated the motivations that ordinary citizens bring to politics. Sometimes, people engage in politics instrumentally, to try to get something for themselves, such as a social service or a tax break. More often, they say they engage in politics to fulfill a civic duty. We act out of civic duty when we try to advance policies or politicians who fit with our vision of the common good.

On serving the common good, see, e.g., Jean-Jacques Rousseau's *On the Social Contract* (1762) and John Rawls, *A Theory of Justice* (1971). On the relationship between duty and a sense of obligation, see, e.g., Andre Blais and Carol Galais, "Measuring the Civic Duty to Vote: A Proposal," *Electoral Studies* 41 (1) (2016): 60–69. On the idea of civic duty being particularly hard in a large country where the relationship between government action and real-life outcomes is sometimes hard to discern, see Robert N. Bellah et al., *Habits of the Heart: Individualism and Commitment in American Life* (Berkeley: University of California Press, 1985). On the relationship between the common interest and self-interest, see Jane Mansbridge et al., "The Place of Self-Interest and the Role of Power in Deliberative Democracy," *Journal of Political Philosophy* 18 (1) (2010): 64–100. On civic education, see, e.g., Peter Levine and Kei Kawashima-Ginsberg, "The Republic Is (Still) at Risk—and Civics Is Part of the Solution," 2017; and Carl Tjerandsen, *Education for Citizenship: A Foundation's Experience* (Santa Cruz, CA: Emil Schwarzhaupt Foundation, 1980).

For scholarly conceptualizations about motivations in politics, consider, for example, a mid-twentieth-century debate about a "Yankee ethos" and an "ethnic ethos." The Yankee ethos, an older, upper-class, Protestant disposition, envisioned political activity as something one does to make the government function well for all citizens. The Yankee ethos was contrasted with an immigrant, poorer, predominantly Catholic, ethnic ethos. The ethnic ethos saw politics as a way to extract government benefits for one's specific community. Scholars tried to understand, from the perspective of each ethos, what was the point of political activity. This division between a disinterested Yankee worldview versus a more conflictual ethnic worldview was a popular concept at the time. (See Richard Hofstadter, *The Age of Reform* [New York: Vintage Books, 1955]; and James Q. Wilson and Edward C. Banfield, "Public-Regardingness as a Value Premise in Voting Behavior," *American Political Science Review* 58 [4] [1964]: 876–87.)

A second academic conceptualization about motivations, which doesn't initially seem related to the first debate, focused on the rationality of voting. One side in a debate thought of voting as something one does to make a difference. Voting is only logical if your vote could influence an election outcome. Since the chance that any individual will cast the deciding vote in a typical election is close to zero, it is therefore irrational to vote. An opposing side replied that casting a decisive vote is not the motivation for voting at all. If nobody voted, then democracy wouldn't function, and so we vote to show our commitment to democracy, even if our one vote isn't going to be decisive. (Benny Geys, "'Rational' Theories of Voter Turnout: A Review," *Political Studies Review* 4 [1] [2006]: 16–35.)

In this debate about voting, the first school of thought is focused on politics as a means to an end. Other political activities, such as lobbying, are also means to an end. One lobbies to influence the government. The ethnic ethos is like this, too: participation is for a specific purpose—to get something tangible for you or for others in your community. The second side in the voting debate thought of a general duty to participate, a view more at home with the Yankee ethos. This ideal of participation also resonated in those amateur Democratic clubs from the 1950s. The club Democrats saw themselves as defending broad principles of good governance against the party machines of the day, which they perceived as protecting their own narrow interests.

These academic debates captured the imagination of scholars until we realized that the divisions, in practice, aren't so clear-cut. When, for instance, wealthy Yankee activists sought to revive inner cities, purportedly for the benefit of the common interest, and incidentally by tearing down poor neighborhoods and displacing their inhabitants, the motivation wasn't entirely disinterested. They were watching out for their own interests at the expense of other's. As for those "ethnic" organizers trying to protect their neighborhoods, they weren't only protecting their own selfish interests. They had as strong a claim as their opponents that they were the ones championing the common good. (See Raymond E. Wolfinger and John Osgood Field, "Political Ethos and the Structure of City Government," *American Political Science Review* 60 [2] [1966]: 306–26. See also the discussion of universalism and particularism with regard to racial politics in Michael Dawson, *Blacks In and Out of the Left* [Cambridge, MA: Harvard University Press, 2013].)

Chapter 1: Refresh the Feed

1 Opposing political views could be given airtime on a program together, or a program with a liberal slant could be balanced by a different program with a conservative slant. The fairness doctrine was eventually revoked because of concerns by the Federal Communications Commission (FCC) that it hindered free speech. With cable TV supplementing the offerings of broadcast, concerns about any one media company having undue influence in its treatment of controversial political issues were mitigated, according to the FCC. Tom Rosentiel, "Is the Fairness Doctrine Fair Game?," Pew Research Center, July 19, 2007, http://www.pewresearch.org/2007/07/19/is-the-fairness-doctrine-fair-game/.
2 Markus Prior, *Post-Broadcast Democracy: How Media Choice Increases Inequality in Political Involvement and Polarizes Elections* (Cambridge: Cambridge University Press, 2007).
3 Ibid.
4 See Ted Brader, *Campaigning for Hearts and Minds: How Emotional Appeals in Political Ads Work* (Chicago: University of Chicago Press, 2006). Even politically unengaged citizens, who do not watch much news, find their way to content with

a dose of incivility to it. Even if they can't follow every political reference, at least they can find entertainment in the drama. See Diana C. Mutz, *In-Your-Face Politics* (Princeton: Princeton University Press, 2015).

5 Jeffrey M. Berry and Sarah Sobieraj, *The Outrage Industry: Political Opinion Media and the New Incivility* (Oxford: Oxford University Press, 2014).

6 Rachel Maddow, "Courts Not Playing Along with Donald Trump's Slowdown Strategy," MSNBC, May 9, 2019, https://www.youtube.com/watch?v= NtFVr0Ul2IM.

7 Berry and Sobieraj, *Outrage Industry*.

8 See A. J. Jatz, "Here's the Median Age of the Typical Cable News Viewer," *Adweek*, January 19, 2018, https://www.adweek.com/tvnewser/heres-the-medi an-age-of-the-typical-cable-news-viewer/355379/.

9 Marc Hetherington and Jonathan Weiler, *Authoritarianism and Polarization in American Politics* (New York: Cambridge University Press, 2009).

10 Self-reported viewership statistics come from an analysis by Jeffrey Berry, Deborah Schildkraut, and James Glaser in the 2018 Cooperative Congressional Election Study. Statistics about overall increase in MSNBC viewership between 2016 and 2018 come from *Adweek*. See https://www.adweek.com/tvnewser/q1-2016 -ratings-msnbc-regains-its-footing-after-poor-2015/288708/ and https://www .adweek.com/tvnewser/q1-2018-ratings-msnbc-posted-a-record-breaking -quarter/360851/.

11 Mark Zuckerberg, "A Blueprint for Content Governance and Enforcement," Facebook, November 15, 2018. The sociologist Zeynep Tufekci has been reporting that social media algorithms drive us to more extreme content, simply because it's the content that piques our interest. See Zeynep Tufekci, "YouTube, the Great Radicalizer," *New York Times*, March 10, 2018.

12 See Deborah J. Schildkraut, Jeffrey M. Berry, and James M. Glaser, "Charge and Retreat: Asymmetric Patterns of Political Engagement among Liberals and Conservatives," Tufts University working paper, 2019.

13 Andrew Guess, Brendan Nyhan, and Jason Reifler, "Selective Exposure to Misinformation: Evidence from the Consumption of Fake News during the 2016 U.S. Presidential Elections," European Research Council working paper, January 9, 2018.

14 See Daniel J. Hopkins, *The Increasingly United States* (Chicago: University of Chicago Press, 2018).

15 Dan Hopkins, "All Politics Is National Because All Media Is National," Five ThirtyEight, June 6, 2018, https://fivethirtyeight.com/features/all-politics-is -national-because-all-media-is-national/.

16 See Timothy B. Lee, "Print Newspapers Are Dying Faster Than You Think," *Vox*, November 2, 2016; Danny Hayes and Jennifer L. Lawless, "As Local News Goes, So Goes Citizen Engagement: Media Knowledge, and Participation in US House Elections," *Journal of Politics* 77 (2) (2015).

17 In the 2016 Cooperative Congressional Election Study, Common Content, 17 percent of non-college-degree respondents versus 28 percent of college-degree respondents said they got their TV news exclusively from national programs.

18 See "In Changing News Landscape, Even Television Is Vulnerable," Pew Research Center, September 27, 2012. See also items on national versus local

news broadcasts by education level in the 2016 or 2018 Cooperative Congressional Election Studies.

Chapter 2: Staten Island, Staten Island, Take Me In

1 Lisa wrote a blog about the encounter, "Niemoeller at Home," Medium, May 13, 2018, https://medium.com/@wilmar1522/niemoeller-at-home-8e1fa30c3eb9.
2 Lisa Mann, "Flossing," Medium, May 17, 2017, https://medium.com/@wilmar1522/flossing-9149ed53b48f.
3 David Broockman and Joshua Kalla, "Durably Reducing Transphobia: A Field Experiment on Door-to-Door Canvassing," *Science* 352 (6282) (2016): 220–24; Joshua Kalla and David Broockman, "Reducing Exclusionary Attitudes through Interpersonal Conversation: Evidence from Three Field Experiments," working paper, 2019.
4 Joshua Kalla and David Broockman, "The Minimal Persuasive Effects of Campaign Contact in General Elections: Evidence from 49 Field Experiements," *American Political Science Review* 112 (1) (2018): 148–66; Eitan Hersh, *Hacking the Electorate: How Campaigns Perceive Voters* (Cambridge: Cambridge University Press, 2015).
5 Quoted in J. Todd Moye, *Ella Baker: Community Organizer of the Civil Rights Movement* (Lanham, MD: Rowman & Littlefield, 2013).

Chapter 3: Rooting for the Team

1 Klar and Krupnikov, *Independent Politics*.
2 Lilliana Mason, *Uncivil Agreement: How Politics Became Our Identity* (Chicago: University of Chicago Press, 2018).
3 Shanto Iyengar and Sean J. Westwood, "Fear and Loathing across Party Lines: New Evidence on Group Polarization," *American Journal of Political Science* 59, no. 3 (2015): 690–707; Shanto Iyengar, Gaurav Sood, and Yphtach Lelkes, "Affect, Not Ideology: A Social Identity Perspective on Polarization," *Public Opinion Quarterly* 76 (3) (2012).
4 The difference between a Democratic Party led by Lyndon Johnson and a Republican Party led by Barry Goldwater was indeed stark, starker than Obama versus Romney. Goldwater opposed the Civil Rights Act, which Johnson championed. Goldwater, unlike Johnson, wanted to increase the use of nuclear weapons in the fight against communism. When called out as an extremist, Goldwater took the opportunity of his speech accepting the Republican nomination to say, "Extremism in the defense of liberty is no vice." Voters recognized the starkness of the choice in 1964 and gave Johnson a resounding landslide against Goldwater.
5 The most common explanation among political scientists for why people saw fewer differences between the parties in the past is that, back in the 1960s, there were lots of conservative Democrats and liberal Republicans. Partisanship wasn't tied closely to ideology. Many Republicans were pro-choice. On matters of racial equality, the most liberal and conservative voters both identified as Democrats. Maybe people didn't see as stark differences between the parties and candidates because conservative Democrats liked Democrats generally but saw

NOTES

something positive in the conservatism of a Republican such as Barry Goldwater. Likewise, liberal Republicans might have liked other liberal Republicans but also saw value in a Democrat such as Lyndon Johnson. Yet, this explanation isn't the whole story. If we just look at survey responses of liberal Democrats and conservative Republicans in 1964 versus 2012, we still see big differences between the two years. Even these kinds of voters were 20 percent more likely to say they cared which candidate won the presidential election in 2012 than in 1964. The stakes weren't higher in 2012 than in 1964. But feelings about the stakes somehow were higher.

6 See Mason, *Uncivil Agreement*.
7 Brian Schaffner and Samantha Luks, "Misinformation or Expressive Responding? What an Inauguration Crowd Can Tell Us about the Source of Misinformation in Surveys," *Public Opinion Quarterly* 82 (1) (2018): 135–47. On affective polarization see also Samara Klar, Yanna Krupnikov, and John Barry Ryan, "Affective Polarization or Partisan Disdain?," *Public Opinion Quarterly* 82 (2) (2018): 379–90; Mason, *Uncivil Agreement*; Stephen N. Goggin and Alexander G. Theodoridis, "Seeing Red (or Blue): How Party Identity Colors Political Cognition," *Forum* 16 (1) (2018): 81–95; Yphtach Lelkes and Sean J. Westwood, "The Limits of Partisan Prejudice," *Journal of Politics* 79 (2) (2017): 485–501. As James Madison wrote in the Federalist Papers, "The most frivolous and fanciful distinctions have been sufficient to kindle [our] unfriendly passions."
8 John M. Carey et al., "An Inflated View of the Facts? How Preferences and Predispositions Shape Conspiracy Beliefs about the Deflategate Scandal," *Research and Politics* 3 (3) (2016): 1–9.
9 Eitan Hersh, "What the Yankees–Red Sox Rivalry Can Teach Us about Political Polarization," *FiveThirtyEight*, August 11, 2016.
10 Avi Selk and Sarah Murray, "The Owner of the Red Hen Explains Why She Asked Sarah Huckabee Sanders to Leave," *Washington Post*, June 25, 2018, https://beta.washingtonpost.com/news/local/wp/2018/06/23/why-a-small-town-restaurant-owner-asked-sarah-huckabee-sanders-to-leave-and-would-do-it-again/.
11 Zack Beauchamp, "Sarah Sanders and the Failure of 'Civility,'" *Vox*, June 25, 2018, https://www.vox.com/policy-and-politics/2018/6/25/17499036/sarah-sanders-red-hen-restaurant-civility.
12 Paul Musgrave and Mark Rom, "Fair and Balanced? Experimental Evidence on Partisan Bias in Grading," *American Politics Research* 43 (3) (2015): 536–54.
13 Andrew Healy and Neil Malhotra, "Partisan Bias among Interviewers," *Public Opinion Quarterly* 78 (2) (2014): 488–99.
14 For instance, in one study, researchers sent fake job résumés out to employers in two counties, one overwhelmingly Republican and one overwhelmingly Democratic. The résumés signaled that the pretend applicant had worked for a partisan campaign and had been a part of the college Democrats/Republicans. In the Republican county, Democratic résumés were slightly less likely to get a callback. In the Democratic county, Republican résumés were slightly less likely. It's hard to know what this tells us. It is possible that a few employers in an overwhelmingly one-sided county think that talking about one's support of the unpopular party just reflects poor judgment on the part of the applicant. The lack of a call-

229

back from the employer might not signal a desire to punish an out-partisan at all. See Karen Gift and Thomas Gift, "Does Politics Influence Hiring? Evidence from a Randomized Experiment," *Political Behavior* 37 (3) (2015): 653–75.

15 Phillip E. Jones, "Partisanship, Political Awareness, and Retrospective Evaluations, 1956–2016," *Political Behavior*, March 23, 2019.

16 Mason, *Uncivil Agreement*; Pew Research Center, "A Wider Ideological Gap Between More and Less Educated Adults," April 26, 2016, https://www.peo ple-press.org/2016/04/26/a-wider-ideological-gap-between-more-and-less-ed ucated-adults/; John R. Zaller, *The Nature and Origins of Mass Opinion* (Cambridge: Cambridge University Press, 1992).

Chapter 4: Precinct 206

1 Daniel Schlozman and Sam Rosenfeld, *The Hollow Parties*, forthcoming.

2 Political science literature on amateur Democrats focuses on different attributes that distinguished amateurs from regulars. Perhaps the most common was on the tension between liberal purism and electability. See Walter Stone and Alan Abramowitz, "Winning May Not Be Everything but It's More Than We Thought: Presidential Party Activists in 1980," *American Political Science Review* 77 (4) (1983): 945–56.

Chapter 5: Voting, or Not

1 Civic-duty question from Pew Research Center for the People and the Press, telephone interview (landline and cell phone), conducted April 4–15, 2012, accessed via Roper Center iPOLL database. Parent question from General Social Survey, conducted February 6–June 26, 2002, accessed via Roper Center iPOLL Database.

2 Stephen Ansolabehere and Eitan Hersh, "Validation: What Big Data Reveal about Survey Misreporting and the Real Electorate," *Political Analysis* 20 (4) (2012): 437–59.

3 "Who Votes for Mayor," Portland State University, March 7, 2019, http://www .whovotesformayor.org/.

4 "Results and Analysis: Where the Democrats Lost Ground," *New York Times*, January 19, 2010, https://archive.nytimes.com/www.nytimes.com/interactive /2010/01/19/us/politics/massachusetts-election-map.html.

5 The Clinton campaign may not have generated as much volunteer enthusiasm as the Obama campaign for other reasons as well, such as a failure on the part of the Clinton campaign to create as robust of a grassroots organization. However, this is a bit of a chicken-and-egg problem: the outpouring of volunteer support for Obama made his campaign's investment in organizing possible.

6 See Jeff Stein, "Clinton's Real Millennial Problem: Young Americans Are Less Loyal to Democrat," *Vox*, September 21, 2016; Jeff Stein, "Hillary Clinton Is Matching Barack Obama with Young Voters," *Vox*, October 25, 2016.

7 Nelson W. Polsby, *Consequences of Party Reform* (Oxford: Oxford University Press, 1983), 169–70.

8 Ibid.

Chapter 6: Voice of Westmoreland

1 Angela Aldous speech, Wisconsin rally, February 26, 2011, https://www.youtube
.com/watch?v=RcBL9atDsR0.

2 See Erica Chenoweth and Marie Berry, "Who Made the Women's March?," in
Meyer and Tarrow, *Resistance*.

3 Alex Gangitano, "Rep. Tim Murphy Admits to Affair with 'Personal Friend,'"
Roll Call, September 6, 2017, https://www.rollcall.com/news/hoh/tim-mur
phy-admits-affair.

Chapter 7: Like, Share, Click

1 Chris Cillizza, "Obama Announces 'Organizing for America,'" January 17, 2009,
http://voices.washingtonpost.com/thefix/white-house/obama-announces-or
ganizing-for.html.

2 Carl Hulse, "'Repeal and Replace': Words Still Hanging over GOP's Health
Care Strategy," *New York Times*, January 15, 2017.

3 See Ari Melber, "Year One of Organizing for America: The Permanent Field
Campaign in a Digital Age," techPresident Special Report, 2010; Sidney
M. Milkis, Jesse H. Rhodes, and Emily J. Charnock, "What Happened to
Post-Partisanship? Barack Obama and the New American Party System," *Per
spectives on Politics* 10 (1) (2012): 57–76.

4 US Census Bureau, Reported Voting and Registration, by sex and single year
of age, November 2008 and November 2010, https://www.census.gov/topics
/public-sector/voting/data/tables.html.

5 See Micah L. Sifry, "Obama's Lost Army," *New Republic*, February 9, 2017.

6 Eitan Hersh and Brian Schaffner, "Postmaterialist Particularism: What Peti
tions Can Tell Us about Biases in the Policy Agenda," *American Politics Research*
46 (3) (2018): 434–64.

7 Jeffrey M. Berry, *The New Liberalism: The Rising Power of Citizen Groups* (Wash
ington, DC: Brookings Institution Press, 1999); Skocpol, *Diminished Democracy*.

Chapter 8: The Russians of Brighton

1 Michael Pahre, "Boston Phoenix and Election Rumor Mill on Wallingford
Road," *Brighton Centered*, September 13, 2007, http://brighton-community
.blogspot.com/2007/09/boston-phoenix-and-election-rumor-mill.html.

2 Yvonne Abraham, "Ward Boss or 'Simple Man,' He Gets Out the Vote," *Boston
Globe*, March 1, 2005, https://rjcf.com/Ball/2009/ballinfo/Naakh.pdf.

3 See Pahre, "Boston Phoenix."

4 See Representative Michael Capuano, "Remarks Honoring Naakh Vysoky,"
Congressional Record 161 (185) (December 18, 2015), https://www.congress.gov
/114/crec/2015/12/18/CREC-2015-12-18-pt1-PgE1837-4.pdf.

5 Sara Rimer, "A Crucial Test for Immigrants to Retain Aid," *New York Times*,
December 23, 1996.

6 Robert Pear, "Administration Welfare Plea Is Scorned," *New York Times*, Feb-

ruary 14, 1997, https://www.nytimes.com/1997/02/14/us/administration-wel
fare-plea-is-scorned.html.

7 See Rimer, "Crucial Test."

8 Robert Pear, "Governors Split over Need for Changes to New Welfare Law,"
New York Times, February 2, 1997, https://www.nytimes.com/1997/02/02/us
/governors-split-over-need-for-changes-to-new-welfare-law.html.

9 Robert Pear, "Governors Limit Revisions Sought in Welfare Law," *New York
Times*, February 3, 1997, https://www.nytimes.com/1997/02/03/gover
nors-limit-revisions-sought-in-welfare-law.html.

10 Robert Pear, "Legal Immigrants to Get Letters on Welfare Cut," *New York
Times*, February 6, 1997, https://www.nytimes.com/1997/02/06/us/legal-immi
grants-to-get-letters-on-welfare-cut.html.

11 Michael Pahre, "Brighton's Russian Jewish Elderly Vote: Menino, Ciommo,
Connolly, Murphy, Arroyo," *Brighton Centered*, September 22, 2009, https://
brighton-community.blogspot.com/2009/09/brightons-russian-jewish-elderly
-vote.html.

Chapter 9: Selfish Donor, Selfie Donor

1 Spencer MacColl, "Democrats and Republicans Sharing Big-Dollar Donors,
DCCC's Million-Dollar Pay-Off and More in Capital Eye Opener: November 10," Open Secrets, November 10, 2010, https://www.opensecrets.org/news
/2010/11/democrats-and-republicans-sharing-b/.

2 Michael J. Barber, Brandice Canes-Wrone, and Sharece Thrower, "Ideologically Sophisticated Donors: Which Candidates Do Individual Contributors
Finance?," *American Journal of Political Science* 61 (2) (2017): 271–88.

3 Seth Hill and Greg Huber, "Representativeness and Motivations of the Contemporary Donorate: Results from Merged Survey and Administrative Records,"
Political Behavior 39 (1) (2017): 3–29.

4 Fredreka Schouten et al., "Joe Biden Dominates, but Pete Buttigieg Makes
Inroads with Obama's Elite Bundlers," CNN, July 20, 2019.

5 Matea Gold, "The GOP Debates Have Become Like Super Bowl Parties for
Top Donors," *Washington Post*, January 19, 2016.

6 Stephen Ansolabehere, John M. de Figueiredo, and James Snyder, "Why Is
There So Little Money in Politics?," *Journal of Economic Perspectives* 17 (1)
(2003): 105–30.

7 Brian Schaffner and I thank Greg Huber for the idea of this survey experiment.
    A party booster would not want to pay a fee to a company for a dinner, but
perhaps a self-interested donor would do so. Maybe the dinner would present a
chance to talk policy even if it was not a vehicle for financial support. But there
is little evidence for this hypothesis. For example, the responses to the two questions are nearly identical (48 percent for party boosting, 35 percent for the event
fee) among retirees (N = 189) who do not have an obvious business interest in an
intimate dinner. This lends more credibility to the idea that the motivation for
paying an event company for dinner with a politician is hobbyism.

8 See "Howard Schultz on Why He Wouldn't Run as a Democrat for President,"

The View, January 29, 2019, https://www.youtube.com/watch?v=RlyQr8h5ZDk.

9 Benjamin-Emile Le Hay, "Friends with Benefits: RSVP Yes to These Upcoming Charity Galas," *New York Observer*, October 31, 2014, https://observer.com/2014/10/friends-with-benefits-rsvp-yes-to-these-upcoming-charity-galas/.

10 On funding the Tea Party movement, see Theda Skocpol and Vanessa Williamson, *The Tea Party and the Making of Republican Conservatism* (Oxford: Oxford University Press, 2012). See also Theda Skocpol and Alexander Hertel-Fernandez, "The Koch Network and Republican Party Extremism," *Perspectives on Politics* 14 (3) (2016): 681–99.

11 Philip Bump, "Bernie Sanders Keeps Saying His Average Donation Is $27, but His Numbers Contradict That," *Washington Post*, April 18, 2016, https://www.washingtonpost.com/news/the-fix/wp/2016/04/18/bernie-sanders-keeps-saying-his-average-donation-is-27-but-it-really-isnt/?utm_term=.af916e2437f9.

12 Sophie Kaplan, "Trump Raised More Dollars from Small Donations," PolitiFact, November 13, 2017, http://www.politifact.com/truth-o-meter/statements/2017/nov/13/kayleigh-mcenany/trump-raised-more-dollars-small-donations/; Matea Gold, "Trump Supporters Eager to 'Drain the Swamp' Help Fill Republican Party Coffers," *Washington Post*, October 6, 2017, https://www.washingtonpost.com/politics/trump-supporters-eager-to-drain-the-swamp-help-fill-gop-coffers/2017/10/05/ec214f22-a53d-11e7-ade1-76d061d56efa_story.html?utm_term=.b56c7aa1b21a.

13 The strongest example of this is a 2015 law in Seattle. Every resident in the city is given a "democracy" voucher that enables them to allocate public dollars to the candidate of their choice. Over twenty thousand Seattle residents returned their vouchers to support candidates. Jennifer Heerwig and Brian J. McCabe, "Expanding Participation in Municipal Elections: Assessing the Impact of Seattle's Democracy Voucher Program" (Georgetown University, Washington, DC: Center for Studies in Demography and Ecology, 2018), https://www.jenheerwig.com/uploads/1/3/2/1/13210230/mccabe_heerwig_seattle_voucher_4.03.pdf.

14 Adam Bonica and Jenny Shen, "How Wealthy Campaign Donors May Reduce Political Polarization and Weaken the Tea Party," *Washington Post*, April 24, 2014, https://www.washingtonpost.com/news/monkey-cage/wp/2014/04/24/how-wealthy-campaign-donors-may-reduce-political-polarization-and-weaken-the-tea-party/?utm_term=.956ec0362404. See also Andrew Hall, "How the Public Funding of Elections Increases Candidate Polarization," working paper, Harvard University, 2014.

15 Tyler P. Culberson, Michael P. M. McDonald, and Suzanne M. Robbins, "Small Donors in Congressional Elections," *American Politics Research*, March 23, 2018.

16 Ari Melber, "Year One of Organizing for America," techPresident Special Report, January 2010.

17 Adam Bonica, "Leadership, Free to Lead," *Boston Review*, July 22, 2011, http://bostonreview.net/bonica-small-donors-polarization.

18 Skocpol, *Diminished Democracy*.

NOTES

PART II

1 Lewis Mumford, *Technics and Civilization* (New York: Harcourt, 1934), 315–16.

Chapter 10: Political Leisure

1 Aristotle, *Politics*, Book VII, 1329b.
2 Lawrence B. Glickman, "Consumer Activism, Consumer Regimes, and the Consumer Movement: Rethinking the History of Consumer Politics in the United States," in *The Oxford Handbook of the History of Consumption*, ed. Frank Trentmann (Oxford: Oxford University Press, 2012).
3 Robert Putnam, *Bowling Alone: The Collapse and Revival of American Community* (New York: Simon & Schuster, 2000).
4 *Oxford Dictionaries Online*, s.v. "Hobby," https://en.oxforddictionaries.com/definition/hobby.
5 Arthur Newton Pack, *Challenge of Leisure* (New York: Macmillan, 1934); Steven Gelber, "Working at Playing: The Culture of the Workplace and the Rise of Baseball," *Journal of Social History* 16 (4) (1983): 3–22; Steven Gelber, *Hobbies* (New York: Columbia University Press, 1999).
6 Austin Fox Riggs, *Play: Recreation in a Balanced Life* (Garden City, NY: Doubleday, Doran, 1935).
7 E.g., "What Will NYT Live Poll GOP Edge Be for TX Senate?," PredictIt, October 12, 2018, https://www.predictit.org/markets/detail/4933/What-will-NYT-Live-Poll-GOP-edge-be-for-TX-Senate.
8 Matthew Yglesias, "Scott Pruitt's Ritz-Carlton Moisturizing Lotion Scandal, Explained," *Vox*, June 7, 2018.
9 Another odd example of political hobbyism as a craft is the computer game *Civilization*. Gamers choose governmental rules, build infrastructure, and wage war. They debate the relative merits of employing fundamentalist, communist, or democratic forms of government for earning points and winning the game.
10 James Q. Wilson, *Political Organizations* (Princeton: Princeton University Press, 1974), 42.
11 Politics can also be a collecting hobby, but it isn't common: ephemera such as campaign pins, signs, photos of politicians, and other memorabilia are collected.
12 Isabelle de Solier, *Food and the Self: Consumption, Production, and Material Culture* (London: Bloomsbury Academic, 2013); Alan Warde, "The Sociology of Consumption," *Annual Review of Sociology* 41 (2015): 117–34.
13 Euny Hong, "Why Some Koreans Make $10,000 a Month to Eat on Camera," January 16, 2016, https://qz.com/592710/why-some-koreans-make-10000-a-month-to-eat-on-camera/.

Chapter 11: Whose Hobby?

1 On leisure time by income, see Table 11a, "Time Spent in Leisure and Sports Activities for Civilian Population by Selected Characteristics, Averages per Day, 2018 Annual Averages," US Bureau of Labor Statistics, https://www.bls.gov

/news.release/atus.t11a.htm. See also Andrea Louise Campbell, "Self-Interest, Social Security, and the Distinctive Participation Patterns of Senior Citizens," *American Political Science Review* 96 (3) (2002).

2 Markus Prior, *Hooked: How Politics Captures People's Interest* (Cambridge: Cambridge University Press, 2019).

3 Ibid.; Markus Prior and Lori D. Bougher, "'Like They've Never, Ever Seen in this Country?' Political Interest and Voter Engagement in 2016," *Public Opinion Quarterly* 82 (1) (2018): 822–42.

4 Analysis of November 2014 supplement of the Current Population Survey, US Census Bureau.

5 Prior, *Hooked*.

6 People in lower-status fields are more likely to choose hobbies that *compensate* for the fact that they might not be in a line of work they particularly enjoy. Unlike higher-status workers, who choose hobbies in which they replicate the skills they use at work but in a low-stakes setting, lower-status workers choose hobbies where they engage skills they do not have the opportunity to engage at work. See Donald E. Super, *Avocational Interest Patterns* (Palo Alto, CA: Stanford University Press, 1940).

7 Mihaly Csikszentmihalyi, *Beyond Boredom and Anxiety* (San Francisco: Jossey-Bass, 2000).

8 Robert Luskin, "Explaining Political Sophistication," *Political Behavior* 12 (4) (1990): 331–61.

9 Alan Gerber et al., "Why People Vote: Estimating the Social Returns to Voting," *British Journal of Political Science* 46 (2) (2016): 241–64; Meredith Rolfe, *Voter Turnout: A Social Theory of Political Participation* (Cambridge: Cambridge University Press, 2013); Torben Iversen and David Soskice, "Information, Social Networks and Interest-Based Voting: Consequences for Distributive Politics," working paper, Harvard University, 2012; Samuel Abrams, Torben Iversen, and David Soskice, "Informal Social Networks and Rational Voting," *British Journal of Political Science* 41 (2) (2011): 229–57; Matthew D. Atkinson and Anthony Fowler, "Social Capital and Voter Turnout: Evidence from Saint's Day Fiestas in Mexico," *British Journal of Political Science* 44 (1) (2014): 41–59; Alan S. Gerber, Donald P. Green, and Christopher W. Larimer, "Social Pressure and Voter Turnout: Evidence from a Large-Scale Field Experiment," *American Political Science Review* 102 (1) (2008): 33–48.

10 Margaret Sheridan, "Wearing Your Opinion on Your Sleeve," *Michigan Daily*, October 24, 2018, https://www.michigandaily.com/section/arts/wearing-your-opinion-your-sleeve.

Is a person who doesn't take any intrinsic interest in an activity but does the activity to convey an image a hobbyist? Probably not. If the activity lacks intrinsic joy, it wouldn't meet our working definition.

11 Amanda Julius, "Brooklynites Crazy for Ukuleles," Huffington Post, April 26, 2010, https://www.huffingtonpost.com/2010/02/24/ukulele-craze-brooklyn_n_474977.html.

12 See John Sides and Lynn Vavreck, *The Gamble: Choice and Chance in the 2012 Presidential Election* (Princeton: Princeton University Press, 2014).

13 See "2016 Republican Presidential Nomination," RealClearPolitics, https://

www.realclearpolitics.com/epolls/2016/president/us/2016_republican_presi
dential_nomination-3823.html.

14 Gelber, *Hobbies*.

15 Sidney Verba, Nancy Burns, and Kay Lehman Schlozman, "Knowing and Caring about Politics: Gender and Political Engagement," *Journal of Politics* 59 (4)
(1997): 1051–72. Some of the differences on surveys between men and women
in how they answer questions about political knowledge are attributable to a
tendency for men to guess at unknown answers versus a tendency of women
to acknowledge they don't know. This difference does not explain the whole of
the gap in political knowledge. See Jeffrey Mondak and Mary Anderson, "The
Knowledge Gap: A Reexamination of Gender-Based Differences in Political
Knowledge," *Journal of Politics* 66 (2) (2004): 492–512.

16 Stephen Ansolabehere and Eitan Hersh, "Gender, Race, Age and Voting: A
Research Note," *Politics and Governance* 1 (2) (2013).

17 Lara Putnam and Theda Skocpol, "Middle America Reboots Democracy,"
Democracy Journal, February 20, 2018, https://democracyjournal.org/arguments
/middle-america-reboots-democracy/; Dana R. Fisher, *American Resistance* (New
York: Columbia University Press, forthcoming).

18 Gelber, *Hobbies*.

19 Katherine Cramer, *The Politics of Resentment: Rural Consciousness in Wisconsin and
the Rise of Scott Walker* (Chicago: University of Chicago Press, 2016).

20 In a famous sociological work about the nature of culture and taste, Pierre
Bourdieu explained, "A work of art has meaning and interest only for someone who possesses the cultural competence, that is, the code, into which it is
encoded. . . . A beholder who lacks the specific code feels lost in a chaos of
sounds and rhythms, colors and lines, without rhyme or reason." See Pierre
Bourdieu, *Distinction: A Social Critique of the Judgment of Taste* (Cambridge, MA:
Harvard University Press, 1984). See also Nicholas Carnes, *White-Collar Government: The Hidden Role of Class in Economic Policy Making* (Chicago: University
of Chicago Press, 2013); Sam Friedman and Daniel Laurison, *The Class Ceiling:
Why It Pays to Be Privileged* (Bristol, England: Policy Press, 2019).

21 See Yochai Benkler, *The Wealth of Networks* (New Haven, CT: Yale University
Press, 2006).

22 Lara Putnam introduced this idea to me, describing it as the "Baumol's cost disease theory of political hobbyism."

23 Henry E. Brady, Sidney Verba, and Kay Lehman Schlozman, "Beyond SES: A
Resource Model of Political Participation (Socioeconomic Status as Explanation
for Political Activity)," *American Political Science Review* 89 (2) (1995): 271–94;
Andrea Louise Campbell, *How Policies Make Citizens* (Princeton: Princeton University Press, 2003).

24 A societal shock to leisure time, such as an economic depression or a technological disruption that puts people out of work, can focus a government's attention on how citizens use leisure time. During the New Deal, for example, the
Civilian Conservation Corps, which employed several million young men to
improve parks and roads, not only supplied food and shelter for the workers but
also inculcated leisure interests and skills, hiring instructors to teach about art,
music, drama, reading, sports, and the outdoors. The Work Projects Administra-

tion, another New Deal program, spent nearly a third of its massive budget on recreation infrastructure. Thousands of swimming pools, playgrounds, skating rinks, and fairgrounds were built by the WPA that still impact how we spend leisure time today. See Susan Currell, *The March of Spare Time: The Problem and Promise of Leisure in the Great Depression* (Philadelphia: University of Pennsylvania Press, 2005), 52. At least in the twentieth century, government and civic leaders took the view that leisure has higher and lower forms. Leisure can be focused on passively soaking up information (movies, radio, online) or alternatively on cultivating interpersonal connections and skills. Behind the Depression-era investment in leisure was an elite judgment that citizens needed to be encouraged to participate in active rather than passive forms of leisure. See also Riggs, *Play*. A British sociologist commented on British governmental advocacy about leisure time, "If people were susceptible to leisure education and state-promoted opportunities, we would now be a nation of church-goers and Shakespeare readers." Ken Roberts, quoted in David George Surdam, *Century of Leisured Masses* (Oxford: Oxford University Press, 2015), 217.

25 Gelber, *Hobbies*.
26 See Gary King, Jennifer Pan, and Margaret Roberts, "How Censorship in China Allows Government Criticism but Silences Collective Expression," *American Political Science Review* 107 (2) (2013): 326–43.
27 See Steven Riess, *City Games: The Evolution of American Urban Society and the Rise of Sports* (Urbana: University of Illinois Press, 1991).
28 Ibid.
29 Surdam, *Century of Leisured Masses*.
30 See Currell, *March of Spare Time*; John Clarke, "Pessimism versus Populism: The Problematic Politics of Popular Culture," in *For Fun and Profit*, ed. Richard Butsch (Philadelphia: Temple University Press, 1990).
31 See also Lewis Mumford, *Technics and Civilization* (New York: Harcourt, 1934).

Chapter 12: Politically Spiritual, but Not Religious

1 For a theoretical approach to "deep" politics, consider Harry C. Boyte and Nancy Kari, *Building America: The Democratic Promise of Public Work* (Philadelphia: Temple University Press, 1996).
2 "For a large swath of human history," writes professor and pastor Elizabeth Drescher, "religion *was* entertainment." It was the reason for a local festival and a source of art and music. Elizabeth Drescher, *Choosing Our Religion: The Spiritual Lives of America's Nones* (Oxford: Oxford University Press, 2016), 98. Not so different is the historical analysis of American political parties, which for decades in the 1800s were a source of local debates, speeches, and spectacles, including boozy Election Day parties. See Elizabeth M. Addonizio, Donald P. Green, and James M. Glaser, "Putting the Party Back into Politics: An Experiment Testing Whether Election Day Festivals Increase Voter Turnout," in *PS: Political Science and Politics* 40 (4) (2007): 721–27; Michael Schudson, *The Good Citizen: A History of American Civic Life* (New York: Free Press, 1998). In a small town, before mass media, religion and politics served not just as forms of culture and entertainment, but as primary forms.

3 Robert Putnam and David Campbell, *American Grace: How Religion Divides and Unites Us* (New York: Simon & Schuster, 2010); Michael Lipka and Claire Gecewicz, "More Americans Now Say They're Spiritual but Not Religious," Pew Research Center, September 6, 2017, https://www.pewresearch.org/fact-tank/2017/09/06/more-americans-now-say-theyre-spiritual-but-not-religious/; Tara Isabella Burton, "'Spiritual but Not Religious': Inside America's Rapidly Growing Faith Group," *Vox*, November 10, 2017, https://www.vox.com/identities/2017/11/10/16630178/study-spiritual-but-not-religious; Christian Smith and Melinda Lundquist Denton, *Soul Searching: The Religious and Spiritual Lives of American Teenagers* (New York: Oxford University Press, 2005).

4 Tara Isabella Burton, "Why 'Secular Lent' Misses the Point," *Vox*, February 14, 2018, https://www.vox.com/2018/2/14/17007284/why-secular-lent-misses-the-point-christian-ash-wednesday.

5 See http://www.rebooters.net/programs.

6 Jonathan Merritt, "Why Christians Need a Church: An Interview with Lillian Daniel," Religion News Service, August 13, 2013, https://religionnews.com/2013/08/13/answering-the-spiritual-but-religious-an-interview-with-lillian-daniel/.

7 Herbert J. Gans, "Symbolic Ethnicity," *Ethnic and Racial Studies* 2 (1) (1979): 1–20.

8 Another writer, Kendra Dean, sets her target on youth mission trips geared toward young people: "These trips' primary beneficiaries are the middle-class teenagers who can afford to take them. Mission is not a trip or a youth activity, a silent cousin to evangelism, or an optional model of youth ministry. Mission is the business that congregations are in." See Kendra Dean, *Almost Christian: What the Faith of Our Teenagers Is Telling the American Church* (Oxford: Oxford University Press, 2010). See also Jonathan Merritt, "Why Christians Need a Church: An Interview with Lillian Daniel," Religion News Service, August 13, 2013, https://religionnews.com/2013/08/13/answering-the-spiritual-but-religious-an-interview-with-lillian-daniel/.

9 Gal Beckerman, "American Jews Face a Choice: Create Meaning or Fade Away," *New York Times*, November 12, 2018, https://www.nytimes.com/2018/11/12/books/review/steven-weisman-chosen-wars.html.

10 Merritt, "Why Christians Need a Church."

11 What one ought not do is what Beckerman describes as "sucking out whatever spiritual or personal sustenance the tradition has to offer and spitting out the pits." The pits are the obligations and the entwinements with other people that raise a person above their own short-term desires. Ibid.

12 See Drescher, *Choosing Our Religion*, for a discussion of the "community" sought out by the religiously unaffiliated.

13 Dennis F. Thompson, "Representing Future Generations: Political Presentism and Democratic Trusteeship," *Critical Review of International Social and Political Philosophy* 13 (1) (2010): 17–37.

NOTES

PART III

1 Charles Duhigg, "The Real Roots of American Rage," *Atlantic*, January/February 2019, https://www.theatlantic.com/magazine/archive/2019/01/charles-duhigg-american-anger/576424/.

Chapter 13: Hobbyist Provocateur

1 "Man needs an antagonist, both for work and for play," writes Arthur Pack in *Challenge of Leisure*.

2 Zuckerberg, "Blueprint for Content Governance."

3 Issie Lapowsky, "Senators Grill Whistleblower on Cambridge Analytica's Inner Workings," *Wired*, May 16, 2018, https://www.wired.com/story/christopher-wylie-cambridge-analytica-senate-testimony/.

4 Issie Lapowsky, "Facebook Moves to Limit Toxic Content as Scandal Swirls," *Wired*, November 15, 2018, https://www.wired.com/story/facebook-limits-hate-speech-toxic-content/.

5 David Freedlander, "How Those Crazy Democratic Fundraising Emails Work," Daily Beast, October 6, 2014, https://www.thedailybeast.com/how-those-crazy-democratic-fundraising-emails-work. See also Michelle Ye Hee Lee and Anu Narayanswamy, "How a Little-Known Democratic Firm Cashed In on the Wave of Midterm Money," *Washington Post*, January 8, 2019.

6 Sarah Jones, "But Their Emails," *New Republic*, June 29, 2017, https://newrepublic.com/article/143615/democrats-emails-strategy-haywire.

7 Simone Pathe, "Unlocking the Truth about 'Matching' Fundraising Emails," *Roll Call*, October 2, 2017.

8 Steve Peoples, "Thousands Protest in Front of Sen. Schumer's Brooklyn Home: 'Chuck's a Chicken,'" NBC New York, February 1, 2017, https://www.nbcnewyork.com/news/local/Sen-Schumer-Battered-by-Both-the-Right-and-Left-in-New-Role--412494133.html.

9 Marc Torrence, "Chuck Schumer Protest at His Park Slope Home: As It Happened," Patch, January 31, 2017, https://patch.com/new-york/parkslope/chuck-schumer-rally-his-park-slope-home-live-updates.

10 Steven Levitsky and Daniel Ziblatt, *How Democracies Die* (New York: Crown, 2018).

11 Colby Itkowitz, "Sen. Klobuchar: Democrats Shouldn't Have Gone 'Nuclear' on Judicial Nominees," *Washington Post*, September 2, 2018, https://www.washingtonpost.com/politics/2018/09/02/sen-klobuchar-democrats-shouldnt-have-gone-nuclear-judicial-nominees/?utm_term=.19187f74e210.

12 Carl Hulse, "Should Democrats Have Saved Their Filibuster for the New Court Fight?," *New York Times*, July 14, 2018, https://www.nytimes.com/2018/07/14/us/politics/supreme-court-filibuster.html.

13 Dahlia Lithwick, "Airless. Insular. Clubby. Smug," Slate, March 29, 2017, https://slate.com/news-and-politics/2017/03/the-grossness-of-neil-gorsuchs-hearings-made-the-democrats-filibuster-possible.html.

239

14 Daniel Hemel and David Herzig, "The Progressive Case against Filibustering Neil Gorsuch," *Vox*, April 4, 2017, https://www.vox.com/the-big-idea/2017/4/4/15168316/filibuster-gorsuch-senate-nuclear-mistake.

15 Oliver Roeder and Amelia Thomson-DeVeaux, "How Brett Kavanaugh Would Change the Supreme Court," FiveThirtyEight, July 9, 2018, https://fivethirtyeight.com/features/how-brett-kavanaugh-would-change-the-supreme-court/.

16 Allahpundit, "Kavanaugh Would Be Done Already If the Dems Hadn't Filibustered Gorsuch, Right?," *Hot Air*, September 27, 2018, https://hotair.com/archives/2018/09/27/kavanaugh-done-already-dems-hadnt-filibustered-gorsuch-right/; Fred Bauer, "How Democrats Overreached on Kavanaugh," *National Review*, October 8, 2018, https://www.nationalreview.com/corner/democrats-overreached-on-brett-kavanaugh/.

17 Chants from protest sheets passed out in Brooklyn. See Torrence, "Chuck Schumer Protest."

Chapter 14: Outrage and Compromise

1 Nolan McCarty, *Polarization: What Everyone Needs to Know* (Oxford: Oxford University Press, 2019).

2 Morris P. Fiorina, *Unstable Majorities: Polarization, Party Sorting, and Political Stalemate* (Palo Alto, CA: Hoover Institution Press, 2017); McCarty, *Polarization*.

3 Matthew Levendusky, *The Partisan Sort: How Liberals Became Democrats and Conservatives Became Republicans* (Chicago: University of Chicago Press, 2009).

4 See, for example, CNN exit polls, 2004 versus 2016, http://www.cnn.com/ELECTION/2004/pages/results/states/US/P/00/epolls.0.html and https://www.cnn.com/election/2016/results/exit-polls.

5 Douglas J. Ahler and David E. Broockman, "The Delegate Paradox: Why Polarized Politicians Can Represent Citizens Best," *Journal of Politics* 80 (4) (2018): 1117–33.

6 Fiorina, *Unstable Majorities*, 88.

7 McCarty, *Polarization*.

8 Eric McGhee, Seth Masket, Boris Shor, Steven Rogers, and Nolan McCarty, "A Primary Cause of Partisanship? Nomination Systems and Legislator Ideology," *American Journal of Political Science* 58 (2) (2014): 337–51.

9 See Andrew B. Hall, *Who Wants to Run? How the Devaluing of Political Office Drives Polarization* (Chicago: University of Chicago Press, 2019).

10 McCarty, *Polarization*; Michael J. Barber, "Ideological Donors, Contribution Limits, and the Polarization of American Legislatures," *Journal of Politics* 78 (1) (2016): 296–310.

11 Hopkins, "All Politics Is National."

12 Analysis of 2016 CCES data shows self-reported out-of-state donors, particularly on the left, are more extreme than in-state donors.

13 Raymond La Raja and Brian Schaffner, *Campaign Finance and Political Polarization: When Purists Prevail* (Ann Arbor: University of Michigan Press, 2015).

14 McCarty, *Polarization*, 67.

15 Julian E. Zelizer, *On Capitol Hill: The Struggle to Reform Congress and Its Consequences, 1948–2000* (Cambridge: Cambridge University Press, 2004).

NOTES

16 Sean M. Theriault, *The Gingrich Senators: The Roots of Partisan Warfare in Congress* (Oxford: Oxford University Press, 2013).

17 Michael Barber and Nolan McCarty, "Causes and Consequences of Polarization," in *Negotiating Agreement in Politics*, ed. Jane Mansbridge and Cathie Jo Martin (Washington, DC: American Political Science Association, 2013).

18 John Hibbing and Elizabeth Theiss-Morse, *Congress as Public Enemy: Public Attitudes toward American Political Institutions* (Cambridge: Cambridge University Press, 1995).

19 Fiorina, *Unstable Majorities*.

20 Frances E. Lee, *Beyond Ideology: Politics, Principles, and Partisanship in the U.S. Senate* (Chicago: University of Chicago Press, 2009); Frances E. Lee, "Two-Party Competition and Senate Politics: The Permanent Campaign on the Floor of the U.S. Senate," working paper; Tim Groseclose and Nolan McCarty, "The Politics of Blame: Bargaining before an Audience," *American Journal of Political Science* 45 (1) (2001): 100–119.

21 McCarty, *Polarization*.

22 Timothy J. Ryan, "Reconsidering Moral Issues in Politics," *Journal of Politics* 76 (2) (2014): 380–97; Timothy J. Ryan, "No Compromise: Political Consequences of Moralized Attitudes," *American Journal of Political Science* 61 (2) (2017): 409–23; Timothy J. Ryan, "Actions versus Consequences in Political Arguments," *Journal of Politics* 81 (2) (2019): 426–40.

23 Charles Duhigg, "The Real Roots of American Anger," *Atlantic*, January/February 2019, https://www.theatlantic.com/magazine/archive/2019/01/charles-duhigg-american-anger/576424/.

24 Marshall Ganz, "Public Narrative, Collective Action, and Power," in *Accountability Through Public Opinion: From Inertia to Public Action*, ed. Sina Odugbemi and Taeku Lee (Washington, DC: World Bank, 2011).

Chapter 15: Bringing Out the Worst in Us

1 My brother-in-law thinks he borrowed this line from a comedian he heard, but isn't sure who it was, and I tried but couldn't track down the source.

2 Political scientists have hypothesized that when citizens get a chance to deliberate respectfully with one another, they become more tolerant, more understanding of where their opponents are coming from, and engage less in zero-sum thinking. Michael Carpini, Fay Cook, and Lawrence Jacobs, "Public Deliberation, Discursive Participation, and Citizen Engagement: A Review of the Empirical Literature," *Annual Review of Political Science* 7 (1) (2004): 315–44. See also Peter Levine, *We Are the Ones We Have Been Waiting For: The Promise of Civic Renewal in America* (Oxford: Oxford University Press, 2013).

3 Dave and his volunteers are doing what the sociologist Arlie Hochschild did when she got to know a community of Trump supporters in rural Louisiana: try to tear down the "empathy walls" that prevent people such as her (a professor living in Berkeley, California) from understanding the position of voters whose experiences are so different (lower-class churchgoers living on the edge of a polluted bayou). Arlie Russell Hochschild, *Strangers in Their Own Land: Anger and Mourning on the American Right* (New York: Free Press, 2016).

4 Dana Fisher, *Activism, Inc.: How the Outsourcing of Grassroots Campaigns Is Strangling Progressive Politics in America* (Stanford, CA: Stanford University Press, 2006).

5 Paul Speer and Hahrie Han, "Re-engaging Social Relationships and Collective Dimensions of Organizing to Revive Democratic Practice," *Journal of Social and Political Psychology* 6 (2) (2018): 745–58; Hahrie Han, *How Organizations Develop Activists: Civic Associations and Leadership in the 21st Century* (Oxford: Oxford University Press, 2014); Adam D. Sheingate, *Building a Business of Politics: The Rise of Political Consulting and the Transformation of American Democracy* (Oxford: Oxford University Press, 2016); Jane F. McAlevey, *No Shortcuts: Organizing for Power* (Oxford: Oxford University Press, 2016); Skocpol, *Diminished Democracy*; Marshall Ganz, "How to Organize to Win," *Nation*, March 16, 2018, https:// www.thenation.com/article/how-to-organize-to-win/; Marshall Ganz, *Why David Sometimes Wins* (Oxford: Oxford University Press, 2009).

Chapter 16: Gateway Slacktivism

1 See "Average Hours per Day Spent in Selected Leisure and Sports Activities by Age," 2018 American Time Use Survey, Bureau of Labor Statistics, https://www .bls.gov/charts/american-time-use/activity-leisure.htm.

2 Ibid.

3 Sidney Verba, Kay L. Schlozman, and Henry Brady, *Voice and Equality: Civic Volunteerism in American Politics* (Cambridge, MA: Harvard University Press, 1995); Steven J. Rosenstone and John Mark Hansen, *Mobilization, Participation, and Democracy in America* (New York: Macmillan, 1993).

4 Showing similar trends, in *Bowling Alone*, Robert Putnam measured that between the mid-1970s and mid-1990s, there was a 40 percent drop in attendance at local public meetings and a 50 percent drop in the number of people taking on leadership roles in civic organizations. As Putnam showed, locally based civic and political activity was replaced by TV (and after TV by the Internet).

The way we interpret volunteer involvement now is also different from in the past, and it renders comparisons with fifty years ago *even more* unfavorable to the present. Already in the 1960s, change was perceptible away from local, federated membership organizations (think Freemasons) that dominated civic life in the 1940s and 1950s to national, top-down advocacy organizations. The advocacy organizations demand little of so-called members. Modern advocacy groups are, as one critic from the sixties called them, pseudo-organizations, run by professionals and consultants. They might have a mailing list and solicit donations from ordinary members, but these are not organizations with regular local meetings where local participants rely on one another for mutual participation. Pseudo-organizations have increased even more since the sixties.

If a survey asks you today if you are a member of an organization, you might say yes but have only a vague relationship to the organization you have in mind. You are less likely to have in mind a local civic club or political advocacy group or a group that is central to your social life. More likely, you have in mind a professional association to which you have no relationship at all except that you attend an annual professional conference that it sponsors. See Daniel J. Boorstin, *The Image: A Guide to Pseudo-events in America* (New York: Vintage Books, 1962); Skocpol, *Diminished Democracy*; Berry, *New Liberalism*. See also Derek Thompson, "The Free-Time Paradox in America," *Atlantic*, September 13, 2016.

5 Kirk Kristofferson, Katherine White, and John Peloza, "The Nature of Slacktivism: How the Social Observability of an Initial Act of Token Support Affects Subsequent Prosocial Action," *Journal of Consumer Research* 40 (6) (2014): 1149–66.

6 Aradhna Krishna, "Can Supporting a Cause Decrease Donations and Happiness? The Cause Marketing Paradox," *Journal of Consumer Psychology* 21 (3) (2011): 338–45. See also Yu-Hao Lee and Gary Hsieh, "Does Slacktivism Hurt Activism?: The Effects of Moral Balancing and Consistency in Online Activism," *Proceedings of the SIGCHI Conference on Human Factors in Computing Systems*, 2013, 811–20.

7 The subjects were mostly women (80 percent). Eighty percent of them were from Kansas, Utah, or Oklahoma. This was a "convenience sample" of willing volunteers but nonetheless a good opportunity to measure how social media affects daily behavior.

8 Jeffrey A. Hall, Michael W. Kearney, and Chong Xing, "Two Tests of Social Displacement through Social Media Use," *Information, Communication & Society*, 22 (10) (2019): 1396–1413.

9 Wendy Willis, "On Political Hobbyism: A Response to Eitan Hersh," Deliberative Democracy Consortium, July 1, 2017, https://deliberative-democracy.net/2017/07/01/on-political-hobbyism-a-response-to-eitan-hersh/.

10 See Hahrie Han and Lara Putnam, "The Best Way for Democrats to Win in 2020? By Ignoring the Candidates for Now," *Washington Post*, April 29, 2019.

PART IV

1 Jane Addams, "Why the Ward Boss Rules," *Outlook* 58 (14) (April 2, 1898). I thank Peter Levine for drawing my attention to this essay by Addams.

Chapter 17: The Dukakis Buffet

1 The neighborhood leader program was inspired by the vision of former Vermont governor Howard Dean, who had recently taken the helm of the Democratic National Committee. Dean focused his tenure on grassroots organizing in all fifty states, a departure from the previous strategy of focusing just on battleground districts in federal elections.

2 Quote from Christopher Edley Jr. in Sifry, "Obama's Lost Army."

3 Schlozman and Rosenfeld, *Hollow Parties*, forthcoming.

4 See also Lara Putnam, "Digital Fixes Won't Solve the Democrats' Problems," *American Prospect*, April 5, 2018, https://prospect.org/article/digital-fixes-wont-solve-democrats-problems.

5 Megan Gibson, "According to Census Data, This Is America's Gayest City," *Time*, August 25, 2011, http://newsfeed.time.com/2011/08/25/according-to-census-data-this-is-americas-gayest-city/.

6 See, for example, Eitan Hersh, "How Democrats Suppress the Vote," FiveThirty-Eight, November 3, 2015, https://fivethirtyeight.com/features/how-democrats-suppress-the-vote/.

7 Massachusetts Democratic Party, "Field Manual for City, Ward, and Town Committee Chairs," 5th ed., May 2011, https://massdems.org/wp-content/uploads/2018/01/chairsmanual2011.pdf.

8 Zeynep Tufekci, *Twitter and Tear Gas: The Power and Fragility of Networked Protest* (New Haven, CT: Yale University Press, 2017).

9 Ibid.; Henry Farrell, "The Consequences of the Internet for Politics," *Annual Review of Political Science* 15 (1) (2012), 35–52; Marc Lynch, "After Egypt: The Limits and Promise of Online Challenges to the Authoritarian Arab State," *Perspectives on Politics* 9 (2) (2011): 301–10; Philip Howard and Muzammil Hussain, "The Role of Digital Media," *Journal of Democracy* 22 (3) (2011): 35–48; Robert Faris and Bruce Etling, "Madison and the Smart Mob: The Promise and Limitations of the Internet for Democracy," *Fletcher Forum of World Affairs* 32 (2) (2008).

10 This was a theme in Jeane Kirkpatrick's 1977 speech to the Democratic National Committee, discussed below in chapter 19.

11 Bruce E. Cain, *Democracy More or Less: America's Political Reform Quandary* (Cambridge: Cambridge University Press, 2014).

Chapter 18: Rage Against the Machine

1 Milton Rakove, *Don't Make No Waves . . . Don't Back No Losers: An Insider's Analysis of the Daley Machine* (Bloomington: Indiana Press, 1975).

2 Ibid., 69.

3 Rakove, *Don't Make No Waves*.

4 Steven P. Erie, *Rainbow's End: Irish-Americans and the Dilemmas of Urban Machine Politics, 1840–1985* (Berkeley: University of California Press, 1988).

5 Ibid.

6 Quote from Jessica Trounstine, "Dominant Regimes and the Demise of Urban Democracy," *Journal of Politics* 68 (4) (2006): 879–93. See also Jessica Trounstine, *Political Monopolies in American Cities: The Rise and Fall of Bosses and Reformers* (Chicago: University of Chicago Press, 2008).

7 Alan Ware, "Anti-partism and Party Control of Political Reform in the United States: The Case of the Australian Ballot," *British Journal of Political Science* 30 (1) (2000): 1–29.

8 Rosenfeld and Schlozman, *Hollow Parties*; William J. Crotty and John S. Jackson, *Presidential Primaries and Nominations* (Washington, DC: CQ Press, 1985).

9 Skocpol, *Diminished Democracy*.

10 See Ware, "Anti-partism and Party Control." See also Richard F. Bensel, *The American Ballot Box in the Mid-Nineteenth Century* (Cambridge: Cambridge University Press, 2004).

11 Hersh, *Hacking the Electorate*; Alexander Keyssar, *The Right to Vote: The Contested History of Democracy in the United States* (New York: Basic Books, 2000).

12 Some states, in this period, also used primaries to elect delegates to national

party conventions to choose nominees for president. But a number of states that initiated presidential primaries in the early twentieth century quickly retreated. By 1924, most states were regularly using primaries for all offices except for the presidency. See Crotty and Jackson, *Presidential Primaries*; Leon D. Epstein, *Political Parties in the American Mold* (Madison: University of Wisconsin Press, 1989).

13 See V. O. Key, *American State Parties: An Introduction* (New York: Knopf, 1956); Seth Masket, *The Inevitable Party: Why Attempts to Kill the Party System Fail and How They Weaken Democracy* (Oxford: Oxford University Press, 2016); Eric Lawrence, Todd Donovan, and Shaun Bowler, "The Adoption of Direct Primaries in the United States," *Party Politics* 19 (1) (2013): 3–18.

14 V. O. Key, *American State Parties: An Introduction* (New York: Knopf, 1956), 96.

15 John Francis Reynolds, *The Demise of the American Convention System, 1880–1911* (Cambridge: Cambridge University Press, 2006); Ware, *Breakdown of Democratic Party Organization*.

16 "Inaugural Message by Governor Robert M. La Follette to the Wisconsin Legislature," Regular Session, 1901. Public Documents of the State of Wisconsin.

17 Crotty and Jackson, *Presidential Primaries*.

18 Said Jacob Gould Schurman, president of Cornell in the early 1900s, "I learned that the system of direct nominations [i.e., primaries], discourages self respecting and independent men from entering the public service and encourages the demagogue, the self advertiser and the reckless and unscrupulous soldier of fortune." Cited in Reynolds, *Demise of the American Convention System*. See Hofstadter, *Age of Reform*.

19 Woodrow Wilson (a political science professor turned US president) offered a progressive vision for government in which "the average man, the plain man, the common man, the ignorant man, the unaccomplished man, the poor man ha[s] a voice equal to the voice of anybody else in the settlement of the common affairs." Ordinary people, he argued, didn't need to cast a ballot the way a party machine instructed them to. If the parties could be moved out of the way, ordinary people would be able enough to cast a ballot perfectly well on their own. Democrat William Jennings Bryan shared this view, that ordinary people are competent enough "to sit in judgment on every question which has arisen or will arise." Quoted in Hofstadter, *Age of Reform*.

20 Michael E. McGerr, *The Decline of Popular Politics: The American North, 1865–1928* (Oxford: Oxford University Press, 1986).

21 Abraham, "Ward Boss or 'Simple Man.'"

22 Crotty and Jackson, *Presidential Primaries*; Rosenstone and Schlozman, *Hollow Parties*.

23 Anirudh V. S. Ruhil, "Urban Armageddon or Politics as Usual? The Case of Municipal Civil Service Reform," *American Journal of Political Science* 47 (1) (2003): 159-70; Pamela Tolbert and Lynne Zucker, "Institutional Sources of Change in the Formal Structure of Organizations: The Diffusion of Civil Service Reform, 1880–1935," *Administrative Science Quarterly* 28 (1) (1983).

24 See *Rutan v. Republican Party of Illinois*, 497 U.S. 62 (1990). See also *Elrod v. Burns*, 427 U.S. 347 (1976).

NOTES

25 See Epstein, *Political Parties.*

26 Rakove, *Don't Make No Waves,* 15. See also Ware, *Breakdown of Democratic Party Organization.*

27 Rosenfeld and Schlozman, *Hollow Parties.*

Chapter 19: The Verbalist Elite

1 William J. Crotty, *Decision for the Democrats: Reforming the Party Structure* (Baltimore: Johns Hopkins University Press, 1978).

2 Sam Rosenfeld, *The Polarizers: Postwar Architects of Our Partisan Era* (Chicago: University of Chicago Press, 2018).

3 Ware, *Breakdown of Democratic Party Organization.* See also Alan Ware, "Why Amateur Party Politics Has Withered Away: The Club Movement, Party Reform and the Decline of American Party Organizations," *European Journal of Political Research* 9 (3) (1981): 219–36.

4 Rosenfeld, *Polarizers.*

5 Sam Rosenfeld and Daniel Schlozman, "The Dilemmas for Democrats in 3 Past Visions for the Party," *Vox,* June 13, 2019.

6 Rosenfeld, *Polarizers,* 138.

7 Rosenfeld and Schlozman, *Hollow Parties.*

8 Byron E. Shafer, *Quiet Revolution: The Struggle for the Democratic Party and the Shaping of Post-reform Politics* (New York: Russell Sage Foundation, 1983).

9 See Rosenfeld, *Polarizers;* Epstein, *Political Parties;* Crotty and Jackson, *Presidential Primaries;* Adam Hilton, "The Path to Polarization: McGovern-Fraser, Counter-Reformers, and the Rise of the Advocacy Party," *Studies in American Political Development,* forthcoming.

10 Polsby, *Consequences of Party Reform.*

11 Crotty, *Decision for the Democrats;* Jeane Kirkpatrick, *The New Presidential Elite: Men and Women in National Politics* (New York: Russell Sage Foundation, 1975).

12 Crotty, *Decision for the Democrats.*

13 Epstein, *Political Parties.*

14 Polsby, *Consequences of Party Reform.*

15 For ways that campaign finance reform has limited the ability of parties to exert control over elections and support pragmatic candidates, see Ray LaRaja and Brian Schaffner, "Want to Reform Campaign Finance and Reduce Corruption? Here's How," Monkey Cage, *Washington Post,* October 26, 2015.

16 Rosenfeld and Schlozman, *Hollow Parties.*

17 Quoted in Rosenfeld, *Polarizers.*

18 See Kirkpatrick 1977 DNC testimony; Rosenfeld, *Polarizers.*

19 Transcript of proceedings, meeting of the Commission on Presidential Nomination and Party Structure, Washington, DC, June 24, 1977, box 1074, Democratic National Committee Records, National Archives, Washington, DC. Digital file of transcript shared by Sam Rosenfeld.

20 Quoted in Rosenfeld and Schlozman, *Hollow Parties.*

21 Quoted in Rosenfeld, *Polarizers.*

22 Fisher, *Activism, Inc.;* Skocpol, *Diminished Democracy;* Berry, *New Liberalism;* Ronald Inglehart, *The Silent Revolution: Changing Values and Political Styles Among*

Western Publics (Princeton: Princeton University Press, 1977); Julian E. Zelizer, "Rethinking the History of American Conservatism," *Reviews in American History* 38 (2) (2010): 367–92.

23 Skocpol and Williamson, *Tea Party*.

24 See Jeffrey Berry, "Tea Party Decline," working paper, 2017.

25 See David Broockman, Gregory Ferenstein, and Neil Malhotra, "Predispositions and the Political Behavior of American Economic Elites: Evidence from Technology Entrepreneurs," *American Journal of Political Science* 63 (1) (2019): 212–33.

26 Geismer, *Don't Blame Us*.

27 Jane McAlevey, *No Shortcuts*.

28 See also work by Nick Carnes, such as "Why Are There So Few Working-Class People in Political Office? Evidence from State Legislatures," *Politics, Groups, and Identities* 4 (1) (2015).

29 Janice Fine, *Worker Centers: Organizing Communities at the Edge of the Dream* (Ithaca, NY: ILR Press, 2006).

Chapter 20: Fear and Fate

1 Diana C. Mutz, "Status Threat, Not Economic Hardship, Explains the 2016 Presidential Vote," *Proceedings of the National Academy of Sciences* 115 (19) (2018): 4330–39; Bethany Albertson and Shana Kushner Gadarian, *Anxious Politics: Democratic Citizenship in a Threatening World* (Cambridge: Cambridge University Press, 2015); Ashley Jardina, *White Identity Politics* (Cambridge: Cambridge University Press, 2019).

2 Those who volunteer today are also disproportionately racial minorities and people from nonwealthy backgrounds. See George Reynolds and Amanda Shendruk, "Demographics of the U.S. Military," *Council on Foreign Relations*, April 24, 2018, https://www.cfr.org/article/demographics-us-military.

3 Ronald F. Inglehart, Bi Puranen, and Christian Welzel, "Declining Willingness to Fight for One's Country: The Individual-Level Basis for the Long Peace," *Journal of Peace Research* 52 (4) (2015).

4 Putnam, *Bowling Alone*. See also, Suzanne Mettler, *Soldiers to Citizens: The GI Bill and the Making of the Greatest Generation* (Oxford: Oxford University Press, 2007).

5 Eitan Hersh, "Long-Term Effect of September 11 on the Political Behavior of Victims' Families and Neighbors," *Proceedings of the National Academy of Sciences* 110 (52) (2013): 20959–63.

6 Robert D. Putnam, "*E Pluribus Unum*: Diversity and Community in the Twenty-First Century: The 2006 Johan Skytte Prize Lecture," *Scandinavian Political Studies* 30 (2) (2007): 137–74.

7 Adam Seth Levine, *American Insecurity: Why Our Economic Fears Lead to Political Inaction* (Princeton: Princeton University Press, 2015).

8 Michael C. Dawson, *Behind the Mule: Race and Class in African-American Politics* (Princeton: Princeton University Press, 1994); Gabriel R. Sanchez and Edward D. Vargas, "Taking a Closer Look at Group Identity: The Link Between Theory and Measurement of Group Consciousness and Linked Fate," *Political Research*

Quarterly 69 (1) (2016): 160–74; Claudine Gay, Jennifer L. Hochschild, and Ariel White, "Americans' Belief in Linked Fate: Does the Measure Capture the Concept?," *Journal of Race, Ethnicity, and Politics* 1 (2016): 117–44; Gabriel R. Sanchez and Natalie Masuoka, "Brown-Utility Heuristic? The Presence and Contributing Factors of Latino Linked Fate," *Hispanic Journal of Behavioral Sciences* 32 (4) (2010).

9 Consider white Democrats who said they weren't particularly interested in politics. They reported on the survey that in the typical day, they spent forty-five minutes on politics. Six percent of them reported that at least some portion of that time was spent on volunteering. The rest of the time was spent consuming and discussing political news. Black and Latino Democrats who were not interested in politics also reported they spent about forty-five minutes a day on politics, but among them 23 percent said some of that time was spent on volunteering, about four times the rate among whites.

10 John Laidler, "And CEO Makes Three: Race for Mayor Heating Up Early," *Boston Globe*, June 14, 2007, http://archive.boston.com/news/local/articles/2007/06/14/and_ceo_makes_three/.

11 Kay Lazar, "Black Malden Charter Students Punished for Braided Hair Extensions," *Boston Globe*, May 11, 2017, https://www.bostonglobe.com/metro/2017/05/11/black-students-malden-school-who-wear-braids-face-punishment-parents-say/stWDlBSCJhw1zocUWR1QMP/story.html.

12 See successes and strategies of nonwhite community organizations, as discussed in Marcela García-Castañon et al., "Democracy's Deficit: The Role of Institutional Contact in Shaping Non-white Political Behavior," *Journal of Race, Ethnicity, and Politics* 4 (2019): 1–31.

13 On power, service, and organizing, see also writing about the Industrial Areas Foundation (IAF), e.g., Mark Warren, *Dry Bones Rattling: Community Building to Revitalize American Democracy* (Princeton: Princeton University Press, 2001).

14 Janelle Wong, *Immigrants, Evangelicals, and Politics in an Era of Demographic Change* (New York: Russel Sage Foundation, 2018); Fine, *Worker Centers*. See also Dara Strolovitch, *Affirmative Advocacy: Race, Class, and Gender in Interest Group Politics* (Chicago: University of Chicago Press, 2007).

15 James Cavendish, "Church-Based Community Activism: A Comparison of Black and White Catholic Congregations," *Journal for the Scientific Study of Religion* 39 (1) (2000): 64–77.

16 Michael Dawson, *Blacks In and Out of the Left* (Cambridge, MA: Harvard University Press, 2013).

17 Peter Murray, "The Secret of Scale," *Stanford Social Innovation Review*, Fall 2013, https://ssir.org/articles/entry/the_secret_of_scale.

18 Michelle Goldberg, "The Millennial Socialists Are Coming," *New York Times*, June 30, 2018, https://www.nytimes.com/2018/06/30/opinion/democratic-socialists-progressive-democratic-party-trump.html.

19 Hayes and Goehl, "Why Is This Happening?"

20 Kwame Ture and Charles V. Hamilton, *Black Power: The Politics of Liberation in America* (New York: Random House, 1967); Peniel E. Joseph, ed., *The Black Power Movement: Rethinking the Civil Rights–Black Power Era* (New York: Routledge, 2006); Rhonda Y. Williams, *Concrete Demands: The Search for Black Power in the 20th Century* (New York: Routledge, 2014).

NOTES

PART V

1 JPS Tanakh translation via Sefaria, https://www.sefaria.org/Isaiah.1?ven=Tanakh
:_The_Holy_Scriptures,_published_by_JPS&lang=bi.

Chapter 21: Learning to Want Power

1 Moye, *Ella Baker*.
2 Ibid.
3 Ibid. See also Barbara Ransby, *Ella Baker & the Black Freedom Movement: A Radical Democratic Vision* (Chapel Hill: University of North Carolina Press, 2003).

Chapter 22: To-Do Lists

1 "Expenditures," Center for Responsive Politics, 2019, https://www.opensecrets
.org/expends/?year=2016.
2 See "Care.com Backup Care Services," in "Care.com Child and Elder Care
2019," Access Tufts, https://access.tufts.edu/carecom-child-and-elder-care.
3 E.g., Betsy Sinclair, *The Social Citizen: Peer Networks and Political Behavior* (Chicago: University of Chicago Press, 2012); Green, Gerber, and Larimer, "Social Pressure and Voter Turnout."

Bibliography

Aalberg, Toril, Jesper Stromback, and Claes H. de Vreese. 2011. "The Framing of Politics as Strategy and Game: A Review of Concepts, Operationalizations and Key Findings." *Journalism* 13 (2): 162–78.

Aarøe, Lene. 2011. "Investigating Frame Strength: The Case of Episodic and Thematic Frames." *Political Communication* 28 (2): 207–26.

Abrams, Samuel, Torben Iversen, and David Soskice. 2011. "Informal Social Networks and Rational Voting." *British Journal of Political Science* 41 (2): 229–57.

Achen, Christopher, and Larry Bartels. 2017. *Democracy for Realists: Why Elections Do Not Produce Responsive Government.* Princeton: Princeton University Press.

Addonizio, Elizabeth M., Donald P. Green, and James M. Glaser. 2007. "Putting the Party Back into Politics: An Experiment Testing Whether Election Day Festivals Increase Voter Turnout." *PS: Political Science and Politics* 40 (4): 721–27.

Ahler, Douglas J., and David E. Broockman. 2018. "The Delegate Paradox: Why Polarized Politicians Can Represent Citizens Best." *Journal of Politics* 80 (4): 1117–33.

Albertson, Bethany, and Shana Kushner Gadarian. 2015. *Anxious Politics: Democratic Citizenship in a Threatening World.* Cambridge: Cambridge University Press.

Aldrich, John H. 1993. "Rational Choice and Turnout." *American Journal of Political Science* 37 (1): 246–78.

Ansolabehere, Stephen, John M. de Figueiredo, and James M. Snyder. 2003. "Why Is There So Little Money in Politics?" *Journal of Economic Perspectives* 17 (1): 105–30.

Ansolabehere, Stephen, and Eitan Hersh. 2012. "Validation: What Big Data Reveal about Survey Misreporting and the Real Electorate." *Political Analysis* 20 (4): 437–59.

———. 2013. "Gender, Race, Age and Voting: A Research Note." *Politics and Governance* 1 (2).

Atkinson, Matthew D., and Anthony Fowler. 2014. "Social Capital and Voter Turnout: Evidence from Saint's Day Fiestas in Mexico." *British Journal of Political Science* 44 (1): 41–59.

Banfield, Edward C. 1968. *The Unheavenly Chorus Revisited.* Boston: Little, Brown.

Barber, Benjamin. 2004. *Strong Democracy.* Berkeley: University of California Press.

Barber, Michael. 2016. "Donation Motivations: Testing Theories of Access and Ideology." *Political Research Quarterly* 69 (1): 148–59.

BIBLIOGRAPHY

Barber, Michael, and Nolan McCarty. 2013. "Causes and Consequences of Polarization." In *Negotiating Agreement in Politics*, edited by Jane Mansbridge and Cathie Jo Martin. Washington, DC: American Political Science Association.

Barber, Michael J. 2016. "Ideological Donors, Contribution Limits, and the Polarization of American Legislatures." *Journal of Politics* 78 (1): 296–310.

Barber, Michael J., Brandice Canes-Wrone, and Sharece Thrower. 2016. "Sophisticated Donors: What Motivates Individual Campaign Contributors?" *American Journal of Political Science* 61 (2): 271–88.

Bellah, Robert N., Richard Madsen, William M. Sullivan, Ann Swidler, and Steven M. Tipton. 1985. *Habits of the Heart*. Berkeley: University of California Press.

Benkler, Yochai. 2006. *The Wealth of Networks: How Social Production Transforms Markets and Freedom*. New Haven, CT: Yale University Press.

Bensel, Richard F. 2004. *The American Ballot Box in the Mid-Nineteenth Century*. Cambridge: Cambridge University Press.

Berry, Jeffrey M. 2003. *The New Liberalism: The Rising Power of Citizen Groups*. Washington, DC: Brookings Institution Press.

Berry, Jeffrey M., and Sarah Sobieraj. 2014. *The Outrage Industry*. Oxford: Oxford University Press.

Blais, Andre. 2000. *To Vote or Not to Vote?: The Merits and Limits of Rational Choice Theory*. Pittsburgh: University of Pittsburgh Press.

Blais, Andre, and Carol Galais. 2016. "Measuring the Civic Duty to Vote: A Proposal." *Electoral Studies* 41 (1): 60–69.

Bond, Robert M., Christopher J. Fariss, Jason J. Jones, Adam D. I. Kramer, Cameron Marlow, Jaime E. Settle, and James H. Fowler. 2012. "A 61-Million-Person Experiment in Social Influence and Political Mobilization." *Nature* 489 (7415): 295–98.

Boorstin, Daniel J. 1962. *The Image: A Guide to Pseudo-events in America*. New York: Vintage Books.

Bourdieu, Pierre. 1984. *Distinction: A Social Critique of the Judgment of Taste*. Cambridge, MA: Harvard University Press.

Boyte, Harry C., and Nancy N. Kari. 1996. *Building America: The Democratic Promise of Public Work*. Philadelphia: Temple University Press.

Brader, Ted. 2006. *Campaigning for Hearts and Minds: How Emotional Appeals in Political Ads Work*. Chicago: University of Chicago Press.

Brady, Henry E., Sidney Verba, and Kay L. Schlozman. 1995. "Beyond SES: A Resource Model of Political Participation." *American Political Science Review* 89 (2): 271–94.

Brennan, Jason. 2016. *Against Democracy*. Princeton: Princeton University Press.

Broockman, David E., Gregory Ferenstein, and Neil Malhotra. 2019. "Predispositions and the Political Behavior of American Economic Elites: Evidence from Technology Entrepreneurs." *American Journal of Political Science* 63 (1): 212–33.

Broockman, David E., and Joshua Kalla. 2018. "The Minimal Persuasive Effects of Campaign Contact in General Elections: Evidence from 49 Field Experiments." *American Political Science Review* 112 (1): 148–66.

Butsch, Richard, ed. 1990. *For Fun and Profit*. Philadelphia: Temple University Press.

Cain, Bruce. 2014. *Democracy More or Less*. Cambridge: Cambridge University Press.

BIBLIOGRAPHY

Campbell, Andrea Louise. 2003a. *How Policies Make Citizens*. Princeton: Princeton University Press.

———. 2003b. "Self-Interest, Social Security, and the Distinctive Participation Patterns of Senior Citizens." *American Political Science Review* 96 (3): 565–74.

Campbell, David E. 2006. *Why We Vote: How Schools and Communities Shape Our Civic Life*. Princeton: Princeton University Press.

Caplan, Brian. 2008. *The Myth of the Rational Voter*. Princeton: Princeton University Press.

Cappella, Joseph N., and Kathleen Hall Jamieson. 1997. *Spiral of Cynicism: The Press and the Public Good*. Oxford: Oxford University Press.

Carey, John M., Brendan Nyhan, Benjamin Valentino, and Mingnan Lie. 2016. "An Inflated View of the Facts? How Preferences and Predispositions Shape Conspiracy Beliefs about the Deflategate Scandal." *Research and Politics* 3 (3): 1–9.

Carmy, Shalom. 2008. "'Yet My Soul Drew Back,' Fear of God as Experience and Commandment in the Age of Anxiety." *Tradition* 41 (3): 1–30.

Carnes, Nicholas. 2013. *White-Collar Government: The Hidden Role of Class in Economic Policy Making*. Chicago: University of Chicago Press.

———. 2015. "Why Are There So Few Working-Class People in Political Office? Evidence from State Legislatures." *Politics, Groups, and Identities* 4 (1).

Carpini, Michael, Fay Cook, and Lawrence Jacobs. 2004. "Public Deliberation, Discursive Participation, and Citizen Engagement: A Review of the Empirical Literature." *Annual Review of Political Science* 7 (1): 315–44.

Cavendish, James. 2000. "Church-Based Community Activism: A Comparison of Black and White Catholic Congregations." *Journal for the Scientific Study of Religion* 39 (1): 64–77.

Cherry, Kevin M. 2009. "The Problem of Polity: Political Participation and Aristotle's Best Regime." *Journal of Politics* 71 (4): 1406–21.

Christensen, Henrik S. 2011. "Political Activities on the Internet: Slacktivism or Political Participation by Other Means." *First Monday* 16 (2).

Cramer, Katherine J. 2016. *The Politics of Resentment*. Chicago: University of Chicago Press.

Crotty, William J. 1978. *Decision for the Democrats: Reforming the Party Structure*. Baltimore: Johns Hopkins University Press.

Crotty, William J., and John S. Jackson. 1985. *Presidential Primaries and Nominations*. Washington, DC: CQ Press.

Csikszentmihalyi, Mihaly. 2000. *Beyond Boredom and Anxiety*. San Francisco: Jossey-Bass.

Culberson, Tyler P., Michael P. McDonald, and Suzanne M. Robbins. 2018. "Small Donors in Congressional Elections." *American Politics Research*, March 23, 2018.

Currell, Susan. 2005. *The March of Spare Time: The Problem and Promise of Leisure in the Great Depression*. Philadelphia: University of Pennsylvania Press.

Curtis, George William. 1894. "The Public Duty of Educated Men," Commencement Address for Union College, June 6, 1877. In *Orations and Addresses of George William Curtis*, edited by Charles Eliot. Norton, NY: Harper and Brothers.

Dalton, Russell J. 2008. "Citizenship Norms and the Expansion of Political Participation." *Political Studies* 56 (1): 76–98.

BIBLIOGRAPHY

Dawson, Michael. 1994. *Behind the Mule: Race and Class in African-American Politics.* Princeton: Princeton University Press.

———. 2013. *Blacks in and out of the Left.* Cambridge, MA: Harvard University Press.

Dean, Kendra. 2010. *Almost Christian: What the Faith of Our Teenagers Is Telling the American Church.* Oxford: Oxford University Press.

DeGrazia, Sebastian. 1964. *Of Time, Work, and Leisure.* New York: Doubleday.

DeNardo, James. 1980. "Turnout and the Vote: The Joke's on the Democrats." *American Political Science Review* 74 (2): 406–20.

De Solier, Isabelle. 2013. *Food and the Self: Consumption, Production, and Material Culture.* London: Bloomsbury Academic.

Drake, Charles Daniel. 1837. "The Duties of American Citizens." Address delivered at the Franklin Society of St. Louis.

Drescher, Elizabeth. 2016. *Choosing Our Religion: The Spiritual Lives of America's Nones.* Oxford: Oxford University Press.

Eliasoph, Nina. 1998. *Avoiding Politics: How Americans Produce Apathy in Everyday Life.* Cambridge: Cambridge University Press.

Enos, Ryan D., and Eitan D. Hersh. 2015. "Party Activists as Campaign Advertisers: The Ground Campaign as a Principal-Agent Problem." *American Political Science Review* 109 (2): 252–78.

Epstein, Leon D. 1989. *Political Parties in the American Mold.* Madison: University of Wisconsin Press.

Erie, Steven P. 1988. *Rainbow's End: Irish-Americans and the Dilemmas of Urban Machine Politics, 1840–1985.* Berkeley: University of California Press.

Faris, Robert, and Bruce Etling. 2008. "Madison and the Smart Mob: The Promise and Limitations of the Internet for Democracy." *Fletcher Forum of World Affairs* 32 (2).

Farrell, Henry. 2012. "The Consequences of the Internet for Politics." *Annual Review of Political Science* 15 (1): 35–52.

Feddersen, Timothy J. 2004. "Rational Choice Theory and the Paradox of Not Voting." *Journal of Economic Perspectives* 18 (1): 99–112.

Ferguson, Todd W. 2014. "The Optimal Level of Strictness and Congregational Growth." *Religions* 5 (3): 703–19.

Fine, Janice. 2006. *Worker Centers: Organizing Communities at the Edge of the Dream.* Ithaca, NY: ILR Press.

Fiorina, Morris P. 1976. "The Voting Decision: Instrumental and Expressive Aspects." *Journal of Politics* 38 (2): 390–413.

———. 2002. "Parties, Participation, and Representation in America: Old Theories Face New Realities." In *Political Science: The State of the Discipline*, edited by Ira Katznelson and Helen V. Milner, 511–41. New York: Norton.

———. 2017. *Unstable Majorities: Polarization, Party Sorting, and Political Stalemate.* Palo Alto, CA: Hoover Institution Press.

Fisher, Dana R. 2006. *Activism, Inc.: How the Outsourcing of Grassroots Campaigns Is Strangling Progressive Politics in America.* Stanford, CA: Stanford University Press.

———. Forthcoming. *American Resistance.* New York: Columbia University Press.

Foley, Edward B. 2015. "Voters as Fiduciaries." Ohio State Public Law Working Paper No. 296.

Fowler, Anthony. 2017. "Partisan Tribalism or Policy Voting?" Working paper.

Fraga, Bernard L. 2018. *The Turnout Gap: Race, Ethnicity, and Political Inequality in a Diversifying America*. Cambridge: Cambridge University Press.

Friedman, Sam, and Daniel Laurison. 2019. *The Class Ceiling: Why It Pays to Be Privileged*. Bristol, England: Policy Press.

Galston, William A. 1991. *Liberal Politics*. Cambridge: Cambridge University Press.

Gans, Herbert J. 1979. "Symbolic Ethnicity." *Ethnic and Racial Studies* 2 (1): 1–20.

Ganz, Marshall. 2009. *Why David Sometimes Wins*. Oxford: Oxford University Press.

———. 2011. "Public Narrative, Collective Action, and Power." In *Accountability Through Public Opinion: From Inertia to Public Action*, edited by Sina Odugbemi and Taeku Lee. Washington, DC: World Bank.

García-Castañon, Marcela, et al. 2019. "Democracy's Deficit: The Role of Institutional Contact in Shaping Non-white Political Behavior." *Journal of Race, Ethnicity, and Politics* 4:1–31.

Gay, Claudine, Jennifer L. Hochschild, and Ariel White. 2016. "Americans' Belief in Linked Fate: Does the Measure Capture the Concept?" *Journal of Race, Ethnicity, and Politics* 1:117–44.

Geismer, Lily. 2014. *Don't Blame Us: Suburban Liberals and the Transformation of the Democratic Party*. Princeton: Princeton University Press.

Gelber, Steven M. 1983. "Working at Playing: The Culture of the Workplace and the Rise of Baseball." *Journal of Social History* 16 (4): 3–22.

———. 1991. "A Job You Can't Lose: Work and Hobbies in the Great Depression." *Journal of Social History* 24 (4): 741–66.

———. 1999. *Hobbies: Leisure and the Culture of Work in America*. New York: Columbia University Press.

Gerber, Alan S., Donald P. Green, and Christopher W. Larimer. 2008. "Social Pressure and Voter Turnout: Evidence from a Large-Scale Field Experiment." *American Political Science Review* 102 (1): 33–48.

Gerber, Alan S., Gregory A. Huber, David Doherty, and Conor M. Dowling. 2014. "Why People Vote: Estimating the Social Returns to Voting." *British Journal of Political Science* 46 (2): 241–61.

Geys, Benny. 2006. "'Rational' Theories of Voter Turnout: A Review." *Political Studies Review* 4 (1): 16–35.

Gift, Karen, and Thomas Gift. 2015. "Does Politics Influence Hiring? Evidence from a Randomized Experiment." *Political Behavior* 37 (3): 653–75.

Gilens, Martin. 2012. *Affluence and Influence: Economic Inequality and Political Power in America*. Princeton: Princeton University Press.

Gladden, Washington. 1902. "Rights and Duties." Address delivered at the Fifty-Eighth Commencement of the University of Michigan. http://www.umich.edu/bhlumrec/c/commence/1902-Gladden.pdf.

Glaser, James M. 2002. "White Voters, Black Schools: Structuring Racial Choices with a Checklist Ballot." *American Journal of Political Science* 46 (1): 35–46.

Glickman, Lawrence B. 2012. "Consumer Activism, Consumer Regimes, and the Consumer Movement: Rethinking the History of Consumer Politics in the United States." In *The Oxford Handbook of the History of Consumption*, edited by Frank Trentmann. Oxford: Oxford University Press.

Goggin, Stephen N., and Alexander G. Theodoridis. 2018. "Seeing Red (or Blue): How Party Identity Colors Political Cognition." *Forum* 16 (1): 81–95.

Green, Donald, Bradley Palmquist, and Eric Schickler. 2002. *Partisan Hearts and Minds: Political Parties and the Social Identities of Voters.* New Haven, CT: Yale University Press.

Green, Donald P., and Ian Shapiro. 1994. *Pathologies of Rational Choice Theory.* Cambridge: Cambridge University Press.

Groseclose, Tim, and Nolan McCarty. 2001. "The Politics of Blame: Bargaining before an Audience." *American Journal of Political Science* 45 (1): 100–119.

Grossmann, Matt. Forthcoming. *Red State Blues: How the Conservative Revolution Stalled in the States.*

Grossmann, Matt, and David A. Hopkins. 2016. *Asymmetric Politics: Ideological Republicans and Group Interest Democrats.* Oxford: Oxford University Press.

Guess, Andrew, Brendan Nyhan, and Jason Reifler. 2018. "Selective Exposure to Misinformation: Evidence from the Consumption of Fake News during the 2016 U.S. Presidential Election." European Research Council working paper.

Hall, Andrew. 2014. "How the Public Funding of Elections Increases Candidate Polarization." Working paper, Harvard University.

Hall, Andrew B. 2019. *Who Wants to Run? How the Devaluing of Political Office Drives Polarization.* Chicago: University of Chicago Press.

Hall, Jeffrey A., Michael W. Kearney, and Chong Xing. 2019. "Two Tests of Social Displacement through Social Media Use." *Information, Communication & Society* 22 (10): 1396–1413.

Hamlin, Alan, and Colin Jennings. 2011. "Expressive Political Behaviour: Foundations, Scope and Implications." *British Journal of Political Science* 41 (3): 645–70.

Han, Hahrie. 2016. "The Organizational Roots of Political Activism: Field Experiments on Creating a Relational Context." *American Political Science Review* 110 (2): 296–307.

Hayes, Danny, and Jennifer L. Lawless. 2015. "As Local News Goes, So Goes Citizen Engagement: Media Knowledge and Participation in US House Elections." *Journal of Politics* 77 (2).

Healy, Andrew, and Neil Malhotra. 2014. "Partisan Bias among Interviewers." *Public Opinion Quarterly* 78 (2): 489–99.

Heerwig, Jennifer, and Brian J. McCabe. 2018. "Expanding Participation in Municipal Elections: Assessing the Impact of Seattle's Democracy Voucher Program." Georgetown University, Washington, DC: Center for Studies in Demography and Ecology.

Hemingway, J. L. 1999. "Leisure, Social Capital, and Democratic Citizenship." *Journal of Leisure Research* 31 (2): 150–65.

Hersh, Eitan, and Brian Schaffner. 2018. "Postmaterialist Particularism: What Petitions Can Tell Us about Biases in the Policy Agenda." *American Politics Research* 46 (3): 434–64.

Hersh, Eitan D. 2013. "Long-Term Effect of September 11 on the Political Behavior of Victims' Families and Neighbors." *Proceedings of the National Academy of Sciences* 110 (52): 20959–63.

———. 2015. *Hacking the Electorate: How Campaigns Perceive Voters.* Cambridge: Cambridge University Press.

Hetherington, Marc, and Jonathan Weiler. 2009. *Authoritarianism and Polarization in American Politics.* New York: Cambridge University Press.

Hibbing, John, and Elizabeth Theiss-Morse. 1995. *Congress as Public Enemy: Public Attitudes toward American Political Institutions*. Cambridge: Cambridge University Press.

Hill, Seth J., and Gregory A. Huber. 2017. "Representativeness and Motivations of the Contemporary Donorate: Results from Merged Survey and Administrative Records." *Political Behavior* 39 (1): 3–29.

Hilton, Adam. Forthcoming. "The Path to Polarization: McGovern-Fraser, Counter-Reformers, and the Rise of the Advocacy Party." *Studies in American Political Development*.

Hochschild, Arlie Russell. 2016. *Strangers in Their Own Land: Anger and Mourning on the American Right*. New York: Free Press.

Hofstadter, Richard. 1955. *The Age of Reform*. New York: Vintage.

Hopkins, Daniel J. 2018. *The Increasingly United States*. Chicago: University of Chicago Press.

Howard, Philip, and Muzammil Hussain. 2011. "The Role of Digital Media." *Journal of Democracy* 22 (3): 35–48.

Huddy, Leonie, Lilliana Mason, and Lene Aaroe. 2015. "Expressive Partisanship: Campaign Involvement, Political Emotion, and Partisan Identity." *American Political Science Review* 109 (1): 1–17.

Hunter, James Davison. 2001. *The Death of Character: Moral Education in an Age without Good or Evil*. New York: Basic Books.

Inglehart, Ronald. 1977. *The Silent Revolution: Changing Values and Political Styles among Western Publics*. Princeton: Princeton University Press.

Inglehart, Ronald F., Bi Puranen, and Christian Welzel. 2015. "Declining Willingness to Fight for One's Country: The Individual-Level Basis of the Long Peace." *Journal of Peace Research* 52 (4).

Iversen, Torben, and David Soskice. 2012. "Information, Social Networks and Interest-Based Voting: Consequences for Distributive Politics." Working paper, Harvard University.

Iyengar, Shanto. 1991. *Is Anyone Responsible? How Television Frames Political Issues*. Chicago: University of Chicago Press.

Iyengar, Shanto, Gaurav Sood, and Yphtach Lelkes. 2012. "Affect, Not Ideology: A Social Identity Perspective on Polarization." *Public Opinion Quarterly* 76 (3): 405–31.

Iyengar, Shanto, and Sean J. Westwood. 2015. "Fear and Loathing across Party Lines: New Evidence on Group Polarization." *American Journal of Political Science* 59 (3): 690–707.

Jardina, Ashley. 2019. *White Identity Politics*. Cambridge: Cambridge University Press.

Jones, Phillip E. 2019. "Partisanship, Political Awareness, and Retrospective Evaluations, 1956–2016." *Political Behavior*, March 23, 2019.

Joseph, Peniel E., ed. 2006. *The Black Power Movement: Rethinking the Civil Rights–Black Power Era*. New York: Routledge.

Kahneman, Daniel. 2011. *Thinking Fast and Slow*. New York: Farrar, Straus & Giroux.

Key, V. O. 1956. *American State Parties: An Introduction*. New York: Knopf.

Keyssar, Alexander. 2000. *The Right to Vote: The Contested History of Democracy in the United States*. New York: Basic Books.

King, Gary, Jennifer Pan, and Margaret E. Roberts. 2013. "How Censorship in

China Allows Government Criticism but Silences Collective Expression." *American Political Science Review* 107 (2): 326–43.

Kirkpatrick, Jeane. 1975. *The New Presidential Elite: Men and Women in National Politics*. New York: Russell Sage Foundation.

Klar, Samara, and Yanna Krupnikov. 2016. *Independent Politics: How American Disdain for Parties Leads to Political Inaction*. Cambridge: Cambridge University Press.

Klar, Samara, Yanna Krupnikov, and John Barry Ryan. 2018. "Affective Polarization or Partisan Disdain?" *Public Opinion Quarterly* 82 (2): 379–90.

Krishna, Aradhna. 2011. "Can Supporting a Cause Decrease Donations and Happiness? The Cause Marketing Paradox." *Journal of Consumer Psychology* 21 (3): 338–45.

Kristofferson, Kirk, Katherine White, and John Peloza. 2014. "The Nature of Slacktivism: How the Social Observability of an Initial Act of Token Support Affects Subsequent Prosocial Action." *Journal of Consumer Research* 40 (6): 1149–66.

Ladd, Jonathan. 2012. *Why Americans Hate the Media and How It Matters*. Princeton: Princeton University Press.

La Raja, Raymond J., and Brian F. Schaffner. 2015. *Campaign Finance and Political Polarization: When Purists Prevail*. Ann Arbor: University of Michigan Press.

Lawrence, Eric, Todd Donovan, and Shaun Bowler. 2013. "The Adoption of Direct Primaries in the United States." *Party Politics* 19 (1): 3–18.

Lee, Frances E. 2009. *Beyond Ideology: Politics, Principles, and Partisanship in the U.S. Senate*. Chicago: University of Chicago Press.

———. 2011. "Two-Party Competition and Senate Politics: The Permanent Campaign on the Floor of the U.S. Senate." Working paper.

Lee, Yu-Hao, and Gary Hsieh. 2013. "Does Slacktivism Hurt Activism? The Effects of Moral Balancing and Consistency in Online Activism." In *Proceedings of the SIGCHI Conference on Human Factors in Computing Systems*, 811–20.

Lelkes, Yphtach. 2016. "Mass Polarization: Manifestations and Measurements." Special issue, *Public Opinion Quarterly* 80:392–410.

Lelkes, Yphtach, and Sean Westwood. 2017. "The Limits of Partisan Prejudice." *Journal of Politics* 79 (2): 485–501.

Levendusky, Matthew. 2009. *The Partisan Sort: How Liberals Became Democrats and Conservatives Became Republicans*. Chicago: University of Chicago Press.

Levendusky, Matthew S., and Neil Malhotra. 2016. "(Mis)perceptions of Partisan Polarization in the American Public." Special issue, *Public Opinion Quarterly* 80:378–91.

Levine, Adam Seth. 2015. *American Insecurity: Why Our Economic Fears Lead to Political Inaction*. Princeton: Princeton University Press.

Levine, Peter. 2013. *We Are the Ones We Have Been Waiting For: The Promise of Civic Renewal in America*. Oxford: Oxford University Press.

Levine, Peter, and Kei Kawashima-Ginsberg. 2017. "The Republic Is (Still) at Risk—and Civics Is Part of the Solution." Medford, MA: Jonathan M. Tisch College of Civic Life, Tufts University.

Luskin, Robert. 1990. "Explaining Political Sophistication." *Political Behavior* 12 (4): 331–61.

Lynch, Marc. 2011. "After Egypt: The Limits and Promise of Online Challenges to the Authoritarian Arab State." *Perspectives on Politics* 9 (2).

Mansbridge, Jane, et al. 2010. "The Place of Self-Interest and the Role of Power in Deliberative Democracy." *Journal of Political Philosophy* 18 (1): 64–100.

Masket, Seth. 2016. *The Inevitable Party: Why Attempts to Kill the Party System Fail and How They Weaken Democracy*. Oxford: Oxford University Press.

Mason, Lilliana. 2018. *Uncivil Agreement: How Politics Became Our Identity*. Chicago: University of Chicago Press.

Mayer, David S., and Sidney Tarrow. 2018. *The Resistance*. Oxford: Oxford University Press.

McAdam, Doug, Robert J. Sampson, Simon Weffer, and Heather MacIndoe. 2005. "'There Will Be Fighting in the Streets': The Distorting Lens of Social Movement Theory." *Mobilization: An International Journal* 10 (1): 1–18.

McAlevey, Jane F. 2016. *No Shortcuts: Organizing for Power*. Oxford: Oxford University Press.

McCarty, Nolan. 2019. *Polarization: What Everyone Needs to Know*. Oxford: Oxford University Press.

McGerr, Michael E. 1986. *The Decline of Popular Politics*. Oxford: Oxford University Press.

McGhee, Eric, Seth Masket, Boris Shor, Steven Rogers, and Nolan McCarty. 2014. "A Primary Cause of Partisanship? Nomination Systems and Legislator Ideology." *American Journal of Political Science* 58 (2): 337–51.

Melber, Ari. 2010. "Year One of Organizing for America: The Permanent Field Campaign in a Digital Age." techPresident Special Report.

Mettler, Suzanne. 2007. *Soldiers to Citizens: The GI Bill and the Making of the Greatest Generation*. Oxford: Oxford University Press.

Milkis, Sidney M., Jesse H. Rhodes, and Emily J. Charnock. 2012. "What Happened to Post-Partisanship? Barack Obama and the New American Party System." *Perspectives on Politics* 10 (1): 57–76.

Mondak, Jeffrey, and Mary Anderson. 2004. "The Knowledge Gap: A Reexamination of Gender-Based Differences in Political Knowledge." *Journal of Politics* 66 (2): 492–512.

Moye, J. Todd. 2013. *Ella Baker: Community Organizer of the Civil Rights Movement*. Lanham, MD: Rowman & Littlefield.

Mulac, Margaret E. 1959. *Hobbies: The Creative Use of Leisure*. New York: Harper.

Mumford, Lewis. 1934. *Technics and Civilization*. New York: Harcourt.

Munson, Ziad. 2009. *The Making of Pro-Life Activists: How Social Movement Mobilization Works*. Chicago: University of Chicago Press.

Musgrave, Paul, and Mark Rom. 2015. "Fair and Balanced? Experimental Evidence on Partisan Bias in Grading." *American Politics Research* 43 (3): 536–54.

Mutz, Diana C. 2015. *In-Your-Face Politics*. Princeton: Princeton University Press.

———. 2018. "Status Threat, Not Economic Hardship, Explains the 2016 Presidential Vote." *Proceedings of the National Academy of Sciences* 115 (19): 4330–39.

Pack, Arthur Newton. 1934. *Challenge of Leisure*. New York: Macmillan.

Polsby, Nelson W. 1983. *Consequences of Party Reform*. Oxford: Oxford University Press.

Prior, Markus. 2007. *Post-Broadcast Democracy: How Media Choice Increases Inequality in Political Involvement and Polarizes Elections*. Cambridge: Cambridge University Press.

———. 2010. "You've Either Got It or You Don't? The Stability of Political Interest over the Life Cycle." *Journal of Politics* 72 (3): 747–66.

———. 2019. *Hooked: How Politics Captures People's Interest.* Cambridge: Cambridge University Press.

Prior, Markus, and Lori D. Bougher. 2018. " 'Like They've Never, Ever Seen in This Country?' Political Interest and Voter Engagement in 2016." *Public Opinion Quarterly* 82 (1): 822–42.

Putnam, Lara, and Theda Skocpol. 2018. "Middle America Reboots Democracy." *Democracy*, February 20, 2018.

Putnam, Robert D. 2000. *Bowling Alone: The Collapse and Revival of American Community.* New York: Simon & Schuster.

———. 2007. "*E Pluribus Unum*: Diversity and Community in the Twenty-First Century: The 2006 Johan Skytte Prize Lecture." *Scandinavian Political Studies* 30 (2): 137–74.

Putnam, Robert D., and David E. Campbell. 2012. *American Grace: How Religion Divides and Unites Us.* New York: Simon & Schuster.

Rakove, Milton. 1975. *Don't Make No Waves . . . Don't Back No Losers: An Insider's Analysis of the Daley Machine.* Bloomington: Indiana Press.

Ransby, Barbara. 2003. *Ella Baker & the Black Freedom Movement: A Radical Democratic Vision.* Chapel Hill: University of North Carolina Press.

Reynolds, John Francis. 2006. *The Demise of the American Convention System, 1880–1911.* Cambridge: Cambridge University Press.

Riess, Steven. 1991. *City Games: The Evolution of American Urban Society and the Rise of Sports.* Urbana: University of Illinois Press.

Riggs, Austin Fox. 1935. *Play: Recreation in a Balanced Life.* Garden City, NY: Doubleday.

Riker, William H., and Peter C. Ordeshook. 1968. "A Theory of the Calculus of Voting." *American Political Science Review* 62 (1): 25–42.

Rolfe, Meredith. 2013. *Voter Turnout: A Social Theory of Political Participation.* Cambridge: Cambridge University Press.

Rorty, Richard. 1999. *Achieving Our Nation: Leftist Thought in Twentieth Century America.* Cambridge, MA: Harvard University Press.

Rosenfeld, Sam. 2018. *The Polarizers: Postwar Architects of Our Partisan Era.* Chicago: University of Chicago Press.

Rosenstone, Steven J., and John Mark Hansen. 1993. *Mobilization, Participation, and Democracy in America.* New York: Macmillan.

Ruhill, Anirudh V. S. 2003. "Urban Armageddon or Politics as Usual? The Case of Municipal Civil Service Reform." *American Journal of Political Science* 47 (1): 159–70.

Ryan, Timothy J. 2014. "Reconsidering Moral Issues in Politics." *Journal of Politics* 76 (2): 380–97.

———. 2017. "No Compromise: Political Consequences of Moralized Attitudes." *American Journal of Political Science* 61 (2): 409–23.

———. 2019. "Actions versus Consequences in Political Arguments." *Journal of Politics* 81 (2): 426–40.

Sanchez, Gabriel R., and Natalie Masuoka. 2010. "Brown-Utility Heuristic? The Presence and Contributing Factors of Latino Linked Fate." *Hispanic Journal of Behavioral Sciences* 32 (4).

Sanchez, Gabriel R., and Edward D. Vargas. 2016. "Taking a Closer Look at Group Identity: The Link Between Theory and Measurement of Group Consciousness and Linked Fate." *Political Research Quarterly* 69 (1): 160–74.

Schaffner, Brian F., and Samantha Luks. 2018. "Misinformation or Expressive Responding? What an Inauguration Crowd Can Tell Us about the Source of Misinformation in Surveys." *Public Opinion Quarterly* 82 (1): 135–47.

Schildkraut, Deborah J., Jeffrey M. Berry, and James M. Glaser. 2019. "Charge and Retreat: Asymmetric Patterns of Political Engagement among Liberals and Conservatives." Tufts University working paper.

Schlozman, Daniel. 2015. *When Movements Anchor Parties*. Princeton: Princeton University Press.

Schlozman, Kay Lehman. 2015. "Creating Participation." In *Creative Participation: Responsibility-Taking in the Political World*, edited by Michele Micheletti and Andrew S. McFarland. London: Paradigm Publishers, 173–83.

Schradie, Jen. 2019. *The Revolution That Wasn't*. Cambridge, MA: Harvard University Press.

Schudson, Michael. 1998. *The Good Citizen: A History of American Civic Life*. New York: Free Press.

———. 2003. "Click Here for Democracy: A History and Critique of an Information-Based Model of Citizenship." In *Democracy and New Media*, edited by Henry Jenkins and David Thorburn, 48–59. Cambridge, MA: MIT Press.

Shachar, Ron, and Barry Nalebuff. 1999. "Follow the Leader: Theory and Evidence on Political Participation." *American Economic Review* 89 (3): 525–47.

Shafer, Byron E. 1983. *Quiet Revolution: The Struggle for the Democratic Party and the Shaping of Post-reform Politics*. New York: Russell Sage Foundation.

Sheingate, Adam D. 2016. *Building a Business of Politics: The Rise of Political Consulting and the Transformation of American Democracy*. Oxford: Oxford University Press.

Sides, John, and Lynn Vavreck. 2014. *The Gamble: Choice and Chance in the 2012 Presidential Election*. Princeton: Princeton University Press.

Siegel, David A. 2009. "Social Networks and Collective Action." *American Journal of Political Science* 53 (1): 122–38.

Sinclair, Betsy. 2012. *The Social Citizen: Peer Networks and Political Behavior*. Chicago: University of Chicago Press.

Skocpol, Theda. 2003. *Diminished Democracy: From Membership to Management in American Civic Life*. Norman: University of Oklahoma Press.

———. 2004. "APSA Presidential Address: Voice and Inequality: The Transformation of American Civic Democracy." *Perspectives on Politics* 2 (1): 3–20.

Skocpol, Theda, and Alexander Hertel-Fernandez. 2016. "The Koch Network and Republican Party Extremism." *Perspectives on Politics* 14 (3): 681–99.

Skocpol, Theda, and Vanessa Williamson. 2012. *The Tea Party and the Making of Republican Conservatism*. Oxford: Oxford University Press.

Smith, Christian, and Melinda Lundquist Denton. 2005. *Soul Searching: The Religious and Spiritual Lives of American Teenagers*. New York: Oxford University Press.

Somin, Ilya. 2013. *Democracy and Political Ignorance: Why Smaller Government Is Smarter*. Palo Alto, CA: Stanford University Press.

Speer, Paul, and Hahrie Han. 2018. "Re-engaging Social Relationships and Collective Dimensions of Organizing to Revive Democratic Practice." *Journal of Social and Political Psychology* 6 (2): 745–58.

Stebbins, Robert A. 1982. *Serious Leisure*. New York: Sage.

Steiner, Jesse. 1933. "Americans at Play: Recent Trends in Recreation and Leisure Time Activities." In *Recent Social Trends in the United States*, Report of the President's Research Committee on Social Trends. New York: McGraw-Hill.

Stone, Walter, and Alan Abramowitz. 1983. "Winning May Not Be Everything but It's More Than We Thought: Presidential Party Activists in 1980." *American Political Science Review* 77 (4): 945–56.

Strolovitch, Dara. 2007. *Affirmative Advocacy: Race, Class, and Gender in Interest Group Politics*. Chicago: University of Chicago Press.

Super, Donald E. 1940. *Avocational Interest Patterns*. Palo Alto, CA: Stanford University Press.

Surdam, David George. 2015. *Century of the Leisured Masses: Entertainment and the Transformation of Twentieth-Century America*. Oxford: Oxford University Press.

Theodoridis, Alexander G. 2017. "Me, Myself and I, D, or R? Partisanship and Political Cognition through the Lens of Implicit Identity." *Journal of Politics* 79 (4): 1253–67.

Theriault, Sean M. 2013. *The Gingrich Senators: The Roots of Partisan Warfare in Congress*. Oxford: Oxford University Press.

Thompson, Dennis F. 2010. "Representing Future Generations: Political Presentism and Democratic Trusteeship." *Critical Review of International Social and Political Philosophy* 13 (1): 17–37.

Thompson, E. P. 1967. "Work-Discipline, and Industrial Capitalism." *Past and Present* 38 (1): 56–97.

Tjerandsen, Carl. 1980. *Education for Citizenship: A Foundation's Experience*. Santa Cruz, CA: Emil Schwarzhaupt Foundation.

Tolbert, Pamela, and Lynne Zucker. 1983. "Institutional Sources of Change in the Formal Structure of Organizations: The Diffusion of Civil Service Reform, 1880–1935." *Administrative Science Quarterly* 28 (1).

Trounstine, Jessica. 2006. "Dominant Regimes and the Demise of Urban Democracy." *Journal of Politics* 68 (4): 879–93.

———. 2008. *Political Monopolies in American Cities: The Rise and Fall of Bosses and Reformers*. Chicago: University of Chicago Press.

Tufekci, Zeynep. 2017. *Twitter and Tear Gas: The Power and Fragility of Networked Protest*. New Haven, CT: Yale University Press.

Ture, Kwame, and Charles V. Hamilton. 1967. *Black Power: The Politics of Liberation in America*. New York: Random House.

Verba, Sidney, Nancy Burns, and Kay L. Schlozman. 1997. "Knowing and Caring about Politics: Gender and Political Engagement." *Journal of Politics* 59 (4): 1051–72.

Verba, Sidney, Kay L. Schlozman, and Henry E. Brady. 1995. *Voice and Equality: Civic Voluntarism in American Politics*. Cambridge, MA: Harvard University Press.

Warde, Alan. 2015. "The Sociology of Consumption." *Annual Review of Sociology* 41:117–34.

Ware, Alan. 1981. "Why Amateur Party Politics Has Withered Away: The Club Movement, Party Reform and the Decline of American Party Organizations." *European Journal of Political Research* 9 (3): 219–36.

———. 1989. *The Breakdown of Democratic Party Organization, 1940–1980.* Oxford: Oxford University Press.

———. 2000. "Anti-partism and Party Control of Political Reform in the United States: The Case of the Australian Ballot." *British Journal of Political Science* 30 (1): 1–29.

Warren, Mark. 2001. *Dry Bones Rattling: Community Building to Revitalize American Democracy.* Princeton: Princeton University Press.

Williams, Rhonda Y. 2014. *Concrete Demands: The Search for Black Power in the 20th Century.* New York: Routledge.

Wilson, James Q. 1962. *The Amateur Democrat: Club Politics in Three Cities.* Chicago: University of Chicago Press.

———. 1974. *Political Organizations.* Princeton: Princeton University Press.

Wilson, James Q., and Edward C. Banfield. 1964. "Public-Regardingness as a Value Premise in Voting Behavior." *American Political Science Review* 58 (4): 876–87.

Wolfinger, Raymond E., and John Osgood Field. 1966. "Political Ethos and the Structure of City Government." *American Political Science Review* 60 (2): 306–26.

Wong, Janelle. 2018. *Immigrants, Evangelicals, and Politics in an Era of Demographic Change.* New York: Russell Sage Foundation.

Zaller, John R. 1992. *The Nature and Origins of Mass Opinion.* Cambridge: Cambridge University Press.

Zelizer, Julian E. 2004. *On Capitol Hill: The Struggle to Reform Congress and Its Consequences, 1948–2000.* Cambridge: Cambridge University Press.

———. 2010. "Rethinking the History of American Conservatism." *Reviews in American History* 38 (2): 367–92.

INDEX

About the Author

Eitan Hersh is an associate professor in the Department of Political Science and at the Tisch College of Civic Life at Tufts University. He researches and teaches about civic participation, US elections, and voting rights. He received a PhD from Harvard University in 2011.z